JOHN LYDUS AND THE
ROMAN PAST

JOHN LYDUS AND THE ROMAN PAST

Antiquarianism and politics in the
age of Justinian

Michael Maas

London and New York

First published 1992
by Routledge
11 New Fetter Lane, London EC4P 4EE

Simultaneously published in the USA and Canada
by Routledge
a division of Routledge, Chapman and Hall, Inc.
29 West 35th Street, New York, NY 10001

© 1992 Michael Maas

Set in 10/12pt Garamond by Witwell Ltd, Southport
Printed and bound in Great Britain by T J Press (Padstow) Ltd, Padstow,
Cornwall

British Library Cataloguing in Publication Data
Maas, Michael
John Lydus and the Roman past: antiquarianism and
politics in the age of Justinian.
1. Byzantine Empire, history, 323–717
I. Title
949.501

Library of Congress Cataloging in Publication Data
Maas, Michael
John Lydus and the Roman past: antiquarianism and politics in the
age of Justinian/Michael Maas.
p.   cm.
Includes bibliographical references.
1. Byzantine Empire–Civilization–Roman influences.   2. Byzantine
Empire–History–Justinian I, 527–565.   3. Lydus, Johannes
Laurentius, 490–ca. 565.   I. Title.
DF572.M34   1992
949.5′01′092–dc20   91–9119

ISBN 0–415–06021–4

For my father
J. J. Maas
and
to the memory of my mother
Dorothy N. Maas

Sitting alone with my slowly moving thoughts, I rediscover many little details known only to myself, details otherwise dead and forgotten with all who shared that time, and I am inclined to linger among them as long as possible.

(Siegfried Sassoon, *Memoirs of a Fox-Hunting Man*, 1931)

. . . με τ᾽ ἀρχαῖα μνημεῖα καὶ τὴ σύγχρονη θλίψη

(George Seferis, "The King of Asine", 1938/40)

CONTENTS

ACKNOWLEDGEMENTS

This book has been written in fits and starts over many years, and it is a pleasure to acknowledge the assistance and encouragement I have received from friends and institutions along the way. A graduate fellowship from the US Social Science Research Council enabled me to spend a year in London in 1981–2, where I wrote an early version of Chapter 7 for my dissertation. I completed most of the research for the present book while a Fellow at Dumbarton Oaks in 1984–5, and I am most grateful to the Director, Dr Robert Thomson, the Librarian, Dr Maury Feld, and their staffs for making my stay so enjoyable. I returned to the project in 1988–9, with a Fulbright Research Fellowship to Great Britain, where I was a Visiting Research Associate at the Department of Classics, King's College, University of London. My warmest thanks go to Captain John Franklin, director of the Fulbright program, and his efficient staff for setting the year on such a smooth course. I am equally grateful to Professor Averil Cameron for including me at King's, only one of her many kind benefactions over the years. I also enjoyed the hospitality of the Library of the Institute of Classical Studies and the Warburg Institute, for which I am deeply appreciative. I wish to thank Allen Matusow, Dean of Humanities at Rice University, who granted me leave and provided additional research funds.

Several friends read this manuscript at different times: I am happy to express my thanks to Peter Brown, a constant source of encouragement and counsel; to Averil Cameron, whose wisdom and practical advice helped me at every turn; to James Caimi, who taught me a great deal about Lydus and saved me from many errors; to Erich Gruen, who pulled no punches; and to Jonathan Shepard, for many thoughtful discussions. So many others made valued contributions that I have room only to mention their names: Tom Brown, Charlotte

ACKNOWLEDGEMENTS

Roueché, Jill Harries, Walter Kaegi, Brian Croke, Art Eckstein, Ken Holum, John Martindale, Michele Salzman, Maria Cesa, James Howard-Johnston, William T. Kennedy, Eddie Flintoff, Professor and Mrs Anastasius Bandy, Mark Whittow, Peter Heather and Gail Sawyer, John Matthews, Renée Friedman, Robert Browning, Philip and Nerissa Wilson, Cathy and Simon Mercer, Russell Schuh, Sue and Mel Melnick, Peter Maas and Lesley Carson, Pericles Georges and Margaret Sinclair, John Callahan, Ira Gruber, Francis Loewenheim, Callie Williamson, Daniel Brener, Christoph Hering, Stephen Greenberg, Christine Kondoleon, Deborah Berardi, John North, Alexander Kazhdan, and Michael Whitby. Without the generous help of Carol Quillen and Paula Sanders, I would not have finished this book; my gratitude is as great as my affection. I am most grateful to Susan Bielstein for editorial expertise on the eve of submitting this manuscript to the press and to Dominic Montserrat for his invaluable assistance in compiling the appendix and checking references. The Interlibrary Loan staff at Rice University have been of enormous assistance, and I wish to thank Douglas Klopsenstein and Jennifer Geran for their labors. Alaric Watson, Joel Walker, Kate Gilliver, and Margherite Debrunner-Hall helped greatly with the bibliography. Leslie S. B. MacCoull compiled the index and made many useful suggestions. Finally, I want to thank my editors at Routledge, Richard Stoneman, Sue Bilton, and Robert Peden, for their exemplary courtesy, attention to detail, and patience.

Houston, December 5, 1990

INTRODUCTION: JOHN LYDUS AND THE SILVER HEIRLOOM

Romans were never indifferent to history. They trusted in precedent, not progress, and self-consciously defined themselves against their past. Throughout the fifteen centuries separating the first Roman emperor from the last, antiquity provided models of correct behavior and conveyed moral and political legitimacy, especially in times of uncertainty and upheaval. This book shows how one late-antique scholar, John Lydus, understood his ties to the past during the reign of the emperor Justinian I, a period of political flux and cultural redefinition of great importance in the development of the Roman state.

Lydus was a disgruntled civil servant and antiquarian who lived during the first half of the sixth century AD, when the late-antique Roman empire based at Constantinople was rapidly moving toward its medieval form.[1] Unlike the western portion of the Empire, however, which under the rulership of Germanic kings could formulate a break with the Roman past,[2] the eastern rump that we call Byzantium always assumed continuity with the Roman past. Even in 1453, when Constantinople, the New Rome, finally fell to the Turks, its inhabitants called themselves *Rhomaioi*.[3] It was an ideal of Rome, however, far more than any accurate knowledge of Roman antiquity, that gradually emerged in Byzantium to become, in Dölger's words, "the center-point of a complex medieval world-view which tied Christ and the church to every aspect of cultural, legal and social life."[4] The status of the Roman past in this emerging Byzantine environment was a matter of debate and invention. Only slowly, and not without conflict, did Byzantium weave a new, Christian myth of its relationship to its subjects, its neighbors, and its Roman past.

Lydus and his antiquarian interests give some small measure of

1

the development of this Byzantine identity in the sixth century because he lets us see how educated men of the administrative elite conceptualized continuity – the crucial issue for a society that characteristically legitimated its response to change in terms of tradition. He felt the pull of tradition in government institutions and in literary culture. The latter was especially sensitive because at stake in Justinianic Constantinople were the last hopes of genuine intellectual pluralism. Who would determine the terms and extent of the relationship of past to present? Who would appropriate the power to define the past and thus control its legitimating force? It is in this historical context that I consider Lydus' three "antiquarian" treatises. They demonstrate not "museumification" of antiquity but current issues cast in historical terms and debate about the status of the past itself. They help us know how and why the past was problematic.

During his reign (AD 527–65) Justinian attempted to identify Christianity with culture in an absolute way. This meant, among other things, approaching the past from a point of view that was at once Christian, Roman, and imperial. In particular, Justinian recast the relationship of the classical heritage to Christianity by creating a sharp distinction between certain aspects of religiously neutral classical culture and paganism, which he sought to eradicate. At the same time, many of his reforms were both justified in terms of Christian ideology and presented in terms of tradition and continuity with the Roman past. He claimed certain legitimizing aspects of the past for himself as emperors had done since Augustus, but in doing so he exploited and exacerbated political problems between the throne and the urban elite that were particular to his own age. The emperor's reduction of the classical heritage for political advantage forced many of his subjects to choose among allegiances that had never before been in such stark conflict.

Consequently, as Justinian formulated his absolutist policies, often couching them in classicizing style, the very terms of the argument, such as "pagan", "Roman", and even "Christian", came under review. There were real ambiguities. To what degree was *Romanitas* compatible with Christianity? In what ways might classical learning be associated with paganism? Lydus provides information about why the relation between Christianity and antique culture was uncertain at this moment. The charge of paganism was frequently heard, but beyond its appropriate application to people who continued to worship the old gods, it also could be confused with other sorts of allegiance to antiquity. Was knowledge about ancient Rome "pagan" ? What made a mode of explanation "Christian" ? Were aspects of the classical legacy that had nothing to do with religious worship suspect? Sorting out one's relation to Justinian's regime entailed more absolute choices than had been necessary in the fourth and fifth centuries, when the Constantinian revolution sank its roots.

Pierre Chuvin has recently chronicled the long decline of paganism in the face of steady Christian pressure; his treatment illustrates again and again the vagaries of policy and personality that made paganism's demise anything but even and straightforward.[5] Nevertheless, general trends appear. Gradually pagans were excluded from public life, while the definition of paganism narrowed to encompass only explicitly religious practice. Christianity set the terms of the conflict, with considerable effect on pagans' views of themselves. Christianity could underwrite a more total view of the world than could pagan cults; it was a good partner for Justinian. But we have to resist the temptation of contrasting paganism and Christianity as complete opposites. If we do so we will not understand Lydus, who did not make the same sharp distinctions as did his emperor. Lydus instead represents a sensibility of the fifth century, which cast the problem of paganism differently.

The fortunes of a few men illustrate the variations and anticipate the Justinianic scene. For example, Proclus, a philosopher and pagan, was the academic godfather to several generations of students, Christian and non-Christian, in Athens, Constantinople, and Alexandria.[6] In this case, paganism was identified with philosophy. His contemporary, Isocasius, was a sophist from Antioch who served as Quaestor in Constantinople in the 460s.[7] Although he had been cured of an illness at the shrine of St Thecla, he remained none the less a pagan until he was publicly denounced; he lived easily in two zones without contradiction. Another man of the age, Cyrus of Panopolis, was "quite simply a cultivated Christian, imbued with classical culture," with the bad luck to be from a town noted as a pagan center.[8] At the height of an illustrious career – he was Praetorian Prefect from 439–41, and then Consul – his popularity earned imperial suspicion. Accused of paganism and removed from office, he became a bishop. After Theodosius II's death Cyrus returned to a secular life at Constantinople.

Justinian's litmus tests, which sought to put an end to such ambiguities, however, were not Lydus', and they need not be ours.[9] From his place on the margins of government and power, Lydus reveals to us a wider range of points of view that still existed in the first half of the sixth century. The patriarch Photius, writing in the ninth century, is the first on record to discuss Lydus' intellectual interests and silence on Christian matters. He rightly noted the difficulty in determining whether or not Lydus was Christian, and the argument has proceeded along these "either/or" lines ever since. Though we can scarcely fault Photius for not understanding the Justinianic cultural scene, we must also understand that trying to pin Lydus down as a pagan *or* a Christian is misleading and anachronistic, for the two were not mutually exclusive. Lydus was Christian, but Christianity in and of itself was not the issue for him. In an age when people increasingly thought of themselves as *pistoi*[10] (that is, faithful Christians) Lydus, though a Christian himself, chose to write in a mode that carefully avoided reference to Christianity.[11] He never betrayed an interest in doctrinal disputes, nor did he address paganism, at least as understood by the palace. He was reacting not to Christianity *per se* nor even to its role in the administration, but to governmental reforms and imperial policies of a narrower sort. Yet, as we will see, he pointedly identified himself politically with a man charged with pagan worship, and he espoused "scientific" positions held by pagan philosophers.[12] His books show evidence of beliefs that had once characterized an anti-Christian pagan polemic but that in his hands now were completely devoid of immediate religious association. What has to be explained is not the religious transformation of the state – there is no question that a "respectable, aristocratic Christianity" [13] existed at Constantinople when Lydus wrote – but his reluctance to admit it, and how that reluctance was conditioned by his understanding of a Roman legacy.

The social identity of a late-antique man like Lydus comprised allegiances to a number of institutions and ideas: Christianity, classical urban culture, a traditional education in rhetoric, philosophy, and possibly Latin, an appreciation of imperial government. In the course of a single day he might read Plato, be healed at a saint's shrine, deliver a panegyric in Latin, praise or criticize the emperor, and sing the Trisagion hymn – without any sense of contradiction. It was not only possible but natural for late-antique Christians to appreciate aspects of the Roman legacy that were not explicitly Christian. Lydus epitomizes this cultural stance. He represents a constellation of commitments particular to the Justinianic era. What distinguishes Lydus from his Byzantine descendant is only the degree to which these different points of reference were emphasized. While aspects of the past such as Greek mythology, Roman law, and antiquarian studies would not disappear in medieval Byzantium, they would lose their independence, always to be understood from a Christian vantage-point.[14] Lydus could not have known that this intermingling of cultural elements would contribute to the survival of the Roman empire in Byzantine garb for another millennium.

Lydus has been called a crypto-pagan, a neoplatonic convert to Christianity,[15] and simply someone whose professional life, culture, and intellectual interests were free of Christian decoration.[16] There is some truth in all these characterizations. As a Constantinopolitan servant of Roman emperors, he cultivated an expertise in Latin and knowledge about Rome, unlike urban intellectuals in the East of earlier epochs who took pleasure in their connections with Greek antiquity.[17] Justinian created an environment that made Lydus' attitudes political, and I will suggest that antiquarianism provided an idiom of resistance to unwelcome realities of the Justinianic milieu.

Lydus' books place him in the long, scholarly tradition of the ancient world that we call antiquarianism.[18] Men who participated in this type of scholarship and collected tomes of abstruse data were interested in the past without being interested in history *per se* – that is, without writing in the normal genre of historiography. Lydus' very distance from the constraints of late Roman historiography – he never set out to write history in the formal sense – in fact helps us understand some of the everyday attitudes toward chronology, causality, and the passage of time that influenced the sensibilities of sixth-century Constantinopolitans. For this reason Lydus' works must be understood as more than sterile fact-gathering. *De Ostentis* (On Portents), *de Mensibus* (On the Months), and *de Magistratibus* (On Magistracies) demonstrate how knowledge of the past played a role in defining social and political identity for Lydus and men of his class. This study views Lydus' attitudes regarding antiquity, particularly the Roman past, as a sensible response to the tensions of the age.

Let us begin with Lydus' perception of the political and cultural issues that plagued Justinianic society. For him, the Roman past did not merge naturally into the Christian *oikoumene*; there was no easy voyage to Byzantium. Lydus perceived overwhelming discontinuities in tradition. On the social landscape he could see only ruin, and he spoke angrily about the changes he witnessed. He asked his readers to imagine that

> a man has a magnificent silver vessel gained not through his own effort but that of his ancestors. He slowly grows poor and, heedless of its strength and beauty, he breaks the vessel to bits.

JOHN LYDUS AND THE ROMAN PAST

He makes many small and fragile pots from it because he thinks
that a very large and ancient vessel contains more silver from its
reduction than from its unity. In the very same way the greatest
magistracy [*sc.* the Praetorian Prefecture] was smashed. Many,
perhaps too many, offices have sprung up in its place, since
Fortune has become displeased with the Poet, who said "The
rule of many is not a good thing. Let there be one ruler." [19]

This allegory provides us with some insight into Lydus' view of the
cultural crisis in the New Rome. Though he meant his silver vessel
specifically to represent the Praetorian Prefecture, the office of state
in which he served for four decades, we may also let the heirloom
stand for his view of society as a whole – that is, the sum of ancestral
achievement now broken and sorely in need of repair. This passage
introduces us to other elements found throughout his books: the
perception of decline; a querulous and defensive spirit; learned
allusions to classical literature; an absence of Christian references. All
these point to sixth-century social issues. The tension between the
debasement of an inheritance and the need for authoritarian rule
reveals a more personal dilemma as well, for Lydus was torn between
his loyalty to the Prefecture and an urban cultural tradition and his
loyalty to Justinian, whose autocratic policies he often found inimical
to those traditions.

Lydus used the image of a broken inheritance again in a far more
intimate and critical way in *de Magistratibus*, as he describes the
brutal treatment of an inhabitant of his home town at the hands of
Justinian's tax collectors:

A certain Petronius in my Philadelphia, a man worthy of
account and distinguished for family, property, and learning, . . .
was the possessor of precious stones from his ancestors which
were numerous and at the same time kept from the sight of
private individuals because of their beauty and size. The Cyclops
[i.e., the taxman[20]] had him seized and had irons put around him
and proceeded to have him scourged.

(*de Mag.*, III.59)

On another occasion he watched an old man, an acquaintance, die
under torture as the Cappadocian's agents sought his gold. With these
gruesome episodes Lydus showed how misrule caused suffering
"beyond the point of tragedy."[21] Yet he could never point an angry
finger directly at Justinian. Even when called upon to lavish praise on
the emperor, as he did with such considerable eagerness that he has

been called a "naiver Jasager,"[22] we will see that Lydus remained deeply ambivalent about the exercise of imperial power and equivocal about the significance of change. He did not react against the imperial ideology of power. In fact, he believed in it. This must be emphasized. What he did oppose were specific, concrete institutional changes and their consequences; he saw signs of decline equally in regalia neglected and in peasants driven from their land.[23] His certain belief that men without the proper education were filling the Prefecture indicates disdain for the new order. Most of all, however, he was disturbed by his own loss of status in the bureaucracy. His devotion to the good old ways stemmed in part from the fact that he had benefitted from them enormously.[24] His crankiness, I believe, was in part a result of personal disappointment; but he was more than a disgruntled favor-seeker. His concerns sprang from immediate, pressing issues that touched his family and friends as well as himself. The innovations and changes to which he objected were part of an imperial policy that attacked men of high office and high culture on the grounds that they were pagans. Justinian's policies affected teaching and curriculum, city government, and the status of local elites – as well as administrative procedure[25] – in what Lydus understood to be a profoundly negative way. As a member of the educated urban elite he was right to feel defensive, for a venerable and coherent way of life was indeed crumbling. For Lydus, despair replaced pride as the promise of his early career and of Justinian's early reign turned sour;[26] the imperial system in which he believed seemed to have betrayed his fondest plans. As he watched from the center of power, he became increasingly disenchanted. He kept one eye firmly on the achievements of the past that seemed sweet in comparison with the bitter present. *De Magistratibus* in particular conveys a feeling of unfinished business, of society's institutions waiting impatiently to be reborn. Lydus' misfortune was not to realize it was too late for the sort of general rejuvenation of institutions and society that he had in mind.

His attitudes represent some portion of the urban aristocracy and administrative elite that felt itself threatened by Justinian's pious social-engineering and by other visible forces in the social and economic order. I say "some portion" because the evidence does not permit us to speak of a uniform opposition to Justinian. We find a sense of a vanishing order in other authors of the day, but none speaks as clearly about decline as Lydus. This reason alone marks Lydus as worthy of rehabilitation.

His analytical and descriptive terms differ from ours, as the example of the silver vessel suggests, but they provide a coherent explanation of a world in transition that *Quellenforschung* cannot supply. We must be alert to a quite different interpretative position that valued precedent and had no ideology of progress. Lydus' fear of loss and concern for restoration represent an extreme expression of a deeply conservative attitude. He operated from a myth of society denied by political and social reality. Yet far from holding him back, his heightened sense of tradition enabled him to concoct some original theories explaining the character of social change and its relation to imperial action. While his contemporary Procopius might posit demonic action as the cause of society's ills,[27] Lydus developed an elaborate theory of the mechanisms of change in the bureaucracy's institutions based on his reading of Aristotle and other philosophers. The fact that Lydus attempted to use philosophical language to explain contemporary affairs is unusual and important, but not surprising, considering his education. We will see how philosophy provided Lydus with a language of explanation alternative to the explicitly Christian or pagan and how the weight of tradition moved him to creativity.

To look for political and social criticism in allegories about heirlooms might strike a modern reader unfamiliar with late antiquity as rather odd. Yet to understand Lydus we must train our eyes to find meaning as he presented it, in veiled allusions to Homer, and also in astrology and a host of other subjects. To fail to do so will lead to the trap that has snared most scholars who have considered Lydus, that of understanding him as the mere proprietor of an exotic pawnshop full of other people's ideas, the relics of other eras, all individually redeemable but collectively somewhat of an embarrassment. A critic once said that Thomas Babington Macaulay "not only overflowed with knowledge, he stood in the slop." [28] In precisely the same spirit, slanders have been heaped on Lydus. While scholars benefit from his learned zeal,[29] they tend to patronize and dismiss the treatises as mere disorganized antiquarianism,[30] as a "nadir of the art of book writing," [31] and Lydus as "only a compiler," [32] "without any understanding of events," [33] and with a "nearly non-existent personality." [34] Such critics have been unwilling to examine seriously the nature of his interest in antiquity: in the age of Justinian the collection of antiquarian knowledge meant something different than it did for Julius Gracchanus in the Republic,[35] or for Ovid, Suetonius, and the many other scholars whom Lydus cited.[36] In short, the context of his

8

antiquarianism needs attention, and his works may be approached (as they have not been previously) as a coherent group, perhaps not unified in theme but certainly sharing a view of the relationships among the political, historical and natural worlds.

To be sure, Lydus represents no milestone in the history of ideas, nor would anyone call him a major figure on the Constantinopolitan political or intellectual scene. His language is often most inelegant. His knowledge of Roman history is highly uneven. He is often vague, diffuse, petty, and short-sighted in his discussion, and he is at his frustrating best dealing with Justinian and the consequences of his reforms. Nevertheless, Lydus deserves to be taken seriously, warts and all, because he offers an invaluable insider's view of Constantinople in an era of crucial change. If we can understand his fears and preoccupations we will have not only a picture of a curiously sympathetic figure but a clearer idea of how at least one Constantinopolitan of the day viewed the transition from Rome to Byzantium.

THE BOOKS

A few preliminary remarks are in order about Lydus' treatises, not all of which have survived. We miss his panegyric to his patron Zoticus (c. 512),[37] his encomium to Justinian (c. 530s),[38] his history of the Persian war that ended in 532,[39] and his poetry.[40] The books that do survive illustrate a preoccupation with ancient knowledge, given life by social and political change. Lydus endeavored to collect material that he feared might be forgotten but that was still useful and relevant. Anticipating an audience that shared his education and interests, he wrote for his peers (*de Magistratibus* records his thanks to his superiors in the Praetorian Prefecture[41]) and for the future. Each of Lydus' three extant books in its own way deals with vanishing knowledge, and a defensive tone pervades them, lending a morbid energy.

De Mensibus collates material about antique festivals and the organization of time in the Roman calendrical tradition,[42] while *de Ostentis* assembles a great deal of information about astrology. It assumes relationships between portents and historical events and demonstrates how divine principles are active in human experience. *De Ostentis* indicates that Lydus saw no break with ancient scientific traditions. The information collected here was, in his eyes, especially useful as new attacks were being mounted against Aristotelian and Ptolemaic cosmology. His third and best-known work, *de Magistratibus*, is a collection of data about the regalia and operation of the civil service – especially his own bureau, the Praetorian Prefecture. It measures the glories of Roman antiquity against the troubles of the present and raises the possibility of a rehabilitated future through a cyclical pattern of generation, decline, and restoration, especially of certain offices of state. Lydus describes the emperor as restorer in unprecedented terms.

Debate about date and sequence of composition has been extensive.[43] Since *de Mensibus* is mentioned twice in *de Ostentis* and nine times in *de Magistratibus*, it was presumably composed first.[44] *De Ostentis* and *de Mensibus* were probably written before Lydus' retirement from the Praetorian Prefecture.[45] The *Suda*[46] tells that the two works were dedicated to Gabriel, presumably the man who was city prefect in 543.[47] Whether *de Ostentis* or *de Magistratibus* was the next to be written remains open to argument,[48] but *de Magistratibus* was probably the final work, for it displays a more thoughtfully developed theory of historical causation, and it also contains references to events later in Lydus' career than those in *de Ostentis*. It is most likely that Lydus completed *de Magistratibus* during his retirement.[49] To judge from the latest references in *de Magistratibus*, he died between 557 and 561.[50] His completed manuscript has not survived in its entirety; it breaks off while describing his hero, the Prefect Phocas.[51]

The chapters of this book deal with the issue of the status of the past in different ways. In Chapter 1, "Changes in the Age of Justinian," I discuss the major cultural and economic shifts of the first half of the sixth century. Chapter 2, "Portrait of a Bureaucrat," presents the known facts of Lydus' life and the highs and lows of his career. Chapter 3, "The Ideological Transformation of Tradition," looks at why control of the past was an important issue for Lydus and Justinian. Chapter 4, "*De Mensibus* and the Antiquarian Tradition," locates Lydus in the antiquarian genre and discusses his different uses of antique knowledge. It explores his ability to use data in an original way as well as his discomfort with some Christian institutions. The connections of antiquarianism to paganism and how Justinian made paganism a political issue are explored in Chapter 5, "Paganism and Politics." Chapter 6, "*De Magistratibus* and the Theory of Imperial Restoration," takes us back to Lydus' work and considers the scheme of imperial restoration he developed. We see what Lydus expected from the emperor but did not get. In Chapter 7, "Lydus and the

Philosophers," I examine Lydus' intellectual debts and see how some of the most important ideas in his theory of restoration fit into contemporary debate about paganism. The "real" issues that divided pagan and Christian are contrasted with the definitions of Justinianic law. Chapter 8, "*De Ostentis*: Portents and the Enemies of Ptolemy," considers Lydus' defensive position regarding Christian attacks on traditional cosmology. It provides more evidence of Lydus' involvement in contemporary debate and helps to explain his custodial attitude toward antiquarian knowledge. The concluding chapter, "Collusion," pulls these various threads together and suggests an explanation for Lydus' ambivalent attitude toward the emperor and his concern for the past.

With this plan in mind, we can now sketch the major changes to which Lydus responded.

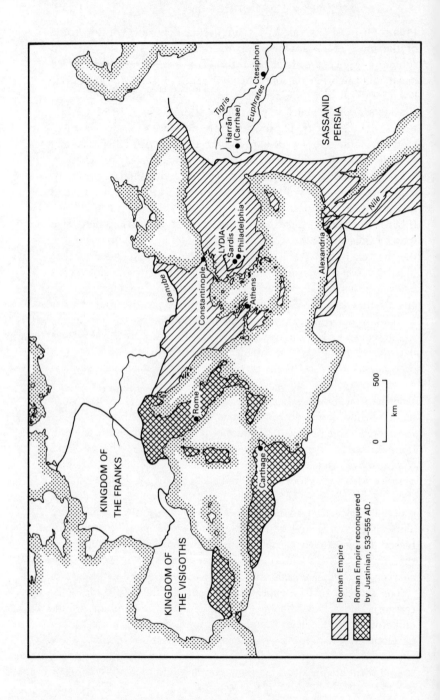

SASSANID PERSIA

Tigris

Euphrates

Ctesiphon

Harrān (Carrhae)

Nile

LYDIA
Sardis
Philadelphia

Alexandria

Danube

Constantinople

Athens

KINGDOM OF THE FRANKS

Rhine

Rome

KINGDOM OF THE VISIGOTHS

Carthage

500

km

0

Roman Empire

Roman Empire reconquered by Justinian, 533–555 AD.

1

CHANGES IN THE AGE OF JUSTINIAN

If Lydus could have looked ahead only a century or two, he would have found a Constantinople that made little sense, in which the antiquity that he venerated was forgotten or changed beyond recognition. To illustrate: the institution with which he identified most closely, his beloved Praetorian Prefecture, would pass out of existence near the end of the next century.[1] Portraits of Christ, whom his writings ignored, would appear on coins. Looking out from the capital city, he would see the end of familiar rhythms of provincial city life as castles, not *fora*, met the needs of the medieval state. Society would become even more militarized at the expense of the civilian bureaucracy that was so important to Lydus.[2] Greek would entirely replace Latin (his field of professional expertise) as the language of law and government,[3] while innocence of antique learning would come to be considered a sign of piety.[4] We need only glance through the pages of the *Parastaseis*,[5] a guide of sorts to the antiquities of Constantinople compiled by "lovers of knowledge"[6] in the eighth century, to see how much of what Lydus took for granted about living as a good Roman in the New Rome would be lost: "take care when you look at old statues, especially pagan ones" admonishes this pious work.[7] Lydus called Time "the creator and destroyer of its own progeny"[8] with good reason. Lydus, of course, could not read the future. He could only feel threatened, and his uncertainty breathes life into his books. This chapter sketches the events and issues that transformed Lydus' world.

The changes that he experienced as attacks fall into three broad categories. First, he responded to the dramatic re-emphasis of the emperor at the ideological and institutional center of society. This development, fostered by Justinian's grandiose ambitions, found expression in the emperor's theories of power and restoration as well as in institutional reforms. Second, economic and religious changes in

13

the cities and the countryside produced unhappy consequences for the urban aristocracy and intelligentsia, and the bureaucracy that drew from them. New routes to power and prestige that had been developing since the fourth century side-stepped the traditional urban arena, forcing what Roueché refers to as the "breaking of the myth of the city." [9] A different, medieval myth of Constantinople grew at the cities' expense, reflecting a more thorough Christianization and the attendant de-emphasis of literary culture, the cornerstone of classical urban life.[10] In this we see a painful redefinition of religion and culture for the urban elite. Third, Constantinople, the imperial center and the focal point of the emperor's activities, took on a more completely Christian garb. That Constantinople should emerge as the symbolic center of imperial power and administration was perhaps inevitable, but the manner in which it became the juncture of divine and human affairs would have been impossible without a Christian influence. In theory, Constantinople and the empire were one.[11] Justinian undertook no major building projects when his troops had recaptured Rome;[12] there could be only one center of empire.

THE EMPEROR AT THE CENTER

During the sixth century the steady centralization of power in the emperor's hands allowed Justinian to define his place between heaven and earth more explicitly in Christian terms. At the same time the community defined itself about him in new ways, for the imperial figure provided a focus for its political and religious devotion and was an element of stability and continuity in this uncertain environment. The emperor linked the community to God,[13] and provided a means of accepting and explaining new circumstance. John Haldon explains:

> In the case of late Roman culture, explanations of change, and attempts to place it within a comprehensible context, were effected through the medium of the imperial ideology, that is to say, the whole symbolic system concentrated around the role of the emperor, his relationship with God and his position as God's deputy on earth, which legitimated for the members of this society – that is to say, which explained in terms of their own subjectively observed social situation – its internal structure. And this ideology was in turn situated within, and received the greater part of its force and relevance from, the general symbolic universe of the Roman world, dominated by

14

the syncretic soteriological theology within which older, now "sub-cultural" symbolic systems were subsumed.[14]

The emperor had been the focus of attention in political theory, of course, since the reign of Augustus, and although Christians since Eusebius had recognized the special role of the emperor in the hierarchy of divine and human power, a Byzantine political rhetoric which could comfortably accommodate Christ and Caesar had still not fully emerged at Constantinople when Justinian came to the throne. This development was neither smooth nor easy, for many precedents of the Roman state upon which the emperor depended for legitimacy, the precedents of world rule with all its attendant rituals of civic life, had never been Christian, and it was difficult to synthesize these distinct aspects of religious and secular expression. The pace of the transformation quickened during the reign of Justinian.

Justinian secured his authority in a variety of new ways that contributed to the Byzantine synthesis: for the first time an emperor claimed to be *nomos empsychos*, the living law – though the idea had been tacitly held for many centuries.[15] He imposed new restrictions on the law schools: after the codification, commentary on the *Digest* was forbidden, and only the emperor kept the authority to resolve ambiguous juridical decisions.[16] In a similar way, as master of the Church he sought to control the definition of orthodox faith. Administrative offices were directly linked to the emperor in their titulature: they were "Justinianic" praetors, proconsuls, and moderators, for example.[17] He insisted on the use of the *Kyrios* title again,[18] and triumphal epithets became more prominent.[19] The protocol of imperial documents also took on a character that would last into the seventh century.[20] Justinian ruled "by the grace of God"[21] and was evidently the first to use the title *Philochristos*.[22] The circus factions were tightly tied to imperial ceremonial.[23] Political theorists acknowledged the emperor's primary, central place as they sketched the ideal reorganization of society.[24] The Deacon Agapetus, for one, urged Justinian to remain an unchanging point of calmness in a world of flux.[25]

The Barberini diptych beautifully expresses these trends, showing for the first time in ivory carving the direct association of classical style and Christian meaning. Its main panel displays a mounted, triumphant emperor typical of representations of the emperor for centuries. The zone directly above the emperor, however, adds something new to this conventional representation: two angels hold a medallion with a bust of Christ, "making imperial authority an integral part of Christian order." [26] We see the same juxtaposition of imperial authority and sanction of Christian divinity in Justinian's theory of legislation found in his provincial reform laws of the 530s.[27]

At about the same time that the Barberini diptych was being carved, the *kontakion*, a poetic form new to the Greek-speaking community, arrived from the Syriac community to take its place at the heart of Byzantine religious celebration.[28] The kontakion accommodated the needs of the regime as well as those of God: "On Earthquakes and Fires," for example, the fifty-fourth kontakion of Romanos the Melode, contains parallels between God, the creator and renewer of the world, and Justinian, rebuilder of Constantinople after the Nika revolt and renewer of the Christian oikoumene.[29] During the reign of Justinian's successor, Justin II, such direct associations of the emperor and Christ would be developed even more fully and deliberately.[30]

Perhaps the most striking evidence of Justinian's pretensions can be seen in the mosaics of his church at San Vitale in Ravenna. Here he stands confidently in the company of Abraham and Christ at the center of the cosmos where he assumes a role in a redemptive, Christian view of the unfolding of history.[31]

Theoretical considerations took concrete form. Justinian undertook extensive building projects throughout his empire. In every corner, churches, bridges, and fortifications were restored or built new. Procopius' *de Aedificiis* lists and praises these many constructions; the important thing is to note the imperial justification it contains for this great effort:

> Then appeared the emperor Justinian, entrusted by God with this commission, to watch over the whole Roman Empire and, so far as was possible, to remake it.[32]

In a more candid moment, when he was writing for another audience, Procopius observed his emperor's intrusive authoritarianism in a different light. He fumed that Justinian always took matters into his own hands to the ruin of his subjects.[33] Justinian wished his projects to be seen as a divinely inspired undertaking to refashion and restore the fabric of the state.[34] God gave him an excellent opportunity to fulfill this responsibility by permitting much of Constantinople to burn to the ground during the infamous Nika revolt of 532. The emperor rose to the occasion and altered the face of his capital by constructing numerous shrines and churches, St Sophia being the grandest.[35]

Under Justinian Constantinople grew as a ceremonial center linked to God through the agency of the emperor's rule.[36]

All these buildings advertised the emperor's omnipresence as well as his piety, and they carried a political message. No observer could have overlooked Justinian's hand in their construction. The Chalke mosaics in the vestibule of the imperial palace in Constantinople (known only from Procopius' description) emphasized the emperor's eternal victory.[37] It was no accident that St Sophia overshadowed in scale the Church of St Polyeuktos built by Anicia Juliana, the last representative of the previous ruling house,[38] for Justinian's buildings stated his supremacy to every rival.

Renewal, that "most praiseworthy achievement of the powerful"[39] in the Roman world, took a prominent place in Justinian's regime. Two traditions of imperial restoration came together while he was on the throne. One derived from the inscriptions that commemorated imperial or private munificence throughout the cities of the eastern empire: their messages of benefaction employed a shared vocabulary of renewal.[40] The second tradition stemmed from Constantine, the first Christian emperor, who contributed to the theme of imperial restoration by grafting Jesus' soteriological functions to concepts of imperial responsibility: like Christ the good shepherd, the emperor would endeavor to restore the souls of his flock to piety and lead them to salvation.[41] Between Eusebius and Justinian this idea did not get translated into non-theological terms. That is, there is no evidence that the Eusebian notion of restoration was ever applied to government. That was Justinian's contribution. During his reign, restoration of Empire in unambiguous administrative terms was fitted into a Christian scheme. In the period before Justinian such terms as *restitutor*, which might suggest that renewal was closely linked with an emperor's responsibilities, are surprisingly absent from panegyric and ecclesiastical historians.[42] *Triumphator, augustus*, and *autocrator* were the frequent imperial epithets. The situation in numismatics was similar. Neither Anastasius nor Justin employed on their coins any of the restoration legends that had begun to appear in the troubled years of the late third century and lasted well into the fifth. Justinian's own coinage – curiously, in light of his other projects and huge number of mints – makes no claims to restoration. In his theory of law, however, as witnessed particularly in his provincial reform legislation of the 530s,[43] the situation was quite different. Before his reign, writers of laws had not addressed the ways in which reform might be achieved in institutional terms.[44] Justinian tried to present the restoration of

17

institutions in a Christian context. The restoration of the state, the reconquest of the western provinces, and the creation of a new law code all were presented as a function of Christian imperium.

CHANGES IN CITY AND PROVINCE

Economic factors

The economic condition of the cities of the eastern empire in the sixth century is difficult to gauge precisely because of the unevenness of archaeological and written evidence. In some regions, such as Syria, Egypt, and Anatolia, there seems to have been a degree of prosperity.[45] In general, however, scholars note stagnation and decline,[46] intensified by the outbreak of the plague in 542.[47] Rouché notes that the picture of urban decline is "full of apparent contradictions," but that "something went wrong in the sixth century" as "the cities lost their resilience," making them vulnerable to whatever brought their final collapse in the early seventh century. Kennedy's observation that in Syria "in the mid-sixth century the classical vision of the city and of urban order was still very much alive,"[48] deserves our attention as much for its suggestion of continuity in attitudes about the shape of urban life as it does for raising the issue of the perception of urban decline. Lydus' fears about change would appear senseless if an idealized vision of the city did not still keep some hold on his imagination as he writes "through public contributions many marvelous things are done in the cities: baths, markets, aqueducts – source of infinite good fortune for the inhabitants."[49] At the same time Lydus shows that the "classical vision" was somewhat at odds with economic and social reality. We must remember that prosperity in a city need not be tied to the ideology of an elite out of step with changes in religion and power structure. It should also be kept in mind that Lydus reveals nothing about those who did make the necessary accommodations with the new, Justinianic establishment and did not see the world as fraught with discontinuities. And indeed I will suggest below that, despite his nostalgia, Lydus' position was *de facto* an acceptance of the new order.

A quite dramatic discontinuity was the end of the city senates. The traditional position of leadership and power of the curial class further eroded during Lydus' lifetime as the cities of the east continued to lose their autonomy.[50] The trend throughout the century was the proliferation of imperial officials, especially provincial governors, bishops,[51] and great landowners – "les forces véritables de l'époque." [52] During the reign of Anastasius (491–518 AD) the city councils ceased to function,[53] although the curial order maintained its many responsibilities including the collection of taxes.[54] De Magistratibus singles out Marinus, Anastasius' Praetorian Prefect, as an enemy of the curial class and the city councils.[55] Lydus noted the end of the councils and added rather wistfully that in the days when the councils functioned – days which he would have remembered from his childhood – the city fathers still wore togas as they performed their duties.[56] He does not, however, claim to be a member of this order or urge its restoration. This may indicate that his family did not belong to the curial class. His career was made possible by ties to highly placed relatives in Constantinople.[57] By the seventh century the cities were no longer self-governing units responsible for collecting revenues for themselves and for the state and had become merely centers of imperial administration which collected revenues and sent them directly to Constantinople.[58] Emperor Leo VI (886–912) issued a law that annulled some of Justinian's legislation on curiales. It explained their diminished circumstances in terms of imperial paternalism:

> because now the law of political matters has undergone a change, and everything depends solely on imperial care and administration.[59]

Justinian, for all his zeal to restore, never attempted to revivify the curial order of which he seemed to have been quite suspicious. His reforms in fact diminished the status of the curials[60] whom he believed to be cruel.[61] He compelled all men of rank to serve in rotation as defensor civitatis, a revived fourth-century office with judicial authority and responsibility to collect taxes, and to guard against possible excesses of provincial governors.[62] Rules were tightened to prevent men from evading these responsibilities.

Procopius felt that the cities were undermined by the emperor's new administrative procedures:

> Furthermore, all the revenues which the inhabitants of all the cities had been raising locally for their own civic needs and for their public spectacles he transferred and dared to mingle them with the national income. And thereafter neither physicians nor teachers were held in any esteem, nor was anyone able any longer to make provisions for the public buildings, nor were the public lamps kept burning in the cities, nor was there any other

consolation for their inhabitants. For the theaters and hippo-
dromes and circuses were all closed for the most part . . . . And
later he ordered these spectacles to close down altogether, even
in Byzantium,[63] so that the Treasury might not have to supply
the usual sums to the numerous and almost countless persons
who derived their living from them. And there was both in
private and in public sorrow and dejection, as though still
another affliction from heaven had smitten them, and there was
no laughter in life for anyone.[64]

Heartfelt as Procopius' groans might have been, the provincial elite
did not vanish or lose its power. The establishment of Constantinople
in the fourth century had created new avenues for men to acquire
prestige and influence that were closely linked to the emperor. By the
late fifth century the ruling elite from the provinces well knew that
the fastest route to power was no longer via traditional urban roles.
Now power was more tightly channeled toward the imperial center at
Constantinople. Prestige was achieved via imperial titles and ranks as
well as civic honors.[65] For example, Roueché cites the case of
Asclepiodotus of Aphrodisias, described not only as "a leader in the
council" of his home town but also as one who "took pride in the
honours and dignities with which the emperor was loading him." [66]
Men eager for a career looked increasingly to the capital – perhaps to
the bureaucracy – for an opportunity to rise. There is some evidence
as well that the leading citizens of the towns were ready "to put their
own interests in direct conflict with those of the city." [67]
Justinian's program of administrative reform, intended to improve
the efficiency and justice of government in the provinces, intensified
dependency upon the throne by increasing its authority over the cities
and countryside. Imperial appointees, especially governors who
embodied the emperor's authority, linked the provinces to the
Constantinopolitan source of power in streamlined fashion. Justinian
had a specific idea of how the governors were to represent him and
how they were to treat the cities and administer justice. He increased
the power of provincial governors and linked them to himself
through new titles,[68] calling them the Justinianic governors, to make
his presence even more tangible to his subjects far from Constantinople. At the same time, he took steps to prevent corruption among his
governors. The careful instructions he gave them indicate a heightened concern for honest administration.[69]
He did not, however, ignore the provincial elites whose support he

needed. The prefaces of his provincial reform legislation show that he cultivated their goodwill by emphasizing in classicizing, historical terms the ancient ties between the provinces and Rome. Ethnic ties, not civic ones, receive emphasis.[70] It is possible, as Rouéché suggests, that the laws themselves were read out before the provincial assemblies that consisted of provincials who held imperial ranks and honors. These assemblies continued to exist well into the sixth century.[71] A law of Justin II's even permitted the provincials (through their assemblies) to nominate candidates for the governorship of their provinces.[72] This concern for the cooperation of the provincial aristocrats, in their civil and clerical capacities, indicates not simply the disappearance of the cities' roles as focal points of local influence, but the emergence of new configurations of authority. How these *honorati* felt about the cities, and to what extent they represent the old urban aristocracy in new guise, we cannot be absolutely certain, though a close identity seems likely.

Lydus (and others like him, we must presume) was reluctant to accept these new facts of life, and so he bears witness to a trepidation about how imperial power might be connected to provincial civic affairs and to how the traditional elites in the provinces might continue to wield their authority locally. At the same time the emperor was searching for ways to deal with an aristocracy that no longer identified completely with the cities.[73]

If the shift from province to imperial center created a sense of dislocation for some, the economic condition of the countryside intensified it. Information is scarce about the countryside in Lydia and the rest of the Diocese of Asia, but Lydus and Procopius describe at least one series of calamities. They describe rotting crops unable to be sold, especially in the inland areas, and harvests plowed back into the soil. They attribute this economic catastrophe in the Diocese of Asia to the economic policies of John the Cappadocian in the 530s and early 540s.[74] The unsold crops resulted from a policy of the commutation of taxes from payment in kind to payment in gold.[75] This saved the imperial government considerable sums because it no longer had to transport the crops to the imperial comitatus.[76] In addition, soldiers were transferred to various battle fronts from their garrison duty in the provinces, which meant that they were not available to help harvest the crops that would have been paid as tax to the government.[77] Lydus, however, was blind to the good intention and perhaps even the occasional good results of this imperial policy.

21

To make matters worse, Justinian required that the tax liability for deserted farms be allocated not only to curials of whose estates the farms had once been a part, but sometimes to landowners who had the misfortune to live in the same census district.[78] The wealthiest curial families managed to avoid the onerous burden while the order in general grew poor.[79]

As the economic situation declined and as the emperor's agents tightened the screws to collect taxes, banditry and lawlessness, always endemic in certain areas of the empire, increased,[80] and a new gendarmerie was established by mid-century to keep the peace in several provinces of the Diocese of Asia, including Lydia.[81] Priests of the oratory of St John in Pisidia petitioned the emperor for protection from brigands, imperial troops, and the magistrates who were seizing their lands.[82] The emperor commanded his representative to arrest, disarm, and punish the mounted, lance-wielding bandits who terrorized the inhabitants of the province of Honorias.[83]

Almost nothing is known of the conditions in Lydus' home town, Philadelphia, beyond the few scraps that he supplies.[84] He mentions in some detail the depredations of Justinian's Prefect, John the Cappadocian, and his evil minions, one of whom he calls "The Laestrygonian, or rather the child-slaying scourge of my native land."[85] His lurid stories of the suffering in Philadelphia have the ring of letters from home:

> This shark-toothed Cerberus, though he was the common plague of all mankind, chewed up my Philadelphia so finely that after him, because it had become bereft not only of money but also of human beings, it could no longer admit any opportunity for change for the better . . . while he remained there, he left behind to none of the inhabitants there any vessel of any kind, any wife, any virgin, any youth unharmed and free of defilement.[86]

Marcus Rautman's recent investigations of the ecology of Lydia around Sardis suggest a dramatic change in the agrarian base of the region in the fifth and sixth centuries. He notes:

> a decline in the cultivation of long term cash crops. Apparently synchronous with this agricultural reorientation occurred a new destabilization of the regional topography, including the accelerated erosion of topsoils and steep slopes previously revetted by terrace farming. A third feature of the fifth century ecosystem involved important changes to the urban water

supply [of Sardis]. The excavated sectors suggest that the flow of water to such public facilities as baths and fountains became increasingly constricted around this time. By AD 600 the supply to a number of buildings and cisterns had shifted from the obsolete high-pressure system to local cisterns and wells, newly installed to serve the needs of the city's [Sardis'] reduced population. The implication of these changes for Sardian urban history reinforces the emerging picture of serious structural problems that undermined the prosperity of the late antique city. In addition to demographic shifts, contributing factors may include marginal climatic fluctuations as well as a breakdown in classical agricultural practices. Recognition of and organized response to these changes appear to have been limited, however, and the decline of the province in the sixth and seventh centuries reflects an inability to maintain its environmental equilibrium.[87]

No comparable study has been carried out in the territory around Philadelphia, the Lydian city that was Lydus' birthplace. Rautman's observations on regional soil changes and water use, however, are most suggestive for Lydia in general. Lydus did not, of course, understand the issues in these terms. He knew that the economy was faltering, but he lacked the conceptual vocabulary to understand the economic causes of this decline. He blamed the rapacity of the government, just as the government, equally aware of dwindling revenues and various manifestations of growing poverty, could only identify causes in terms of corrupt or inefficient administrators. Because Constantine Porphyrogenitus failed to enter Philadelphia on his list of the twenty leading cities of Asia,[88] we may guess that in the next century Philadelphia declined somewhat more precipitously than other cities in the region.

The plague

The factor most disruptive of urban and rural life was the great bubonic plague that ravaged the empire in the 540s.[89] Estimates of the casualties vary, but perhaps as many as 244,000 died in Constantinople alone, about half the city's population.[90] The most recent estimate for the overall mortality rate for the eastern empire suggests that about one-third of the population may have fallen victim.[91] The social and economic effects of this tragedy cannot be overestimated:

deserted farmlands, dramatic reduction of revenues, difficulty in military recruitment[92] – these were only some of the more obvious consequences. The legislation passed in the immediate aftermath of the plague's first assault indicates economic confusion. It dealt with the collection of loans, the heirs of debtors, inheritance and related matters.[93]

We must assume that the plague hit the cities of the empire as hard as Constantinople, and that Lydia suffered like the other provinces of the East, but precise data are unobtainable.[94] Trombley has provided some evidence that the countryside was less affected than the cities.[95] Before the plague, despite other economic setbacks, there is no reason to think that the population of the cities of the east had diminished significantly.[96] Probably more than any other factor, the plague weakened the urban fabric of the east and paved the way for the crises of the seventh century when the Persians and then the Arabs caused so much destruction. By the end of the century the economic deterioration of the cities was marked.[97]

Christianization

Rapid Christianization profoundly affected the cities of the eastern empire and the surrounding countryside. Dagron has sketched the process of Christianization of early Byzantine cities.[98] He notes the "conquête du centre,"[99] a trend visible especially in the sixth century in which ecclesiastical buildings, representative of the established church, began to dominate the urban centers. Though neither obligatory nor constant,[100] the phenomenon does reflect the growing power of the bishops in the towns of the east.[101] Public ceremonial in the cities came to center on the Christian liturgy. Christian festivals dominated public life even at the expense of imperial ceremonial, which became more and more associated with Constantinople alone,[102] the possessor of many important holy relics.[103] In Constantinople the reconstruction of St Sophia facing the palace demonstrated at the highest level the interlocking nature of imperial and ecclesiastical power. The relationship between these two structures formed the basis of the urban plan of the capital.[104] The plans of the lesser cities as well demonstrate the presence of the Christian church and the clergy at the heart of urban life.[105]

These changes were not limited to an increase in monumental Christian architecture. In daily life as well, urban space began to be used differently. A law of Justinian, for example, permitted burial

24

within the city walls of Constantinople contrary to the old Roman requirement of burial outside of the city.[106]

In the same way churches and Christian shrines replaced pagan sites in the countryside;[107] often the new Christian buildings were constructed from building materials robbed from the pagan cult centers they sought to replace. Pagan buildings gradually disappeared through general neglect, and zealous peasants led by their priests chopped down sacred trees.[108] In this regard, Justinian's enormous building program was particularly destructive. During Lydus' lifetime fierce campaigns were undertaken against the pagans surviving in the countryside, and although Justinian's efforts at universal conversion were not entirely successful (recent research has demonstrated that the pagan presence was still quite visible in parts of the empire[109]), they definitely changed the character of rural life.

Christianity had a profound effect on traditional education, too. Although classical oratory was practiced in provincial capitals and in Constantinople into the second half of the sixth century,[110] the emperor did little to promote its growth. Justinian cut off public funds for rhetorical training,[111] and education fell increasingly to the churches and monasteries.[112] By the end of the century literary life diminished, perhaps quite quickly,[113] and Latin faded from the scene.[114] Latin ceased to be the language of legislation, and more than once Lydus drew attention to an oracle of Fonteius that predicted the empire's collapse when the ancestral language should be abandoned.[115] There is also some reason to think that book production declined during the reign of Justinian. A survey of papyri and manuscripts that can be attributed to the period from the end of the fifth century to the end of the sixth has led one recent writer to the conclusion that already under Justinian fewer books were being copied.[116] Book production ground down as readers disappeared, and there was a shift to ecclesiastical production of books and libraries.[117]

CHANGES IN CONSTANTINOPLE

In Constantinople, where Lydus spent his adult life, the changes are better documented. Consequently they give the illusion of greater complexity. Economic distress brought an influx of poor and dis-possessed into the city,[118] which the imperial government tried to deal with in several ways. Justinian created the office of the Quaesitor in 539 as head of a new constabulary to monitor all new arrivals in the city and to make sure that they returned to their homes as soon as their business was completed.[119] Despite the efforts of this officer, however, the city population swelled with poor immigrants.[120] Some of them had come to petition their masters, who now lived at court as absentee landlords, yet another reflection of the heightened centralization of Justinian's system.

Justinian's legislation recognized the presence of the poor in his city and empire[121] as a problem rooted in the abuses of provincial governors and the excesses of the great urban aristocrats of his empire, including those of Constantinople. His laws repeatedly address economic problems resulting from the flight from the countryside to the cities and the administrative abuses that contributed to it.[122] His legislation also facilitated his own political objectives and reflects in part the considerable influence of the Church upon social legislation.[123] In this regard it is useful to emphasize the well-articulated belief in imperial responsibility for the health of the social order – admittedly far from a novel idea but now emphatically restated in this new legislation and directed toward immediate problems.[124]

Recent work by MacCormack shows how Constantinople developed new rhetorical and visual images in the course of the sixth century as public ritual gradually became court ritual. Her study of accession ceremonial reveals that a theory of power and rule developed which placed Constantinople, not Rome, at its very center. And at the heart of Constantinople stood the Hippodrome, the site of the ritual re-enactment of imperial victory in the races and site of public acclamations and imperial ceremonial. Corippus called the Hippodrome an image of the cosmos. Constantinople, now the home to emperors for several generations, began to take on a symbolic value as the center of the empire. In the new urban-based imperial ideology, the emperor, with his unique ties to God, linked the city and the world, heaven and earth. As one of the ritual acclamations put it, "the city desires you, the oikoumene desires you." [125] The power which passed to him from God enabled the emperor to rule the city, the empire, and by implication, the world. By the reign of Heraclius, imperial accession was described only in terms of the emperor's relationship to God and his struggle against the forces of evil.[126] Panegyric spelled out these theories, ceremonial enacted them, urban architecture gave them formal setting, works of art depicted them – and the citizens of Constantinople accepted them as useful representations of the hierarchy of power in the world. The emperor embodied the empire.[127]

CHANGES IN THE PRAETORIAN PREFECTURE

Besides the curial class, the other victim of the reforms, in Lydus' eyes, was the Praetorian Prefecture.[128] The reforms in the provinces were enacted by John the Cappadocian, Justinian's extremely unpopular Prefect. Provincials hated him because of his ruthless methods. His subordinates within the Prefecture (if Lydus may be taken as a representative case) objected to changes in procedure brought about as part of the reforms. In particular a tightening of the mechanisms of appellate procedure, intended to reduce the flood of cases from the provinces and free the legal staff for more important matters, left the Prefect's staff with longer hours and lower fees.[129] Lydus deeply resented it when the Prefecture lost control of the post and the manufacture of arms to the rival bureau of the Magister Officiorum,[130] and he felt insulted that a man from this bureau was given the top job in the Praetorian officium.[131] Other simplifications of administrative practice within the bureau, including the abandonment of Latin,[132] enraged Lydus, who could not see beyond the habits of administrative routine to the advantage gained for the empire as a whole. It was a sad irony that he remained hostile to John the Cappadocian, Justinian's minister, who sought to make the empire more efficient, albeit through ruthless centralization and fiscal policy that relied on the brutal collection of taxes and strict controls of public funds.[133] When the Cappadocian fell in 542 hopes for real reform foundered;[134] Lydus was left with fantasies.

In the next chapter we will examine Lydus' career against the background of these changes and see that his life mirrored the instability of the society in which he lived.

2

PORTRAIT OF A
BUREAUCRAT

Scarce information limits the scope of a biography of Lydus. What personal data we have derives entirely from his own books. Later writers who discussed his work or mentioned his name seem to have had no independent information about him.[1] In this chapter I examine Lydus' career, for connections exist between the events of his professional life and the development of his attitudes about politics and government.

When he was 21 in the year 511, Lydus, like many other ambitious young men from the provinces, went to Constantinople to seek his fortune. He did not attain the throne as did Justinian, an Illyrian, or become the Praetorian Prefect as did John the Cappadocian, or become a historian, like Procopius from Caesarea, or a writer of hymns, an architect, or even a champion charioteer. Instead, he found a niche in the imperial bureaucracy, as a middle-level functionary in the Praetorian Prefecture. He served there with uneven success for forty years, retiring disillusioned and disappointed in late 551 or early 552[2] at the age of 61 or 62.

His career spanned the reigns of Anastasius, Justin, and Justinian, men of markedly different temper and ambition. As a functionary at the heart of the administration, Lydus understood the intricacy of court life and observed the impact of imperial personalities on the shaping and implementing of policy in Constantinople and in the lesser communities of the empire. Lydus' career began well with Anastasius (whom he praised for his concern for the welfare of teachers)[3] and continued satisfactorily with Justin, but Justinian's adventures caused fiscal chaos and indirectly brought an end to Lydus' public life. Justinian's presence in *de Magistratibus* is so obtrusive – and ambiguous – that it is necessary to remind ourselves of Lydus' first successes in previous reigns. His concern for the proper

28

management of the empire took on a particular edge in response to Justinian. Lydus' idealized version of bureaucratic history[4] caused him to see the state in a condition of decline, and he expected the emperor to rectify the situation. We will see in *de Magistratibus* a direct correlation between Lydus' pessimistic view of contemporary society and events and the failure of the emperor to act appropriately.

Lydus was also a man of letters. For the last several decades of his life he taught at the imperial school at Constantinople, although he never devoted himself exclusively to scholarship. That sort of man he felt to be somewhat impractical and out of touch with reality.[5] Instead, Lydus represents another type on the Constantinopolitan scene – the bureaucratic eruditi, civil savants we might say, educated in rhetoric and Latin, philosophy and law, men with the habit of combining traditional education and public service[6] – and in Lydus' case, at least, fussiness about filling out government forms correctly.[7] There was nothing extraordinary about a high civil servant having a good classical education. In 360 the emperors Constantius and Julian had decreed:

> No person shall obtain a post of the first rank unless it shall be proved that he excels in long practice of liberal studies, and that he is so polished in literary matters that words flow from his pen faultlessly.[8]

This goal does not seem always to have been met, but it never lost appeal.[9] In the fifth and sixth centuries there continued a strong link between *philosophia*, *philologia*, and the offices of state. Lydus, like his more illustrious contemporaries Cassiodorus and Peter the Patrician, had intellectual commitments beyond his administrative career.[10] Lydus is unusual for being the only bureaucrat on record to have been awarded a teaching post by the emperor.[11]

In Lydus' eyes, literary success was tightly bound to public service. He took pride in his learning and literary skills which had a recognized place in the imperial administration and which in his case won imperial patronage. In addition to philosophy, Lydus had a special interest in knowledge about the past. In this guise he was part of the "antiquarian" tradition. He collected information about the past, as had many others before him. This tradition of learning made it possible to create the illusion of continuity with antique success and fitted neatly into his views about the character of proper administration. He viewed good government as an endangered species, and tied its demise to administrative decline.

Lydus received a classical education in his birthplace of Philadelphia, of the sort which for centuries had been preparing the sons of the local aristocracies throughout the empire for public service. Presumably it was here he learned Latin.[12] In Kaster's words, "Whatever its other shortcomings, the grammarian's school did one thing superbly, providing the language and mores through which a social and political elite recognized its members."[13] His family was presumably at the top of the city's social pyramid, and evidently Christian. His father, Laurentius,[14] had, after all, given his son a Christian name. The family was also well connected in Constantinople, and, with string-pulling at exalted heights, Lydus eventually entered the imperial service. That he managed to remain at his post, despite anti-pagan purges and a general atmosphere of intolerance during the reign of Justinian furthers the impression that formally, at least, Lydus accepted the Christian faith. Christianity, however, did little to shape the views expressed in his surviving works. At school he absorbed from his teachers the idea of guardianship of a precious literary heritage, as well as a broader and perhaps less well-articulated sense of an urban tradition.[15] Service in Constantinople in a bureau with proud and ancient traditions further reinforced Lydus' custodial interest in the past; *de Magistratibus* is a monument to the history and procedural habits of a great bureaucratic office. His long years in the Prefecture may well have been as influential as his classical education in shaping his conservative point of view.

Though he spent most of his life at the center of the empire, Lydus retained considerable pride in and affection for his home town, Philadelphia,[16] especially for its ties with pagan antiquity, even going so far as to claim that it had been founded by Egyptians.[17] He records as well a word in the "ancient Lydian tongue,"[18] and asserts that the idea of honoring the year as a god began in Lydia, as well as giving other bits of Lydian mythology.[19] This wealthy city, an Attalid foundation with impressive Hellenistic walls and parapets, traditionally controlled the Cogamis Plain and the hilly land to the northeast[20] from its vantage point on a spur of the Tmolus range. The area was known for its earthquakes, and Lydus describes a festival for avoiding such disasters.[21] The city had been especially prosperous in the third century[22] and won the extremely prestigious title "Temple Warden of the Augusti,"[23] indicating its role in the provincial imperial cult.

By the fifth century Philadelphia had earned special distinction for its temples and festivals. Lydus fondly remembered the age-old festival of Janus celebrated at the new year.[24] The students of Proclus referred to Philadelphia as a "Little Athens," because the city with its festivals and beautiful temples had once made their master feel at home during a period of political danger at Athens,[25] a fact that Lydus reported with pride. He also boasted of Philadelphia's reputation as a center for learning. His frustration and outrage at the harsh treatment of Philadelphia and Lydia at the hands of Justinian's fiscal ministers[26] demonstrates that he was well aware of the ways in which provincials, both well-born and poor, could suffer at the hands of imperial administrators. While he remained blind to the faults of his own class and tried to distance himself from the abuses of the bureau in which he served and prospered, he showed concern for the thousands of impoverished countrymen who thronged to the slums of the capital.[27] No such sentimental recollections ever color his mentions of Constantinople, however; he knew the disappointing reality of the capital only too well.

Lydus initially found it slow going upon his arrival at Constantinople. Competition was quite keen for the post he sought, that of *memorialis*, a secretarial post in the *sacra scrinia*,[28] and he found himself with free time as he waited to be accepted into that bureau.[29] Studious soul that he was, Lydus began attending the lectures of Agapius, a neoplatonic philosopher then in vogue in the city. Agapius, a student of Proclus,[30] was evidently an effective teacher, for Lydus later filled his books with philosophical material of various sorts. *De Magistratibus* would be shaped by philosophical theories.[31]

A change in administration put an end to Lydus' formal studies: when another Philadelphian, Zoticus, became Praetorian Prefect in 511[32] the young man's career began to take off. The Prefect found him a position in the Prefecture as an *exceptor*, a shorthand secretary, the starting point for all careers in that bureau.[33] The post and the influence to peddle that came with it proved extremely lucrative. In his first year Lydus earned in addition to his normal salary over 1000 solidi in fees.[34] Full of gratitude to Zoticus, Lydus composed a panegyric in honor of his patron. A suitable reward followed: Zoticus gave him a solidus per line from the public treasury.[35] At the encouragement of another highly placed relative, Ammianus,[36] Zoticus arranged a suitable marriage for his young protégé. In *de Magistratibus* Lydus remarked upon his bride's good character and dowry of 100 pounds of gold[37] – and never mentioned her again.

At some point during this same first year Lydus received an additional prize. He was enrolled among the *adiutores* of the *ab actis* – that is, he became an assistant to the official who dealt with civil cases and held responsibility for keeping judicial records.[38] He was given the title of "first" *chartularius*, the normal nine-year probationary period being waived.[39] Not only did he not purchase this appointment as was customary, he received an additional annual salary of 24 solidi. This appointment was even more remarkable because of his youth, and Lydus himself called the appointment unprecedented.[40] His two colleagues were old men who had bought their positions and drew no salary but made their livelihood from fees.[41]

When Lydus started his career, Latin was still used to some extent as the official language of government in the Greek east, though the precise degree is difficult to determine.[42] Within the offices of the eastern Prefecture, however, Latin had been abolished by Cyrus (Prefect 439–41),[43] much to Lydus' dismay. He thought the Prefecture had lost its good fortune when decrees appeared in Greek,[44] and several times he cited an oracle that predicted the fall of the Empire when the ancestral language should be abandoned.[45] By the time Lydus began his career, full control of the ancestral tongue had become a specialist's tool, and Lydus' linguistic training proved of considerable value. Imperfect as his knowledge may have been,[46] Lydus advanced partly on the basis of knowing Latin. From his first promotions to the imperial commissions of his mature years, he worked in offices in which knowledge of Latin was essential.

Lydus' skill at Latin was of utmost value in fulfilling the responsibilities of *chartularius*. He composed in Latin the legal briefs (*suggestiones*) for cases referred to the Senate[47] on appeal. He drew up the registers of cases and persons (the *cotidiana* and *personale*) to appear before the court of the Praetorian Prefect.[48] In addition, he assisted other *adiutores* who worked in the palace on legal matters, performing his tasks so successfully that "as though equipped with wings" he rose to the ranks of the *a secretis* at court.[49] The precise responsibilities of the post in the palatine bureaucracy during the Justinianic period are not known; in the preceding century, however, the *a secretis* were the pool of secretaries to the *consistorium* from among whom the emperors chose their particular secretaries.[50] The position of imperial *a secretis* conferred more prestige than being a mere *praefectianus*.[51]

Also during the reign of Anastasius, Lydus served as *chartularius* of the *scrinium* of the *commentarienses*, possibly in 517.[52] The emperor entrusted the *commentarienses* with confiscations and banishments;[53] from the earliest stages of his career Lydus knew the cost of imperial disfavor, for he was actively engaged in implementing such imperial decisions. Victims included men of similar background to Lydus.[54] We may suspect a conflict of loyalties.

At some point Lydus abandoned his double career by giving up his tasks in the palace and devoting himself full-time to the Praetorian Prefecture.[55] The reasons for this decision are not clear.[56] Caimi suggests probably the best one. In December 524 the emperor Justin prohibited with few exceptions the holding of two or more public offices.[57] Lydus had to choose between the two posts and decided to stay in the Prefecture.[58] He subsequently felt he had made the wrong decision:

> Since I was expecting far greater things to come to me as time went on, I abstained from my zeal for the court and devoted my whole life to the service.[59]

The note of disappointment in his voice is real, for his career never flourished again as it did in those early years. He continues:

> When in all respects public affairs had been brought to such a state as this account has recorded, and when in addition fortune was showing disfavor to men of literary attainment, something that had not happened before, I came to hate the service.[60]

The sequence of his narrative is confused and perhaps misleading, for some important and positive things did happen to him between the time he "devoted his whole life to the service" and the time he "came to hate" the Prefecture. In particular, Lydus' knowledge of Latin and reputation for scholarship was brought to the attention of Justinian. The emperor invited his learned servant to deliver a panegyric in Latin before an assembly of visiting dignitaries from Rome.[61] He also requested that Lydus prepare a history of the most recent Persian war which had witnessed the valiant and successful resistance by the fortress of Dara of a Persian siege, probably in 530.[62] The peace treaty was concluded in the spring of 532.[63] It seems most likely that the imperial commission to write the history, now lost,[64] should be dated to the spring or summer of 532. Phocas, the aristocratic Praetorian Prefect for whom Lydus showed great respect,[65] held office at this time, and we may suppose that Phocas sponsored Lydus. This suggests a date between January and October 532 for his commission.[66] Such imperial favors do not suggest a faltering career. In Lydus' mind, Phocas' months in the Prefecture were a period of favor for literati. It was the time when Lydus received his important commissions. During these months immediately following the Nika revolt, Justinian attempted to cultivate the political support of the conservative, educated elite.

In October, however, Justinian felt secure enough again to dismiss Phocas, and the Cappadocian returned to the Prefecture. It was probably at this time that Lydus felt that "fortune was showing disfavor to men of literary attainment," and he "came to hate the service and turned all [his] attentions to literary efforts." [67] Caimi points out that there are no firm chronological points to which his dramatic change of heart toward the Prefecture may be connected, [68] but the second Prefectureship of John the Cappadocian is indicated. Whether Lydus was reacting to the growing influence within the Prefecture of men with expertise in finance but not of high culture or whether he was feeling the lack of sponsorship of Zoticus or Phocas, it was during the second Prefectureship of John the Cappadocian that Lydus' career slowed. The dates of composition of *de Ostentis* and *de Mensibus* further this argument. As we have seen, *de Ostentis* was compiled in reaction to the Persian sack of Antioch in 540, [69] and both books were dedicated to the Prefect Gabriel who held office in 543. The mid-to-late 530s and early 540s were presumably the years in which Lydus devoted his free time to private literary projects.

In *de Mensibus* Lydus mentions a visit to Cyprus; [70] perhaps this was in connection with the provincial reform of 536 which made Cyprus part of the new Prefecture of Scythia, [71] cutting it off from the Prefecture of the East. A special law court was established, and Lydus may have been involved in its organization. [72]

A few years later, sometime between 539 and 541, a legal reform earned Lydus's resentment. Justinian changed the structure of the *iudices pedanei* [73] to the great disadvantage of the professional rhetors who practiced in this court [74] where Lydus served for an unspecified time as a *matricularius*, or "custodian of the registers." [75] Lydus objected that the position was no longer lucrative because important business was no longer being transacted there. [76] He blamed John the Cappadocian for these changes. [77] Even though the Cappadocian lost his post in 541, the position of men with literary training continued to deteriorate. [78] In the mid-to-late 540s Justinian began to conduct purges of intellectuals and rhetors. In 545–6 Phocas was publicly disgraced and driven to suicide. [79] If Lydus' period of disenchantment began at the end of Phocas' consulship, it is tempting to wonder if Lydus meant to associate literary attainments and paganism in some way.

While Lydus complains of "hating the Prefecture" and points to the anti-intellectual position of the government, it is clear that his own career proceeded apace. He did not lose imperial favor. Justinian acknowledged Lydus' literary efforts with a letter to the Praetorian Prefect that was intended to confirm Lydus' standing and service in the *officium* of the Prefecture. It commended his scholarship, literary skills, and erudition proven in the course of the decade and awarded him a teaching post at the imperial school in Constantinople.[80] The date of this appointment to the professorship is uncertain. Perhaps *de Ostentis* and *de Mensibus* had become known and enhanced his literary reputation. Lydus implies that the professorial appointment was part of the reward for his literary services. Lydus does not choose to comment on the fact that his prestigious new job came at a time when other literati were being purged. Perhaps only overtly pagan scholarship was singled out, but this seems unlikely, for Justinian's attack on traditional education was not presented as an anti-pagan endeavor, and Lydus speaks of erudition, not pagan erudition. Because in 543 the urban prefect was Gabriel to whom *de Mensibus* and *de Ostentis* were dedicated,[81] it has been suggested that Lydus' appointment to the school occurred at this time.[82]

Lydus reproduced Justinian's letter:

> We are conscious of the fact that the most learned John's education in scholarship, both his precision in language matters and his grace among poets, and the rest of his erudition are, indeed, extensive; and that, in order to render by his own efforts the language of the Romans more dignified, although he is properly discharging the service in your Excellency's courts of justice, he has chosen along with it both to spend his life among books and to dedicate his whole self to scholarship. Therefore since we judge it to be unworthy of our times to pass over unrewarded one who has ascended to such a degree of excellence, we instruct your Excellency to present him . . . a grant from the public treasury. Let the aforementioned most wise man know, however, that we will not stop at this but will reward him with both dignities and greater imperial liberalities, because we consider it absurd for such eloquence to be deemed worthy of so small a reward, commending him if he should impart also to many others the skill which he possesses.[83]

Accordingly, Lydus began to teach in the Capitoline school without surrendering any of his other responsibilities to the Praetorian Prefecture.[84] It is likely that he continued to receive a salary for his work in the Prefecture, without the fees that were an additional benefit of that position.[85] Presumably he held the post until his retirement. The precise nature of his teaching responsibilities is unknown, though perhaps like his colleague Eugenius, a grammarian and poet who taught at the imperial school late in the fifth and early in the sixth centuries, his lectures included metrics, orthography, and lexicography.[86] It has been suggested that the material compiled in his books originated as his "lecture notes," but this sort of information would have fitted awkwardly into the usual curriculum.

De Magistratibus telescopes the rest of his career, and the next thing about his service he mentions with any enthusiasm is the ceremony marking his retirement from the Prefecture in late 551 or early 552.[87] On that occasion the Prefect Hephaistus[88] read a decree full of praise, the terms of which show how Lydus wished to be honored and remembered. It says that Lydus preferred the sobriquet "most learned" to all his formal titles and that his erudition won him the admiration of his students. His involvement in civil affairs – that is, his service in the Praetorian Prefecture – was accomplished in harmony with his studies. The letter ends with a comparison to the emperor Justinian who

> in addition to his other excellences is obviously also a lover of
> learning, time having effected this well in our own time in order
> that our august ruler might lead also the rest of our entire
> political order to something more illustrious.[89]

This letter is instructive. It shows that in the 550s the pursuit of learning was still represented as an imperial virtue, even after the purge of rhetors and intellectuals a decade earlier.

His rank at retirement may have been *cornicularius* (if he had become an *augustalis* due to his reputation), but Lydus did not mention that he himself held this rank in any of the numerous mentions of *cornicularius* in *de Magistratibus*,[90] an uncharacteristically modest oversight. More likely he held the lower rank of *primiscrinius*.[91] At retirement he obtained two new titles, *tribunus et notarius vacans* and *comes primi ordinis*.[92] And then as he put it, "I went on again with my books."[93]

Lydus was a particularly Constantinopolitan variety of bureaucrat.[94] His ideas of service to the state and its ruler as well as to his bureau are compatible with the New Rome at mid-sixth century. Though Lydus deplored the mismanagement in the provinces, he never doubted the need for a centralized, effective government run by a well-educated bureaucracy and guided from the top by a learned emperor. While nostalgic for vanished curial institutions, he never suggested that they be restored. He objected to administrative reforms that would have improved conditions in the provinces because they diminished somewhat the primacy of the prefecture. In his deliberate grafting to the imperial figure aspects of learning that had been the preserve of traditional education throughout the cities of the empire, he implicitly diminished the distance between the center and the outlying regions. Perhaps most indicative of a Constantinopolitan point of view, he bound magistracies to imperial power by tying the growth of the Roman state to the development of its offices.[95] The Constantinopolitan character of his interests is important because it points to the success of Justinian's centralization and the emergence of the Byzantine myth of society. That Lydus complains about changes and anti-intellectual sentiments in the Prefecture even as his own career advanced suggests that he may have felt guilty about his service in this bureau. His conservative tendencies emerge quite strongly in his complaints about change, but he survived quite well. It is time now to turn to the idea of tradition itself, to see how and why it was important in Lydus' day.

3

THE IDEOLOGICAL TRANSFORMATION OF TRADITION

When Symmachus made his case to the Emperor Valentinian II in 384 to have the Altar of Victory restored to the Roman Senate House, he argued that regular sacrifice at the altar had made Rome great by guaranteeing victory to her rulers and peace to her subjects. He asked for tolerance of the pagan cults by the Christian emperor, suggesting that age-old rituals and ceremonies might be discontinued only at the peril of the state.[1] A few years later the Christian Prudentius scoffed at this opinion. In his tract *Contra Symmachum* he explained that Roman customs and rituals in fact had changed to the benefit of society,[2] and that it was only reasonable to follow the new, divinely revealed teachings of Christianity.[3] This exchange neatly encapsulates two late-antique approaches to the idea of continuity with the past, one idealistic in its emphasis on uninterrupted rite, the other pragmatic about human dependence on custom and the desirability of change, but both confronting altered circumstance through a historical lens and both prepared to find value in the lessons of antiquity. The two opposing camps recognized antiquity's power to anchor legitimacy, but in this instance Symmachus' plea for pluralism fell on deaf ears.

During the age of Justinian these alternatives were finally resolved. Under the aegis of a Christian emperor, a belief in the efficacy of maintaining Roman traditions combined with recognition of the desirability of change. At Justinian's court sensitivity to antiquity was transformed into an ideological tool of both imperial *sollicitudo* and aristocratic self-definition, and for a while it provided the idiom of political argument between them. Justinian's administrative reforms provoked political opposition. Though still couched in pagan-vs-Christian rhetoric and concerned with explaining change, the pressing issues became the nature of imperial power and what role the past should play in justifying the new Justinianic political order. The result

38

was one of the major developments in sixth-century political theory, in which motifs and ideals were integrated to form an essentially Byzantine idiom of history and power.

For the synthesis to be successful, several things were required. Justinian had to affirm and clarify connections with the secular past in his role of Emperor of the Romans. He had to establish himself formally as the guarantor of continuity with his great predecessors, with his victories seen as an extension of all the triumphs that had made Rome great. It was necessary to demonstrate that his exercise of power through laws and arms conformed to ancient practice and were not innovations but restorations of the Roman order. (These elements will be discussed below in the section "Justinian cultivates the past.") He also needed to develop a theory of power in Christian terms that rationalized the need for change within the state; thus, explanation of reform sought a place in a completely Christian hierarchy of power and in law. This is evidenced in the new theory of legal sanction introduced by Justinian that elaborated the origin of imperial power in the Christian God. In this role the emperor was at once the incarnate law and sole lawgiver, the chief magistrate of the state, and the chosen representative of heaven on earth. (This material will be discussed below in the section "Justinian the Christian restorer.")

In the midst of these developments Lydus stood very close to pagan thought. We shall see through comparison with the pagan Zosimus how he perpetuated an idea of maintaining links with the past through continuity of "rite" – not sacrificial but administrative and so devoid of religious association. Lydus' theory of magistracies made change necessary and desirable. In this effort he paralleled developments generated by the palace. Unlike the imperial makers of propaganda, however, Lydus carefully avoided Christian expression. He could not accept their synthesis of Roman power and Christian sanction, and so, in the long term, his theories could not enter the mainstream of Byzantine political expression. His handbooks would be only museum catalogues. The imperial position clarified by Justinian, on the other hand, would be at the center of society, joining not only heaven and earth, but also past and present in the Christian empire.

JUSTINIAN CULTIVATES THE PAST

The weight of tradition

Byzantine society's awareness of its ties to the past is a vexing issue. Many scholars have regarded such ties as retardant;[4] but Edward Shils suggests more positively that traditionalism can become self-aware and productive:

> The traditional transmission of beliefs and knowledge is not one that is sought. . . . The "search for a usable past" is something quite different. . . . The drumming up of tradition . . . or the recommending of the observance of traditions which were no longer being generally received, represents an ideological transformation of tradition. It is certainly quite remote from the process of traditional transmission.[5]

We may expand this idea to suggest that the idea of "drumming up" connections with the past – not merely the transmission of ideas through time – may be useful in describing social activity. Such was indeed the case during Lydus' lifetime; in Justinian's Constantinople consciousness of tradition did not retard political development, though there was no consensus on the identity of tradition. In the absence of a developed ideology of progress to legitimize change, the force of tradition directed attention to antiquity, and arguments about ties with the past fuelled political debate.[6] Justinian, Zosimus, and Lydus "drummed up" tradition in different ways.

Which past to choose?

The sixth century held no unified view of the past. Many pasts, Greek, Roman, local and civic, Biblical and New Testament, tied to different literary and cultural traditions competed for the attention of sixth-century theorists.[7] One's access to these pasts was determined by one's education and the simple sense of belonging to a cultural or political tradition.[8] With no priesthood or synods to determine and protect doctrine and dogma, the non-Christian past was passive, to be approached and recast by anyone with the interest and education to do so. The educated elite of the sixth century had to make the effort of confronting the past and incorporating it into their theories, to choose an historical point of view. They did so with the help of intense training in rhetoric and classical literature, yet Zosimus, Lydus, and Justinian all did so in different ways. Since historical knowledge was often inexact, a creative ideologue was relatively free to cast history and traditions as necessary to further his theories or claims to authority.

It is necessary to point out that not only were there different pasts available, but each carried different internal dynamics. Choosing one over another meant adopting a specific attitude toward historical interpretation and so toward analysis of change and, indirectly, toward imperial power. For someone who accepted Christian history, for example, events in the past could take on prophetic meaning for the present. The elaborate constructs of patristic typology let the past be brought into the present in non-linear ways: witness Abraham, Melchizedek, Justinian, and Christ all co-temporally present in the San Vitale mosaics. Without strain Malalas began his Chronicle with Adam, not Romulus. Cassiodorus made Joseph the first Prefect – in Pharaoh's court.[9] From a consciously pagan point of view, events in the past had a quite different value, and continuity could be valued for little more than its own sake or as an insurance policy against disaster. Zosimus, for instance, believed wholeheartedly that the empire had fallen into ruin because of the abolition of the secular games. Though there were many pasts, I shall focus here on only one, the Roman past, especially as it was tied to the imperial office.

The importance of the past to the expression of imperial power

When scholars discuss early Byzantium's perception of imperial power they tend to isolate several conflicting sources of legitimation for imperial activity: first, the authority that comes from God, next, that which comes from the senate and people, and finally that conveyed through the army.[10] The first avenue of legitimation might be called "sacerdotal" and the latter two "magisterial." The former refers to Christian attitudes about sovereignty that had been developing since the time of Constantine and Eusebius. These made the emperor the sole delegate of God on earth,[11] a divinely selected and protected gift to humanity.[12] The "magisterial" refer to Roman political attitudes that had developed prior to the addition of Christian motifs to the ideological repertoire. They derived imperial power from certain institutions: those of the republic, which made the emperor the chief magistrate,[13] and those of the army, which reflect the realities of the third century in particular. Since the fourth century there had been a tension between sacerdotal and magisterial avenues of legitimation, and their relationship has often been studied and is well understood.[14] Though this "magisterial/sacerdotal" model can be quite useful in understanding the sixth-century issues that confronted Justinian and Lydus, it is incomplete, since it does not adequately

41

account for another legitimizing force, namely that conferred by the past, through the invocation of tradition.

The exercise of power in practical day-to-day terms does not always conform to theory. It is the job of theory, rather, to put the best face on immediate circumstance or to analyze and justify after the fact. So when we consider Justinian's search for legitimation, we should look beyond the confines of "constitutional theory" to see what other devices could be useful to the emperor.

The past could legitimize imperial action in several ways, for political change might be validated through appeal to a past that provided exempla of successful rule. The emperor accordingly had a vested interest in appropriating the legitimizing aspects of antiquity, if for no other reason than to facilitate his own policies. Admitting to innovation remained taboo, but the need to react to changed circumstance never went away, as Prudentius understood and as the new legal theory developing during Justinian's reign established. Justinian's bringing the legitimizing forces of antiquity into the imperial orbit should be understood as a calculated attempt to exploit certain predispositions of a political group for political purposes early in his reign.

To clarify this point, it is useful to consider the past in two regards, as an indicator of social and professional identity, different for emperor, bureaucrats, and aristocrats, and as an element in political struggle. No one advocated innovation, but the call for restoration raised questions about what to restore and how.

First, the Roman past could be a peg of identity for the urban elite schooled in the classics. For Lydus and other similarly educated men to feel that they participated in and protected the traditions of antiquity gave meaning to social life. Classical culture was part of what they were. But by the reign of Justinian it was also something of which they had become artificially aware, and so it was to a degree dissociated from them. To write in a classical style or describe a defunct civic ritual or feel a particular allegiance to some imagined past conditions, was something that one might choose to do, as Lydus chose to collect data on magistracies, calendars, and portents. Such self-conscious effort suggests a proprietary and custodial attitude, and at the same time reveals a sense of discontinuity from the past and disengagement from the present.

With regard to the bureaucracy, Lydus' effort in *de Magistratibus* to demonstrate the antiquity of the Praetorian Prefecture and its singular importance to the Roman state implies a like-minded audience within that bureau. These are the peers he thanks for encouragement and support in his literary efforts.[15] Obviously the members of this particular branch of the civil service took pride in their office. Perhaps there were even "in-house" histories of the office in the archives from which Lydus drew. Certainly the functionaries of the Praetorian Prefecture were well aware of the historical importance of their bureau. We may suppose the other great offices of state had similar traditions and strong allegiances; Peter the Patrician, for instance, wrote a history of the Master of Offices, which unfortunately is now lost. *De Magistratibus* shows that an historical point of view was central to a conception of bureaucratic practice and proper government.

Since, for the emperor, identification with Roman antiquity constituted yet another technique for the expression of imperial power, the "search for a usable past" entered the realm of policy-making and propaganda. By distinguishing pagan cult from classical learning and ceremonial, as his laws clearly do, Justinian liberated the material from pagan associations. He was now a bit freer to appropriate what he wished of the past. The imperial office thus emerged as a point around which these disjointed bits of the past might find a new orbit, even though the church sometimes frowned or turned a blind eye. The emperor would put himself forward as the special preserver of antique traditions. And so the Vota and the Brumalia continued to be celebrated by the palace as late as the tenth century.[16]

Such imperial self-aggrandizement posed a threat to Lydus and like-minded men of his class who by training, education, and conservative instinct identified closely with antiquity. It was their own tradition, urban not imperial, that was being taken in hand by an overbearing parvenu. If he were to assume these custodial associations with the past, what would be left for them to protect? Yet in *de Magistratibus* Lydus provides the very handbook for an emperor bent on restoration, and he concocts an elaborate philosophical theory to enable the act of restoration. In this light it is not coincidental that Lydus stresses knowledge of the past as an imperial attribute.

The role of the past took a place, then, in a subtle struggle between the emperor and the mandarinate, both concerned with self-definition, the latter with survival as well. Uncertainty gave the past a high profile and politicized the possibility of association with it. The new *arcanum imperii* – and the real threat to men like Lydus – was the compatibility of the secular tradition with Christianity.

Classical emphasis

As Averil Cameron has shown, "Any notion of Justinianic classicism as a simple or unified phenomenon must be rejected. The concept has no explanatory force; on the contrary, it must itself be explained." [17] One part of an explanation comes from seeing how Justinian exploited associations with the past. Rather than suggest a general "classical revival" for the reign, it seems better to argue that at different times in his reign cultivating an association with classical antiquity became a special part of his imperial program. These connections never stood in the way of the emperor's Christian propaganda. They always were tied to up-to-the-minute expressions of the emperor's authority as a Christian ruler.

One period of political classicizing began in the immediate aftermath of the Nika revolt. This ill-fated insurrection had been caused by a number of factors.[18] Though the sources are somewhat hazy, it seems that many nobles were involved who were angry at the fiscal policies of Justinian's Prefect, John the Cappadocian. They also disliked the quaestor, Tribonian, whose reforms did away with certain tax-exemptions and reorganized the laws of inheritance and succession.[19] The spark was struck when crowds in Constantinople took to the streets, eager for vengeance on the City Prefect, Eudaimon, who had ordered some lynchings. At the same time, perhaps even orchestrating the insurrection from behind the scenes, an aristocratic claque led by Justinian's nephews attempted to seize the throne.[20] The crowd demanded that three officials be removed, Tribonian, Eudaimon, and John the Cappadocian, and gained a temporary victory with their dismissal, and the emperor nearly fled the city. As is well known, the insurrection was cruelly suppressed. Thirty thousand or more perished at the hands of Justinian's bodyguards. Nevertheless, Justinian acceded to some of the demands, and removed the three officials from office. The new Prefect, Phocas, a well-regarded patrician, had been suspected of paganism a few years earlier, but his pedigree made him acceptable to the angry aristocrats and his service to the state and willingness to cooperate made him acceptable to the emperor. Not all the aristocracy wanted to remove Justinian. The choice of Phocas is the first indication that Justinian was willing to cultivate the goodwill of the aristocracy up to a point in choosing the replacement for the Cappadocian and that appeal to the past might be a way to assuage their fears. (The laws to which the nobles objected

stayed on the books.[21]) In this instance it was no coincidence that the
new minister was classically trained.

By the middle of the decade a classicizing mode had come into
vogue. A detail of court panoply illustrates a delight in archaizing
details. Lydus explains that the *Excubitores*, Justin and Justinian's old
unit, "still" wore the uniform which Romulus had established, himself
following Aeneas.[22] Though Lydus knew that this corps had been
established by the Emperor Leo,[23] the conceit is indicative of current
pre-occupations. After the unexpectedly sudden victory of Belisarius
over the Vandals in 534, imperial propaganda began to present the
campaigns in the west as a mission of restoration of the old imperial
domains.[24] The original excuse for the invasion had been the restoration of orthodoxy to the Arian Vandal kingdom in north Africa.[25]
The triumph accorded to Belisarius upon his return to Constantinople
(and, interestingly enough, orchestrated by Tribonian[26]) was perceived by Procopius, an eyewitness, to have had archaizing features.
As McCormick has shown, however, even these elements were firmly
subordinated to imperial authority.[27] Belisarius no less than the
vanquished Vandal king ended the triumphal parade grovelling at the
emperor's feet. But the tone of restoration had been set: "To Rome
Justinian restored what was Rome's," recalled Lydus two decades
later.[28] In contrast, when another triumph was celebrated in 559 to
mark the victory of Belisarius over a group of Huns, the archaizing
elements had vanished.[29]

JUSTINIAN THE CHRISTIAN RESTORER

It is the series of reform laws enacted between the years 535 and 538,
however, that best exemplifies the careful cultivation of antiquity for
propaganda purposes and its integration into a Christian theory of
kingship and law.[30] The reform legislation was intended to eliminate
corruption, redefine the relations between civil and military administrators, improve appellate procedure, and enhance the power of
provincial governors. By ensuring the well-being of his subjects,
Justinian hoped to win the favor of God; by casting the reforms in
antiquarian terms of restoration, he hoped to win the favor of the
classically educated administrators; by directly linking provincial
history to the capital, he side-stepped the cities and centralized his
power.[31] The prefaces of these laws strove to create the illusion that
the contemporary reforms merely built upon ancient precedent. For
this reason they contain a great deal of historical information, often

highly contrived, that purported to connect past and present. For example, Justinian's Novel 25 (May 535) begins:

> We have thought it right to adorn the nation of Lycaonia with a greater form of government than its present one since we have considered those first beginnings from which comes the present nation of the Lycaonians, according to those who have written about ancient matters. They have informed us that the Lycaonian nation is most closely akin to the Roman people and, on the same evidence, practically wedded to it. Long ago Arcadia in Hellas was ruled by Lycaon, and he began the settlement of the territory of the Romans. After he had seized the land of the Oenutrians he gave a beginning to the Roman empire. We are speaking of times far more ancient than those of Aeneas and Romulus. When a colony was established there he seized a large portion of Pisidia, which he named after himself, calling the land Lycaonia. Hence it is only just that the administration of this province should be ornamented by investing it with a sign of the ancient Roman magistracies. And now its current administrators, that is, the civil and military governors, should be joined into one office and decorated with the title of Praetor. This title is part of the patrimony of the Roman people.[32]

This explanation garbles legend and completely overlooks the true historical connection of the two nations. The emperor's need to join the civil and military administrations found its true justification, in fact, in the dual nature of the praetorship itself.[33] This antiquarian pose found expression in a new theory of legal sanction that invoked Christian divinity in a more complex way than had ever been done before. Justinian understood his rule to govern every aspect of his subjects' lives:

> The legislator (we mean the one invested with sovereignty) of a government should direct his attention everywhere, should see that everything is properly conducted and that nothing is neglected.[34]

Such watchfulness was necessitated by random, unpredictable changes in society. In the theory of legislation developed in Justinian's *Novels* and also in the *Code*, the idea of Nature as a disruptive force in society to which the emperor must respond in his guise as lawmaker gained a prominence lacking in the prior legal tradition.[35] As Novel 84 (AD 539) explains:

46

Nature, everywhere inclined to the production of numerous innovations (this prelude has often been employed in legislation but will constantly be repeated as long as Nature persists in these practices), has induced us to enact many laws.[56]

The state of flux that characterizes human society required constant legislation, for no law

has ever been sufficient to provide for all cares, but . . . laws have need of much correction in order to be adapted to the inconstancy and perversity of Nature.[37]

Thus Justinian found justification for all his activities, including the purges. God had given to him alone the capacity to make law and mend society, but he must never innovate or be rash himself in his legislation, for

it is certainly not the part of a well-established and powerful government without good cause to alter and divide what for a long time has been settled and confirmed.[38]

In this way historical precedent took a heightened role; restoration, a propaganda byword of Justinian's early reign, found a place in legal theory in a new way. The consequence of just administration by the emperor would be God's favor for mankind;[39] it was not necessary to spell out the cost of weak and ineffective rule. God would judge the emperor and punish him if he did not meet the challenges caused by Nature. He needed the legitimation of the past to be a proper Christian monarch. This complex interplay of Roman past, imperial legislation, and divine sanction in Christian terms was new in Roman legal theory.[40] Complementing these developments in legal theory are such figural representations as the Barberini ivory, dated to this period,[41] that shows the emperor on horseback in the centuries-old triumphal posture, but now beneath a medallion of Christ. The well-known equestrian statue of Justinian (now lost) suggests the same idea and emphasizes further the new order based at the New Rome. As MacCormack puts it, "An old iconography, that of the mounted, triumphant emperor, riding, usually, over a fallen enemy, had been used in a new context, where movement had become localised in one place, in Constantinople."[42] Divine favor had enabled the reconquest of Vandal Africa and the early victories in Italy.

The momentum did not last forever, and this officially sanctioned cultivation of the classical past fell out of sustained use after a decade when the disappointments in the west and the shock of the plague turned Justinian's attentions to other matters. Classical culture never regained this officially sanctioned resiliency.[43] The classicizing, imperial idiom did, however, have an afterlife. Lydus' concern with restoration kept in step with the expectations that the imperial propaganda had raised and tried to exploit in the 530s, but which remained only as disappointed dreams when he wrote *de Magistratibus* in the 550s.

FROM ZOSIMUS TO LYDUS

Lydus was not the first writer in the Greco-Roman world to have believed that his was an age of decline; such a gloomy view doubtless was already old when Hesiod wrote. The idea of decline played a special role in Roman society where the past in general was so overvalued that conformity to precedent became the measure of accomplishment. By late antiquity, belief in contemporary decline had become not merely a literary topos or simply a reflection of the contemporary political scene. In the wake of the loss of Roman political control over what had been the western provinces and the consequent fierce debate between pagans and Christians about the reasons for the sad state of affairs,[44] the notion of contemporary decline took on an added vigor and a special importance. In the fifth and early sixth centuries Romans of both east and west speculated about the significance of calamitous events; Saint Augustine's *City of God* was certainly the most influential response, Justinian's ambitious schemes of reconquest and reform arguably the most dramatic – and without doubt the most expensive. It must be stressed that a shared belief in "living in an age of decline" need not require shared agreement on why or how that decline had come about, or even whether or not it was irreversible. Contemporary decline (as they saw it) so upset some fifth-century writers that they composed elaborate apocalyptic visions imagining the impending end of the world.[45] Yet their predecessor, the embittered historian Ammianus, scorned men who believed "the state was never before overspread by such a dark cloud of misfortune."[46] Among philosophers the theme of living in a corrupt state was a commonplace as well, stretching back to Plato's *Republic*; in Lydus' day the neoplatonist Simplicius elaborated on this theme, making clear allusions to contemporary circumstances.[47] Procopius' *Historia Arcana* complains of the destruction of the empire under the demonic rule of Justinian,[48] and Justinian, of course, saw the empire in need of correction. Lydus' lacrimose attitudes find a place in the context of contemporary disillusionment. *De Magistratibus* would never have been written if Lydus had been less haunted by ruin. That Lydus explains decline not from a theological or geopolitical but from a bureaucratic point of view makes his criticism especially timely and helpful in understanding the transformation of society in the Justinianic empire. As Justinian and his purges mark a highpoint of anti-pagan repression in the sixth century, Lydus stands at the end of a diminuendo of pagan polemic against Christianity and Christian intolerance. Though the bureaucrat never attacked Christianity directly or advocated pagan worship, we hear in his political expression the echoes of an angry tradition. In that long argument between pagan and Christian a simple formula had given shape to the recriminations on both sides: failure to act properly resulted in divine disfavor. The issue had become responsibility for decline and the misfortunes of the empire.[49] Through comparison with the attitudes of his near-contemporary, the pagan polemicist Zosimus, we can see how Lydus adapted certain anti-Christian attitudes to his own theory of decline.

The pagan historian Zosimus wrote a *New History* in the early years of the sixth century.[50] This book lamented the barbarization of the empire and the decline of pagan worship.[51] It is difficult to gauge the degree to which his belief in decline was accepted by his peers, for his book did not receive much attention from other writers. Only the church historian Evagrius, who wrote in the second half of the century, shows that Zosimus' work had gained some currency as a pagan attack on Christianity.[52] Evagrius attempted to refute Zosimus' criticism of Constantine and the church for causing Roman decline. Certain similarities between Zosimus' arguments about decline and those found in *de Magistratibus* help show how the transition from a pagan interpretation of imperial decline to Lydus' stance, with its implicit acceptance of Christianity, was possible. Though separated by nearly a generation – Zosimus was active chiefly in the reigns of Anastasius and Justin – the two men seem cut from the same cloth. Both belonged to the imperial civil service in Constantinople, where Zosimus served as a treasury advocate.[53] They speak for a world of Constantinopolitan functionaries upon whose shoulders ultimately fell the mundane tasks of implementing the policies of their superiors. Both expressed great fondness for tradition and felt sharply Rome's decline. Both discussed Roman history from a vantage point of deterioration, and they shared a concern for the decline of the Praetorian Prefecture. Like Lydus, Zosimus occasionally gave glosses on the origins of different magistracies.[54] These similarities reveal their experience in the civil service. On the issue of continuity and decline, though, they illuminate an important aspect of sixth-century social change.

Though much of his polemic was absolutely standard, Zosimus deviated from the polemical tradition by ignoring the religious policies of Julian and by failing to criticize any specific doctrines.[55] He placed great importance on the performance of rite and believed that the empire had lost divine protection by neglecting pagan ceremonies.[56] This emphasis on performance of rite warrants attention, for his concern for the precious links between divine aid and proper forms of worship was a fundamental prop of his understanding of the operation of the human and political universe. In Zosimus' scheme, the proper observance of rite guaranteed Rome's rise. His paganism was based on cultic observance and found meaning and expression in his analysis of history. Proper observance enabled the success of the Roman government. Precisely the same issues, as we have seen above, goaded Justinian into action, though his equation of course expressed itself in Christian terms.

Goffart correctly points out "the preoccupation of sixth century Byzantium with understanding the relation between past measures and present problems," [57] but he does not emphasize sufficiently the shared faith of Lydus and Zosimus in the importance of continuity,[58] as evidenced in Zosimus' words "As long as the above was performed precisely . . . the Romans kept their empire . . . but, the rites having been neglected . . . the empire gradually ebbed." [59] Goffart stresses Zosimus' belief that the abandonment of the ancient rites of worship of the pagan gods was a chief cause of the fall of the empire:

> [Zosimus] did not miss the ancient gods. Instead he castigated the innovation that consisted in abandoning the gods. Their abandonment summed up to him the multitude of innovations . . . that were responsible for bringing about the desolation he saw about him. Far from being a pagan votary, Zosimus invoked the worship of the gods chiefly as a symbol of the secret of Empire. Empire like religion is a ritual with unchanging forms; religious repetition of the ritual assures eternity. . . . Faithlessly the Romans departed from ritual; they innovated and disaster ensued. This is the message of Zosimus.[60]

The same might be said of Lydus as well – once the overtly pagan references were taken away. Lydus shares Zosimus' belief in the necessity of maintaining traditional forms, but does not deal with the same subjects. He focusses exclusively upon aspects of administrative procedure. This fascination with regalia and procedure should not be lightly dismissed as mere antiquarianism; throughout *de Magistratibus* such information had a real importance as the physical expression of an office's essential identity and historical career. Lydus believed in the maintenance of proper regalia and nomenclature of offices, for these were the tangible expressions of a magistracy's existence; he distinguished magistrates from the offices they held. Maintenance of regalia was necessary so that the office would not be forgotten. For Lydus, maintaining or dismissing these rites and regalia determined the office's continued existence. Thus the tangible symbols of office must be protected if continuity is desired. Lydus illustrated this principle with the career of the tyrant Domitian:

> Domitian . . . came near to wiping the memory of the Master of Horse clean away, by not leaving axes, standards or even the so-called rods to the office.
>
> (*de Mag.*, II.19)

Why had decline set in? Zosimus and other pagans saw Constantine's conversion of the empire to Christianity as the beginning of the end.[61] Zosimus and Lydus continue in this fashion, accusing Constantine of immoderate and innovative taxation and of erroneous frontier policy.[62] Zosimus devotes a long passage to Constantine's division of the magistracy of the Praetorian Prefecture into four regional prefectures and his removal of military authority from the Prefect's area of responsibility.[63] Lydus also pointed to this decision of Constantine as the first step in the Prefecture's demise, though he was careful to explain the military and economic reasons that forced his hand. While Zosimus criticized Constantine's Christianity, Lydus made no direct attack. Most Christian writers, on the contrary, saw Constantine's reign as the end of the beginning, as it were. The Theodosian Code began with the legislation of Constantine. And even if they were forced occasionally to be desperate about the turn of events, Christians could be optimistic in their woe; for them history had a definite direction toward the end of days and final vindication, the Last Judgment.[64] Justinian blamed the sloth of his predecessors for the empire's woes.[65]

Lydus differed from all these interpreters. Unlike his Christian and pagan peers, he gave no active role to gods or to human worship, remaining as mute about contemporary pagan rite as he was about

Christian theological controversy. The gods were completely dissociated from his interpretation of events and natural phenomena. For him, generation, decline, and regeneration constituted a constant, natural pattern manifest in human activity. When he talked about the *aitiai*[66] of the Praetorian Prefecture's decline, his explanations were based upon an analysis of economic factors, combined with a belief in the importance of human decision-making and human virtues – or lack of them. Proper government had become, in effect, the "sacral act" [67] that must be performed for the well-being of the state. Lydus expected the emperor, not the gods, to be the restorer of magistracies and the guarantor of prosperity. His sense of antiquity, his interpretation of historical causality, his conscious debts to antique knowledge all stand independent of overt pagan association. By limiting his subject matter to the operation of magistracies in history he could side-step the sore points of Christian–pagan debate.

There is, however, one major issue over which Zosimus and Lydus would disagree: that the empire had ended. Just as it was basic to Zosimus' arguments that Rome had fallen and that his world was that of a "successor state,"[68] so it was essential to *de Magistratibus* that the empire was still very much a going concern, even though it might be in a state of *phthora*. The right emperor – perhaps Justinian – could set things straight again. This, of course, was the operative premise of Justinian's policies, at least in the early years of his reign.

Three points of view, then, depended upon the interpretation of continuity. Justinian's position tied Roman history to Christian sovereignty: guarding and maintaining tradition took a formal place in imperial ideology. For Zosimus, a pagan bureaucrat, it was the continuity of pagan rite that guaranteed the prosperity of the state; he would have agreed with Symmachus. Lydus, finally, tried to have it both ways: he was close to pagan thought in his silence concerning Christianity and his emphasis on the need to maintain traditions, yet he accepted Justinian's desire to restore the empire. In the next chapter we will see how Lydus fitted into the antiquarian tradition and used antique knowledge in a variety of ways that were not so directly touched by ideological concerns.

4

DE MENSIBUS AND THE
ANTIQUARIAN TRADITION

> The attention therefore to Erudition is also beautiful, which
> Pythagoras expended, in order to correct the order of mankind.
> (Iamblichus, *Life of Pythagoras*, ch.12, trans. T. Taylor, London,
> 1818)

"Time is the creator as well as the destroyer of its own progeny,"
states the first chapter of *de Mensibus*, and the introduction of *de
Magistratibus* tells us that "time is the creator and concealer"
of human works. With these clichés Lydus articulates his fear of
discontinuity with the past and justifies his erudite endeavors.[1] How
Romans and other peoples organized time into its various units is the
general subject of *de Mensibus*, the most straightforwardly antiquarian of his works – and least revealing of sixth-century ideas
beyond the fact of its composition. Need we assume that Lydus
practiced what he described? Did the antique data have only a
museum value for Lydus by the time he collected it, making the
treatise primarily a custodial venture? Or may we find Justinianic
Constantinople in its pages?

Addressing the slippery character of sixth-century antiquarianism,
Herbert Hunger posits a running battle between the champions of an
intellectual paganism and those of Christianity, fought in part on the
field of antiquarian studies, and he locates Lydus in this context.[2]
Momigliano called Lydus "altogether a representative of that revival of
interest in old Roman customs and institutions which is characteristic
of Justinian's reign."[3] These scholars outline the broad problem for
discussion, but do not explain Lydus' fascination with antiquarian
material. What does Lydus' choice of topic reveal about himself and his
milieu? In Paolo Mastandrea's words, cultivation of the past in late
antiquity was not "a response to the whim of a fatuous public concerned

only with bizarre curiosities, but [was] obedient to a precise historical and cultural choice."[4] What choices does *de Mensibus* represent?

The social tensions and dislocations of the Justinianic period provide a general context for the work. Quite naturally men like Lydus sought reassuring evidence of continuity. Compiling anti-quarian handbooks was one among many small ways to shore up the present. Affecting a classicizing literary style such as we see in Procopius' imitation of Thucydides,[5] insisting upon the continuity of administrative procedures – as Lydus does in *de Magistratibus*, dressing palace guards in costumes from a mythical past,[6] and resurrecting a venerable ceremony such as the triumph,[7] were all efforts to bring the past tangibly into everyday life.

As a collection of calendrical material, *de Mensibus* reflects a different contemporary expression of uncertainty – a strong interest in chronology and methods of recording dates.[8] In the course of the century, Christian schemes of reckoning came to the fore in different areas. Christian chroniclers following in the footsteps of Eusebius established a dating system that integrated antique history with a Christian scheme of time.[9] The "anno mundi" style of reckoning time came into vogue at Constantinople while the old Roman system of giving the date by kalends, nones, and ides gradually fell into disuse; Heraclius' laws were the last to give a date in these terms.[10] Novel 47 of Justinian required that indictional dating be given on all official documents, as well as his regnal year and the consul's name (until consular dating was abandoned in 541).[11] Various coins of the period indicate indecision about conventional methods of indicating the date.[12] The religious calendar of the church required classification and regulation as well, with considerable debate about the proper date of Easter. In the course of this discussion, Dionysius Exiguus, a Roman cleric, devised the now-familiar system of dating "anno domini," although it did not come into general use for some centuries.[13] We may infer Lydus' misgivings about calendrical changes from his hostile remark that Theodosius II had put an end to Olympic dating; he used the verb *neoterizo*, which carried the negative association of unwelcome innovation.[14]

It is easy to sneer at *de Mensibus* as trivial and to forget the pedigree of such an antiquarian endeavor, however; for many years before Thucydides created political history, Greeks had been writing "systematic treatises"[15] about different aspects of antiquity. No precise ancient term existed for this enterprise; *"archaiologia"* probably comes closest to our "antiquarianism."[16] Lydus never explicitly placed himself within this tradition [17] but his readers would have understood. He knew at first or second hand the works of dozens of antiquarian writers[18] and was proud of his erudition. The first paragraph alone of *de Magistratibus* mentions Capito, Fonteius, Varro, Sallust, and Gracchanus. He drew from the collections of Aristophanes of Byzantium,[19] Athenaeus,[20] and Diogenianus the Lexicographer,[21] as well as the better-known treatises of Varro[22] and Cato.[23] Lydus used second-hand references to books lost in his own day that were of special importance to his research, such as *On the Office of the Praetorian Prefect* by Aurelius Arcadius Charisius.[24] His familiarity with such an array of writers was in part due to his own industry and in part to his grammatical and rhetorical training: antiquarian expertise was necessary for any orator who wished to dazzle his audience.[25] His peers shared the education and interest, and some composed antiquarian books, too, on a wide range of subjects. Closest to home was his contemporary Peter the Patrician, who wrote about the history of the Master of Offices.[26] We may also point to Hesychius of Miletus' lost biographical dictionary of pagan writers and scholars;[27] the geographical lexicon of Stephanus of Byzantium, an epitome of which was created almost immediately and dedicated to Justinian;[28] the anonymous handbook on political theory, in which two high state functionaries talk as comfortably about the proper relations between the emperor and the senate as about military tactics in ancient Greece, to name only a few.[29] Other writers affected antique language, which was difficult for the unschooled to understand, and included in unsystematic fashion details about the past.

This learned fascination with the past can be partly explained by their education in classical literature and their reverence for – and delight in – antique forms. At first glance *de Mensibus* would seem to do no more than this. Unlike *de Ostentis* and *de Magistratibus*, *de Mensibus*, the earliest of Lydus' monographs, addresses no issues of Justinian's court directly nor does it attempt to explain current phenomena. At least as the text stands today, without a formal statement of purpose, it seems that Lydus only intended *de Mensibus* to relate information about the weeks and months of the year and that he wanted to provide an extended commentary on aspects of the ancient Roman calendar as many other writers had done in earlier centuries. The book's odd array of calendrical data can have had little religious significance to Lydus, for it does not describe the calendar used at Constantinople in the mid-sixth century. Instead, *De*

Mensibus focusses exclusively on the non-Christian past. To some extent, this reflects the elite's pleasure in and curiosity about the traditions of their ancestors. It is the past at its least political – the acceptable face of classical learning.

In a recent discussion of the ritual calendar in the late republic and the early empire, Beard suggested that "the ritual calendar as a whole can be seen as a conceptual pageant of Rome and of what it was to be Roman . . . not a fixed, unchanging view of Romanness, it incorporated new, changing, divergent images of what Rome was." [30] She stressed that the calendars were produced by men who "practiced or observed the rituals" and insisted rightly on "tak[ing] the rituals and the preserved exegesis together . . . as an important part of a religious discourse." [31] We may, in similar fashion, find some ways to understand Lydus' idea of "what Rome was" from *de Mensibus* in its original arrangement and treatment of material.

ORGANIZATION AND DESCRIPTION

Perhaps the most remarkable thing about *de Mensibus* is its organization. The book consists of four major sections, or books, that treat different aspects of the calendar. The first is fragmentary, but seems to deal with the oldest Italian calendars and the institutions of Numa. The second book deals with the days of the week, the third with the months in general, and the fourth with the months in sequence, listing holidays and festivals. No precise models for this arrangement survive. None of the sources that Lydus mentions on festivals, as far as we can tell, dealt with the week as part of the Roman year. Fasti dealt with the year as an entity; as we will see, this type of source is mirrored in his Book IV. It cannot be proven from silence, but the structure of *de Mensibus* appears to be highly original.

Book I

A modern reader will be hard-pressed in the face of the mutilated condition of the text to discover the precise topic of the first book.[32] It may have been intended as a general introduction to the work, though not to the year as a whole.[33] Wuensch, its most recent editor, argued in 1898 that the fragments contribute to a consistent argument and theme: namely, how the earliest religious customs pertaining to the calendar came to Italy from Lydia, the author's homeland.[34] Lydus describes the solar year which Numa instituted and the lunar system it replaced,[35] but not until Chapter 13 does he mention Aeneas, who brought calendrical data to Italy. Chapter 14 describes Romulus' foundation of Rome, states the city's birth horoscope, and gets *de Mensibus* off to its proper start with Romulus' establishment of a ten-month calendar that began in March. Chapter 15 discusses the numerical significance of the number 10. Such numerological comments play a highly visible, though subordinate, role in *de Mensibus*.[36] Soon we hear how King Numa began the twelve-month year.[37] Numa is described as a contemporary of Pythagoras (a very old tradition), thus bringing together a "historical" figure, Numa, and a mode of analysis, numerology. The subsequent chapters of Book I have little relevance to an explicitly calendrical theme.

Book II: the days of the week

Substantive discussion in Book II commences in the second chapter with the times of day at which Babylonians, Egyptians, Hebrews, Umbrians, Athenians, and finally the Romans of antiquity as well as of Lydus' own day considered the natural day to begin and end.[38] Lydus next offers several explanations for the number of days in the week: the seven rhythms of the movements of the planets and the number of the planets.[39] The remainder of the book discusses each day of the week in turn, including when the day began,[40] the name of each day, the relationship of each day with a planet, and the numerical significance of each day. Scholars have noted many errors.[41]

For his discussion of the days of the week, Lydus marshalled information from many sources, and his treatment is notable for the original application of his information, particularly numerological lore. He is concerned with pagan myth, and though he never mentions Christian subjects, he reveals a dependence on Christian structures.

Lydus' week is especially noteworthy because it begins with Sunday: he followed the Christian system.[42] The week had come into widespread use in the Mediterranean world only during the first and second centuries AD. Its origins in the Roman world lay not in the Jewish week of seven days that would become an influence through Christianity, but in the so-called planetary week of seven days which took its arrangement from the seven planets.[43] Different astrological schemes, however, produced different arrangements of the planets, and different sequences of the days' names were followed in different parts of the empire for reasons still not clearly understood.[44] Sunday gradually became the first day of the Christian week, and when Constantine recognized Sunday officially as the day of rest in 321,[45] the victory of the Christian week was assured. Despite the opposition of church leaders, however, the pagan names of the days were commonly used by Christian worshippers, particularly in the western part of the empire. In the east planetary names of the days never caught on, as witnessed still in Greece.

That Lydus started with Sunday and followed the sequence of days preserved in our calendar[46] is not surprising, of course, since he was a Christian, but it does indicate the artificiality of his presentation of antique data. Though he avoided Christian reference, Lydus did not attempt to resurrect any archaic pattern of the week. In fact, he gave no indication that he was aware of any alternatives, and he avoided the opportunity to discuss the matter in the fourth chapter of Book II where the origin of the week is considered and where such a treatment would have been appropriate. At this point in the text, we learn only that the Chaldeans and the Egyptians established the seven-day week based on the number of planets. And "they called the first day 'one' from the monad . . . [and they] associated [it] with Apollo, that is, the sun." [47] Lydus' tacit acceptance of the week as it had taken shape and gained respectability in Christian hands demonstrates the thorough penetration of Christianity into the most mundane levels of daily life.

The second striking aspect of his discussion of the week is his application of old, but still useful, numerological science to the days of the week. When he tells us that the sun, like the monad, is simple, masculine, and productive (II.6) or that the number 2 is female, has sides of uneven length, is impure and empty (II.7) he speaks from a millennium-long tradition of arithmetical investigation.[48] Allegedly begun in the fifth century BC by Pythagoras, this system of knowledge, while enduring many interpretations, amplifications, and changes, had become widely diffused in popular thought as well as in the formal philosophical speculation of Christians and pagans alike. The fourth century AD witnessed a renewal of interest in Pythagorean teaching; the neoplatonists Porphyry and Iamblichus both wrote about Pythagoras.[49] Pythagorean teachings constituted an important fund of knowledge still applied in Lydus' century,[50] and Michael Psellus would excerpt Iamblichus' *On Pythagoreanism*[51] in the eleventh century. Lydus' knowledge of this field, then, is unremarkable.

Numerology, as the variations of "Pythagorean" doctrines are commonly called,[52] considered arithmetical relationships and numbers to be manifest in the organization of the cosmos and to be an attribute of divinity – if not divinity itself.[53] Despite their different formulations of the number's relationship to divinity, the different philosophical schools shared some beliefs: exterior to human experience there were principles thought to be operable both in the non-sensible spheres above the moon and on our physical world as well. Reality was derived from these numerical principles.[54] Philosophers were charged with the task of exploring and explaining the arithmetical principles, for numbers could reveal the secrets of nature and even divinity. This venerable tradition of investigation and explanation took different shapes, ranging from what seem to us to be the more genuinely "scientific" enterprises of mathematics and astronomy, to less easily accessible areas of arithmology,[55] astrology, and the occult in which numbers have "qualities that are not in any sense mathematical." [56] This more "mystical" approach to numbers won immense popularity.[57] That we find Lydus closer to this "non-scientific" pole should not blind us to its respectability. His numerical explanations were neither "antiquarian" in a pedantic sense, nor did they represent a "superstitious" break with a more "rational" tradition.

Among Lydus' works, numerology is limited to *de Mensibus*, and there almost exclusively in the second book, where he discussed the numerical significance of each day of the week. These passages diverge from mainstream arithmetic theory in ways that illustrate Lydus' ability to adapt the source to the requirements of his own text. Each day took the number of its sequence in the week. That number associates the day with a series of phenomena in which the number is also manifest and which Lydus listed. For example, he associated the fourth day with the fourth planet; philosophers linked it to the tetrad; Pythagoras said the soul has four straight sides; there are four foundations of the soul, four positions of the sun, and four phases of the moon (II.9). We see that every day took significance like other phenomena of the natural world, as it manifested qualities of a number.

Though Lydus cited many different philosophers associated with numerological investigation, including the legendary Pythagoras himself, Philolaos, Timaeus, and Nicomachus of Gerasa, that most important figure at the heart of all mathematical knowledge in the late empire, in fact his material came primarily from one source, a first-century neo-Pythagorean compendium which had wide influence in subsequent centuries in different recensions.[58] Philo had depended on a quite similar edition,[59] while Nicomachus, Macrobius, Theon of Smyrna, and others drew from more distant versions.[60] Lydus cited some of these writers on occasion. Thus sources which Lydus may have known independently of the primary source were themselves indebted to it.

Where comparison is possible, it appears that Lydus alone applied his data to the weekdays with consistency. Philo, for example, in *de Opificio Mundi*, the work that shows the clearest traces of a source similar to Lydus', comments upon fewer numbers.[61] Nicomachus did not turn his attention to weekdays and numbers in either his *Introduction to Arithmetic*, which survives,[62] or in his *Theologumena Arithmetica*, which we know from Photius and various fragments.[63] Christian writers, just as easily seduced by the interpretive and symbolic values of numbers, on occasion could dabble in number theory in describing the importance of certain days of the week – but not in the fashion of *de Mensibus*.[64]

We may be fairly secure that Lydus' source on numerology presented its information in elucidation of the first ten numbers, not in terms of a seven-day week. The decad was the basic number sequence, often discussed and generally accepted as containing all the basic information about numbers.[65] In his presentation of the week, Lydus offered information about numbers 1 through 7, and 10. We find data about 8 and 9 in Book IV in the discussion of the eighth and ninth months, the only two months discussed in numerological terms. Evidently Lydus had a source that dealt with the decad, not the week, and he also did not want any of his research data to be wasted.

The conclusion must be that while there was precedent for using numerical analysis to understand the week, Lydus followed his own star in applying number data to the weekdays.

Book III

In the third book of *de Mensibus*, Lydus offers a wealth of general information about the length, names, divine and numerological associations, and chief festal divisions of the Roman months. He compares Roman and non-Roman material, and he demonstrates an interest in the relationship of these data to theories of generation.[66]

It should be mentioned that the introductory chapter of Book II appears to be out of place and might serve better here:[67]

It seems necessary to me to speak about the months, from what source and how each of them took its name, and in what way each was observed religiously by the Romans – at least as far as we can gather such information from the Roman historians. [I also wish to speak] about the differences of the years, periods, and times, and the hour of dawn, in ancient times. My hope is that these observations will fall sweetly on the ears of my readers.

After the lunar month is mentioned (III.3), Lydus refers to the *Timaeus'* theory of generation, which returns our attention to the Platonic influence on his works.[68] A long discussion follows of the cyclical nature of the number 10 (i.e., in a ten-month year, the year always begins again from the same spot at which it ended). Next comes a learned disquisition upon the number of months in calendars of the Egyptians, Arcadians, Sicyonians, Latins, and Romans both ancient and modern.[69] Here the theme of generation reappears to tie the moon firmly to all generated life that we know. Numa then is described as establishing the twelve-month year, following Pythagorean theory, and giving each month three festivals, the kalends, ides, and nones. This is followed by a long discussion of the gods with which the kalends, ides, and nones are associated as well as methods of computing the days between them, and the number of days in individual months. Lydus gives an explanation of the great year and the cycles of the planets.[70] He provides a list of the names of the twelve months among the Greeks, Athenians, Hebrews, Egyptians, and Romans, and what each people considered to be the first day of the year. He describes Rome's three New Years – priestly (in January), national (in March), and the cyclical or political (in September).[71]

Book IV

This final section of *de Mensibus* possesses the most interesting structure, for Lydus uses calendrical fasti as a model, and it contributes to our understanding of the ambiguous character of old festivals that had lost their association with pagan cult, but which in later times the Church would see in sharper contrast to a more thoroughly Christianized environment.

As Ovid composed his *Fasti* in verse, so Lydus in Book IV gives his readers in prose a description of a year's festivals and related information. The organizational scheme of his "prose calendar" is repetitive. Each month is presented in sequence, beginning with January.[72] Lydus starts the discussion of every month with a treatment of its name. If a name derives from a god or goddess, Lydus explains the deity's name as well as the astrological associations of the planet that bears the divinity's name. If an emperor has given his name to the month, we learn something of his career and accomplishments. When the month's name is derived simply from its ordinal rank in the year, Lydus explains that the count began in March, with the old Roman New Year (IV.122, p.158). He takes the trouble to include this information only through October. By November he brusquely notes his earlier explanations of the same point. Sometimes the numerical significance of each month's position is explained.

From early times the Romans had worked to explain and discuss their calendars,[73] and *de Mensibus* belongs in this tradition. The fourth book of the treatise derives ultimately from two approaches to the calendar. The first consists of commentaries upon the year and its festivals.[74] Some Roman authors wrote fasti that included grammatical and historical explanations of the days.[75] Lydus knew at first or second hand the most important of the commentaries, especially that of Varro, the polymath of the age of Julius Caesar.[76] Most of the works of Varro and other writers that he mentions are now lost, for example Anysias' *On the Months* and two different books, both called *On Festivals*, by Cincius[77] and Phlegon of Tralles.[78] He knew Cornelius Labeo's *Fastorum Libri*, referred to in *de Mensibus*,[79] but not Suetonius' *On the Roman Year*, now lost. Lydus cited Ovid once in *de Mensibus*[80] and may have known other poetic works of commentary, but no clear links are evident. Since Lydus often gave the name of authors cited by an intermediary without naming the intermediary[81] and since very little of this material survives in any case, it is difficult to determine precisely which were Lydus' chief influences. The issue is further confused by the fact that the main works constituted the nucleus of a fairly fixed corpus from which many authors quoted by Lydus themselves freely drew.

Laterculi fasti, graphic charts of the year, are the second source for Book IV. We possess two relatively late examples, the fasti of Furius Dionysus Filocalus (354 AD) and of Polemius Silvius (448–9 AD).[82] While there is no indication that Lydus knew either of these, he was familiar with similar calendars through his research. Roman scholars had always taken it for granted that calendars had to be explained, and Lydus shared this interest in interpretation. We may consider the calendars of Filocalus and Polemius Silvius as the two extant, graphic equivalents of the "prose calendar" of Book IV. A brief description of them will help us understand Lydus' work.

The fasti of Filocalus are presented in the usual fashion of Roman calendars. Days are arranged in parallel columns, with each day noted on a separate line. In its first three columns are the usual nundinal letters marking out the sequence of the days of the month. The fourth column numbers each day according to the kalends, ides, and nones. In the fifth column appears special information: the games, days on which the senate might meet, festivals, and imperial birthdays. The position of the sun with regard to the zodiac also appears for each month. Though every day of the month is indicated, not every day receives annotation. No Christian data are recorded on this calendar, even though Filocalus certainly was a Christian, as indicated by his association with the Pope.

The calendar of Polemius Silvius, composed nearly a century later, follows roughly the same arrangement. Polemius probably consulted the calendar of Filocalus.[83] Following the name of each month and above the parallel columns, Polemius Silvius gave the names by which the month was called among the different nations (Hebrews, Egyptians, Athenians, other Greeks) and sometimes inserted a very brief comment. Below this, the first column numbers each day beginning with the kalends. The second column provides data about special days; both Christian and pagan festivals appear, as well as imperial birthdays, days of civil importance such as the designation of consuls and praetors, and occasional lengthier notes explaining a day's importance in slightly greater detail. A third column lists weather conditions.[84] As in the Filocalan calendar, not every day received comment, but Polemius Silvius' purpose was different from Filocalus'. He was less concerned with interpreting the fasti than with noting additional information on Roman themes that he felt to be worth remembering, such as the birthdays of Cicero and Virgil. Polemius Silvius drew this information from his own research and not from calendars of the public year or of the Christian year.[85] In this way he expressed academic and custodial concerns beyond those normally found in a calendar.

These older fasti that include varied historical and explanatory material anticipate Book IV. Polemius Silvius' very willingness to incorporate Christian and non-Christian material represents fifth-century realities, just as Filocalus' choice to ignore Christianity reflects the circumstances of his own day. In contrast, Lydus' calendar is a mirage, mirroring neither past nor present. The fourth book of *de Mensibus* was not intended to be a calendar in the formal sense of the fasti, but nevertheless, its silence on contemporary matters is unsettling.

Like these fasti, *de Mensibus* follows the order of the months and days, though it does not comment on every day. As previously noted, Lydus included a wealth of information on many subjects. His treatment of festivals should be singled out.

The celebration of religious festivals lay at the heart of urban life in the Roman empire. Their processions, sacrifices, and history – some were of great antiquity – contributed to a city's identity. They filled the calendar and gave a pattern to the year and to one's life in the city.[86] Christianity's impact on these urban rhythms was profound; suppressing the festivals was not easy for they were so absolutely a fact of urban life. In time, the Church could offer a well-developed system of festivals and rituals as an alternative and then as a substitute.[87] As we will see in the next chapter, a half-way solution undertaken by Christian regimes was to permit festivals as long as no sacrifices were offered, for sacrifice was considered to be definitive of paganism. In some places pagan festivals still took place openly. In other towns, festivals continued as they always had, though emasculated without sacrifice; living in a city required them. In the sixth century the situation had not been settled once and for all. We need to know much more about these festivals in Lydus' day, for they measure the degree of Christian penetration of traditional urban life.

In Book IV Lydus limited himself almost exclusively to festivals from pagan Roman antiquity. Trajan is the last emperor mentioned by name,[88] and at least a third of the festivals described took place in the city of Rome itself.[89] There are no references to Christian celebrations, and we find no mention of the great festivals of the city of Constantinople, such as its birthday on May 11.[90] Lydus did, however, mention some festivals of antiquity, such as the Vota and the kalends, which continued to be practiced at Constantinople with the full approval of Justinian because they had lost – or because it was possible to ignore – their pagan origins. We may rightly conclude that *de Mensibus* was not written to defend pagan rites or to argue for their restoration. Instead, it shows how pagan rite had been transformed into a more acceptable, if still ambiguous, practice.

Lydus' description of the Brumalia, however, hints that the situation was not in fact quite so simple.[91] This popular holiday, celebrated between November 24 and December 17, was a time of dinner parties and wishing one's friends "vives annos." [92] It had an extremely long history connected with the celebration of the winter solstice, and Lydus gives many details of the pagan rites associated with it in antiquity. The holiday continued to be celebrated in Lydus' time, for he notes that "to greet someone by name during the Brumalia is a rather recent development," and more pointedly, "the truth of the matter is that people call this the festival of Cronos; consequently the Church shrinks away from this affair." [93] He goes on to tell about Cronos and the association of chthonic demons with the festival. If it were not for the mention of ecclesiastical disapproval, we would not know that the festival had any contemporary dimension at all. This is all the stranger because Agathias reported without censure of any sort that the Brumalia was being celebrated by the citizens of Constantinople at the time of a great earthquake in 577. [94] Malalas also described the contemporary imperial celebration without flinching. [95] We know that Justinian celebrated the Brumalia on a lavish scale with banquets and spectacles throughout the empire, as Choricius of Gaza's *Oration* attests. [96] In 521 Justinian had inaugurated his first consulship with magnificent entertainments during the Brumalia (on the day that began with the first letter of his name). [97] As spelled out in Novel 105 some years later, this was in accordance with his attitude about the ceremonial responsibilities of the consulship to provide parades, games, and theatrical productions for the populace. [98] The pious emperor felt no impropriety in celebrating the Brumalia together with the consulship. In another law concerning pagan worship, Justinian reiterated the idea that ancient festivals might be celebrated by his subjects – as long as no pagan sacrifices were performed. [99] We see here the grounds on which he was prepared to celebrate time-honored festivals. He was no more concerned about the "paganism" of the Brumalia than he was about that of the consulship. Both were simply part of the secular ceremonial of everyday late-antique life, as far as the palace and the public were concerned. On one level *de Mensibus* can be seen as a simple expression of this interest and of the acceptance of certain civic celebrations.

Lydus' comment on ecclesiastical disapproval, however, suggests a more complicated situation and requires that we look to a later period. Such ceremonial did not forever remain immune from charges of religious impropriety. By the end of the next century, attitudes would change considerably. The Quinisextum Council ("in Trullo") held in Constantinople in 692 proscribed in its sixty-second canon celebrations of the kalends, Vota, Brumalia, and Panegyris, [100] festivals going on in Lydus' Constantinople and all described in *de Mensibus* as they existed in Roman antiquity.[101] Pagan associations that the church found merely objectionable in Lydus' day assumed greater significance in the seventh century. Why did Lydus make a point of the church's censure when the Brumalia was being celebrated without comment by the emperor and devout Christians? He evidently recognized its pagan (as opposed to merely antique) history, but did not wish to elaborate further. Perhaps the antiquarian material had not been completely neutralized after all.

This chapter has shown how Lydus participated in several traditions of ancient learning: calendrical commentary, numerological lore, and discussion of festivals. We saw how he unwittingly applied his data to structures that were already Christian, though he affected to ignore that fact. We saw how he used some of his knowledge to his own ends, thus demonstrating flexibility and originality within the antiquarian tradition. He provides no hint that he may have practiced any of the pagan rites he described; even if he were not a Christian, the material in *de Mensibus* for the most part does not reflect sixth-century conditions. Some of the material clearly has only "museum value" for him, while other information he finds current and useful. No political message lurks within *de Mensibus*. Devoid of outspoken political or religious comment, the book illustrates the acceptable, living face of ancient learning. We will see in the next chapter how other sorts of knowledge fell under imperial ban.

5

PAGANISM AND POLITICS

De Ostentis begins with a discussion of signs and portents among the Hebrews, using the story of Moses and the Exodus as illustration. Someone other than Lydus at some later date, however, must have added this prooemion to the manuscript, for its definitions of signs (manifest in comets) and portents (earthly phenomena that transcend nature) bear no resemblance to those employed by Lydus in the remainder of the text. In fact, in none of his works does Lydus display any significant interest in the Bible. To have begun *de Ostentis* with such a nod toward Christianity would have been entirely out of character for him. The same is true of *de Mensibus*. At the end of Lydus' treatment of traditional January celebrations (none of them Christian), there has been added a quotation from Isaiah proclaiming that God abominates such festivals and sacrifices.[1] Once again we confront a sentiment utterly at odds with the intellectual outlook evidenced in the rest of the book.

My purpose in this chapter is not to discuss the manuscript tradition of these works of astrology and ancient religious practice or to speculate when the biblical passages were added.[2] Instead, I examine the political consequences of Justinian's simplification of culture. If a pious copyist at some later time felt compelled to add biblical passages to the manuscript, Lydus in his own day did not. How should his silence on Christian matters be understood? I believe that Lydus' avoidance of Christian reference was as much a political as a literary issue, for although it is true that feigned ignorance of Christianity characterized the classicizing writings of some of Lydus' contemporaries, Justinian's virulent anti-paganism (manifest in part in attacks on traditional education), coupled with his efforts to legitimate some of his projects by reference to the Roman past, produced an environment in which one's stance toward antiquity could be a delicate matter. Lydus' works are a kind of barometer of the pressures on the intelligentsia.

Imperial policies of repression can tell us much about the status of the antique under Justinian, for at this time cultural identification became a political issue for several interrelated reasons. First of all, Justinian staked a claim to the legitimizing aspects of antiquity. Emperors since Augustus had sought to anchor their regimes in this fashion. For Justinian, the issue was complicated by a classically trained elite that defined itself in terms of association with antiquity and felt threatened by his economic and anti-intellectual policies, and by certain ambiguities surrounding the definition of paganism. Justinian faced the need to dissociate "useful" aspects of the past from paganism. The custodial attitude toward the classical past that through education and conservative instinct had been characteristic of an aristocratic point of view now became the subject of conflict and competition. Thus, in delineating proper connections with antiquity, imperial action helped shape a particular palace-centered view of society and history that threatened an entrenched establishment. Second, in a sudden, drastic tightening of the rules of acceptable religious activity, Justinian renewed attacks on pagan belief.[3] As Chuvin puts it, "From Justinian on, all pagans were condemned to civil death." [4] Paganism, which in earlier reigns had been tolerated to some extent among professors and high court functionaries,[5] was anathema to the emperor. Justinian's intertwined goals of eliminating wrong belief and removing his political opponents frequently merged under the aegis of anti-pagan persecution, and this gave allegiance to the classical past a new, political dimension. Lemerle writes:

> The invectives against the "madness of the impious Hellenes" had mostly been until then the work of Christian polemicists: the emperor and the State took them over and adopted, as a principle of government, the intolerance which was in the very nature of Christianity.[6]

Yet, as we will see, the definition of this "impious madness" remained uncertain, and so a volatile political issue. We must ask what aspects of the past were problematical and to what degree was association with non-Christian antiquity tolerated. How were the issues defined? Lydus' political beliefs and writings take us to the very middle of these issues. What place was there in the midst of Justinian's purges and persecutions for books that ignored Christianity and took pains to associate themselves with archaic and arcane sources of information? With opposition to the throne liable to be branded paganism, Lydus' freedom to treat antiquarian topics helps mark out the limits of Christian and non-Christian discussion; and since Lydus remained an active participant in Justinianic society, his writings show the acceptable limits of challenging the spirit of the regime. The place to begin is with the treatment of pagans during the reign of Justinian, when Lydus was at his desk.

THE OFFICIAL VIEW OF PAGANISM

We know how the palace viewed pagans. Justinian inherited with the Theodosian Code a full range of anti-pagan legislation accumulated since Constantine – from periods, it is important to note, in which Christianity was less firmly established and domestic politics had a different character.[7] These laws provided the justification for Justinian's first purge of pagans in 528–9, the year following his formal accession to power.[8] The Code prepared by his lawyers that appeared in 534 reduced the number of laws against pagans, but the emperor enforced them with a severity missing in the reigns of his immediate predecessors.[9]

The definition of paganism provided by the Code was clear and simple: anyone who performed rites – sacrifices, libations, or divination – in honor of gods (whose names we are not told) or financed pagan worship, or abetted it in any way, would suffer the full force of the emperor's anger and the law. He called the practice of pagan cult a public crime[10] and imposed harsh penalties. If a baptized Christian were found in pagan worship, he would forfeit his life. Non-Christians could not hold public office, teach, or possess property, but Justinian allowed a three-month period during which pagan offenders might accept Christian orthodoxy and so keep their offices and lands. Those who failed to accept Christianity lost their property at the end of the three months, with backsliding to cultic practice punishable by death.[11] On the other hand, violence was forbidden against pagans who stopped their cultic worship but did not become Christians – as long as they lived quietly and within the law.

Forced abandonment of rites was in no way inconsequential. Harl has recently emphasized the importance in late-antique pagan worship of sacrifice as the medium that enabled communion between mortals and gods. Ritual sacrifice was understood by pagans to benefit the state.[12] Justinian was no less certain that pagan worship was injurious to the empire; he continued to call pagan worship a public offence. Sacrifice was the crucial issue, as witnessed by the emperor's readiness to permit traditional holiday festivities to continue as they had for centuries. His Code retained an old law and its important proviso:

> The convivial pleasures of the people shall be conducted in accordance with ancient customs, but no sacrifices and no damnable superstition observed.[13]

By so neatly excising sacrifice from the festivals (and cultivating popular goodwill), Justinian "de-fanged" one form of pagan worship, leaving only age-old public social forms. Such disengagement of cult from culture was nothing particularly new. The legal definition of paganism had focussed upon ritual sacrifice since the beginning of anti-pagan legislation, providing a comfortable way for Christianity to blend with the surrounding culture. In the next century even these neutered festivals would be challenged by ecclesiastical authority.[14]

Sacrifice, however, despite the attention paid it in imperial legislation, was not the only indicator of pagan belief. Notably absent from Justinian's formal definition of paganism was any thought that specific doctrines or attitudes might be considered pagan. This is surprising, because it was on specific topics such as the creation of matter and the eternity of the world that pagan intellectuals distinguished themselves from Christians and that any genuine debate took place in the sixth century.[15] In other words, Justinian's legislation avoided significant issues by focussing its objections on sacrificial rite and by considering pagan worship only in terms of public welfare. Justinian's own legislation oversimplified and misrepresented the situation in Constantinople, for the language of the laws was in fact not adequate to the task of defining or describing accurately the complex character of paganism in the capital. Thus, if understood only from the vantage point of the persecutor, the reality of paganism will be distorted.

THE PURGES

There were three major persecutions of pagans during the reign of Justinian. These occurred at intervals of about twenty years – scarcely what could be considered unrelenting oppression, but frequent enough to keep anxiety on a low boil. The first came in 528–9, shortly after Justinian assumed the purple.[16] Anastasius and Justin had not gone out of their way to stamp out paganism, and the purge

70

caused great fear. The emperor set up a panel of bishops and officials to investigate pagan practices.[17] The victims of the first purge known by name were highly placed officials in Constantinople. Among those caught were Macedonius the Referendarius and Pegasius of Heliopolis, whose fates are not known; Asclepiodatus the Eparch, who took his own life; Phocas the Patrician, who was charged but cleared of suspicion and later replaced John the Cappadocian in the midst of the Nika revolt; and Thomas the Quaestor.[18] We may be certain, however, that men of the same status were attacked elsewhere in the empire, for Justinian instructed his agents to investigate all his cities.[19] An inscription from Sardis, for example, dated to the 530s[20] indicates that far from the capital "unholy and abominable pagans" felt the emperor's anger. At least one unfortunate soul found himself "interned in a hospital for ten years," [21] a punishment not mentioned in the laws. Malalas, speaking of this first persecution of 529, tells of tortures, whippings, arrests, and confiscations of property.[22] Since he was a Christian, there was little reason for him to have exaggerated the brutality of the persecution, but other authors, less sympathetic to imperial policy, do not corroborate all of these details.[23]

In 545–6 a new persecution began, this time led by a Monophysite monk, John of Amida, who would one day be bishop of Ephesus. He returned to the capital fresh from successful campaigns of forced conversions and church building, subsidized by the emperor in Lydia, Caria, Asia, and Phrygia.[24] In this second purge, the intelligentsia of Constantinople suffered especially.[25] John boasts that many noble and illustrious men fell through denunciations and torture. Grammarians, sophists, lawyers, and doctors fell victim, and some high officials, too. Phocas, Lydus' patron, who had survived the inquisition of 528–9, again found himself accused of pagan worship. Disdaining the public execution that was the penalty for backsliding, he took his own life. At the emperor's command, Phocas was buried like a donkey, without prayer or ceremony of any sort.[26]

The last major intensification of anti-pagan activity instigated by Justinian occurred in June 562.[27] Malalas tells us that "pagans were arrested and paraded around. Their books were burned in the kynegion [sc. the theater for animal hunts],[28] together with images and statues of their loathsome gods." [29] The *Life* of St. Simeon Stylites describes the appointment of the new imperial official, Amantios, to Syria. Finding the leading citizens of Antioch "involved in heresies, paganism, and astrology, [Amantios] carried out a swift and severe repression in which books . . . were burned in the kynegion and their

71

idols hung up in all of the public squares. The offenders were imprisoned, then tried and sentenced." [30] Michael the Syrian, a twelfth-century chronicler drawing upon sixth-century sources,[31] adds that officials seized five pagan priests, one at Athens, two in Antioch, two in Baalbek; significantly, however, he mentions none arrested at Constantinople. The fires consumed about two thousand books.[32]

WHO WERE THE PAGANS?

These attacks of Justinian (and later purges begun by the Emperors Tiberius and Maurice)[33] suggest the continued presence in the sixth century of a substantial and easily identifiable non-Christian population in the urban centers (including Constantinople) as well as in the countryside. Undoubtedly Christianity had not reached all corners of the empire, and in some rural areas pagan worship continued more or less openly during and even well beyond our period.[34] John of Amida's campaign of mass conversion, for example, exposed many thousands of non-believers.[35] In Constantinople, however, the face of paganism was less visible.[36] We know of individuals who took part in public affairs and who wrote and thought about political affairs in explicitly pagan terms in the fifth century, when paganism rapidly declined. Pagan intellectuals in particular devoted their energy to discussion of the fall of the western empire.[37] After the age of Justinian, however, such independent voices cannot be heard in the capital. We are accordingly drawn to wonder about how they came to be muted. How can we estimate the "pagan" presence in Constantinople?

Several factors compound the difficulty of ascertaining the shape of pagan belief in Constantinople. Except for the doctrines of those self-admitted pagans, the philosophers[38] (who anyway were fish out of water in the Christian capital), we know very little about the beliefs of the individuals who worshipped secretly at Constantinople. The emperor's laws lumped all pagans together, but in fact, we cannot rely on the legal definition to distinguish among all those people who were not Christians or not yet sufficiently Christian to satisfy the authorities. All pagans, furthermore, did not consider it necessary or desirable to perform sacrifices, as we know from Damascius' account of the piety of Asclepiodatus of Alexandria.[39] It is possible, though no evidence survives to support the notion, that other pagans also did not perform sacrifices in Lydus' Constantinople. There was neither a specifically pagan agenda nor a well-defined group of pagans to endorse it, and yet, curiously, the idea of paganism retained a high political and symbolic value.

Open worship had ceased in the reign of Theodosius I.[40] By the reign of Justinian cultic paganism in the capital necessarily would have gone underground, and we do not know what form their rites took. There remains, furthermore, no physical evidence of pagan cult, temples, or priesthoods at Constantinople in the sixth century.[41] Procopius reveals that "Hellenes" performed their rites in secret:

> But even those among them who had decided to espouse in word the name of Christians, seeking thus to arrest their present misfortunes, these not much later were seized at their libations and sacrifices and their unholy acts.[42]

Justinian's code recognized that some may have continued in pagan worship after perfunctory baptism.[43] Pagan teachers who accepted Christianity were required in addition to have their families baptized in order to demonstrate the sincerity of their decision.[44] This note of uncertainty suggests that it was not always easy even for the emperor to be positive about who was a pagan and who was not.[45]

The difficulty of determining pagan identity made the accusation of paganism an effective political tool.[46] The charge of paganism was widely and loosely applied in the sixth century, as a rather imprecise term of political invective. Many different sorts of men found themselves suspected of paganism, which clearly had the very general sense of being dangerous and subversive. Pauline Allen has rightly called the accusation a great "bogey." [47] The tool was not the sole property of Justinian. A few examples can illustrate this point. The *Suda*, drawing on an unnamed sixth-century source, tells us that Tribonian the Quaestor was a pagan.[48] Why he was so accused we do not know. Certainly Justinian would not have tolerated a pagan in charge of his legal projects. Perhaps because he was "steeped in the non-Christian past" [49] the Quaestor fell foul of his critics. Procopius gossips that John the Cappadocian muttered pagan prayers under his breath while in church.[50] Somewhat after Justinian's reign, in 579 the citizens of Antioch accused even their own Patriarch Gregory of performing pagan rites.[51] Other aristocrats and intellectuals were also charged with pagan worship.[52]

IMPERIUM AND RESPONSIBILITY: IDEOLOGICAL AND POLITICAL REASONS FOR THE PURGES

Ideological reasons

The persecutions sprang from both Justinian's notion of Christian imperium and the political environment attendant upon each purge.

Justinian's anti-paganism was not an isolated concern, but part of a wider effort to impose uniformity upon every aspect of his empire. Seen in this context, the persecutions take on a slightly different color from those of his predecessors. They symbolize a new sort of imperial solicitude, for Justinian had been able to formulate more thoroughly and completely a doctrine of imperial authority that incorporated divine sanction in Christian terms with a particular attitude toward antiquity.[53]

Paganism may no longer have been a threat to Christianity, but Justinian considered its presence even in pathetically diminished form a threat to his power and so took pains to eliminate it. This is not to suggest a political opposition with a pagan rallying-cry. Far from it; Justinian's problems were not Theodosius II's.[54] To understand the character of the threat he perceived and his motivations for enforcement of orthodoxy, we must appreciate a late-antique attitude toward an old issue – the function of the celebration of religious rite. By whom and in what manner would divine favor and protection of the gods be assured? Roman religious thought found the answer to this question in the public performance of well-defined rituals. But what rites were necessary and who would perform them? Late-antique pagans, as we have noted, had come to identify ritual sacrifice with the public weal. In analogous fashion, Justinian understood the act of ruling as a sort of sacral rite that required uniformity of belief from his subjects and relentless correction of error on his part,[55] hence the symbolic value of the persecution. He understood the responsibility of empire to be his alone. In his eyes, the "sacral rite" of rulership was a uniquely imperial act of correct government. Let us look closely at this aspect of his autocratic measures.

The purges, though separated by several decades, had several things in common. They embraced the entire empire, finding victims in the countryside as well as the major cities. They were part of a much broader assault upon all forms of non-orthodox belief in the empire. The fact that Manichaeans, heretics, and homosexuals suffered in these purges demonstrates that it was not simply paganism *per se* to which Justinian objected, but deviance of any sort from the legally determined norm.[56] As Honoré points out:

> The laws against heretics, pagans, and male homosexuals were of long standing and, in the former case, frequently renewed. But no serious attempt had hitherto been made to purge the central or local administration of officials with unorthodox

beliefs or sexual tastes, still less to rid the empire of them altogether. Justinian did not view either of the classes of dissenters with tolerance. On the contrary, he thought that laxity or delay in enforcing the rigour of the law would bring God's wrath on himself and the empire.[57]

The persecutions stemmed from Justinian's understanding of his responsibilities to his subjects and to God. Political action was predicated as much upon divine – or demonic – sanction as upon legal force. First and foremost, Justinian saw himself as a Christian monarch. The formal expression of his power was always in terms of his relationship to Christian divinity even as he strove to maintain a legitimizing association with Roman antiquity.[58] To put it quite simply, Justinian understood his imperium to be God's gift to him alone. To maintain the throne, the sign of God's favor, Justinian was obliged to govern his subjects fairly, and like a good doctor cure all their afflictions.[59] This took the shape of implementing uniform belief throughout the empire, for any uncorrected deviance contradicted his claims to universal authority and gave evidence of the imperfect performance of his obligations as ruler. By eradicating deviance particularly in the structure of government, Justinian was able to demonstrate his loyalty to God and his worthiness to rule. With the stakes so high, the impulse for coercion and forced conversion was very great.[60]

Justinian's legislation concerning the interpretation of law and teaching by pagans in 529 must be considered as an enactment of this ideology.[61] He did not forbid the teaching of "pagan" philosophy, only instruction in it by non-Christians.[62] Only orthodox Christians – that is, orthodox by the emperor's definition – were permitted to be government officials.[63] By the same reasoning, only the emperor would be permitted to interpret the law, as he alone was the *nomos empsychos*.[64] Justinian felt obliged to display to God his effort to establish uniform belief. Hence the purges, the prohibition on teaching and interpretation of law by pagans, and the public burning of books and destruction of pagan statues, specially imported to Constantinople at the emperor's orders.[65] The entire edifice of the state must be built of blocks of equal purity.

The purges, then, may be understood as an attempt to purify the state. The first purge, at the outset of his reign, indicates Justinian's desire to ensure the success of his rule. He had in mind ambitious plans of conquest and reform and wanted to be able to count on divine support. The second purge makes sense as a response to the plague. Calamity in the empire could be interpreted as a punishment for some impropriety in the act of government. When in 541 a strain of the bubonic plague appeared in the east, riots broke out against "pagans" in the countryside. The disease reached Constantinople by 542, taking a toll in lives estimated at half the city's population.[66] We may assume that Justinian responded to the disaster as had the rustics in his eastern provinces – by a reinforced policy of religious persecution and purification. Justinian gave his imprimatur to the missionary activities of John of Amida in an effort to restore God's favor and so bring an end to the pestilence. When the missionary returned to the capital the second purge began. It is also possible that Justinian encouraged John, a known Monophysite, in order to foster unity between Monophysites and Chalcedonians. The final purge in May 562 responded to political, not natural, hardships. The months preceding the purge witnessed street-fighting in Constantinople and elsewhere between Blues and Greens, widespread arson in the capital, a revolt of troops and Hun incursions in Thrace, and the dismissal of Zemarchus the *curator domus Placidiae*.[67] In the autumn the grain supply failed because of bad weather, and several court officials attempted to kill Justinian.[68] Crisis signalled impurity to Justinian, and pagans were a cause to be rooted out.

Political reasons

The purges must also be investigated as a response to immediate political and practical difficulties most of which, unfortunately, we can only dimly perceive. The fact that so many of the purges' victims were aristocrats or officials high in the government encourages us to seek political motivations behind the accusations. This is not to suggest that accusations were totally cynical; Justinian easily understood his enemies to be the enemies of God. Pagans were not Justinian's only target, however. He also struggled with an entrenched aristocracy angered at the growth of his power at their expense. Justinian often accused his enemies of paganism as an excuse to confiscate their property,[69] to mention just one outrage. Procopius' *Historia Arcana* precisely represents the hostility of men at odds with the emperor. Landholders, burdened with heavy taxes necessitated by the emperor's projects and wars, grew angry and frustrated.[70] But to translate this discontent into a coherent picture of political opposition is extremely difficult: we have no reason to assume a uniform opposition. Those men whose power Justinian challenged were also the men in whom reverence for the high culture of antiquity was most deeply ingrained through education and social custom and was an important part of their self-awareness. In an age of blurring boundaries, *reverentia antiquitatis* could also be confused with pagan worship. Justinian took advantage of this to ferret out not only secret pagans but others who did not fit into his absolutist schemes – rhetors, doctors, civil servants. Thus, we find different configurations: some men, like Lydus, had an abiding interest in antiquity, even in antique religious celebration, but were also Christians and good servants of the state. Others, like Phocas (as we will see below), were highly educated men of impeccable social background, who rose to the highest office but fell for worshipping pagan gods in secret. Pagan philosophers and rustics · attempted to follow old ways, but Justinian's long arm sought them out. The ambiguous meaning and uncertain applicability of "paganism" in educated circles made it an easy charge to be exploited for political ends. In fact, so flexible was the charge that even clergy and Justinian's own ministers could be accused of being pagan, as we have seen.

I would suggest that by the insistence upon a strict distinction of Christian and pagans, Justinian's purges imposed an artificial polarization upon the Constantinopolitan elite, which was to some degree more prepared than he to tolerate an intellectual or religious pluralism. The word "pagan" (or "hellene") no longer constituted a complete intellectual, social, or political identity.[71] The charge of paganism was part of the rhetoric of imperial power and persecution. The official view lumped together all who did not accept Christianity (except for Jews, Samaritans, and heretics), but in the educated strata of society we must not assume distinct pagan and Christian worlds, as was the case in remoter regions of the empire far from politics and high culture where older gods were still openly worshipped.[72] We must not play Justinian's intolerant game but should expect to find instead in Constantinople an uneasy cultural ground of common interests, values, and education shared below a veneer, not necessarily hypocritical, of Christian conformity – the ingredients of a many-faceted social identity. This group was shaken as its attitudes became politicized by imperial edict. Surprisingly enough, the dry and pedantic realm of antiquarianism is of important diagnostic value in this environment, for antiquarianism provides a key to the middle ground between Christianity and paganism. In this context Lydus' interests are significant far beyond their value as collections of information from antique authors. Antiquarianism provided a vehicle free of Christian association. His deliberate avoidance of Christian terminology and topics went beyond the stylistic; it was a political statement in reaction to Justinian's treatment of classical culture.

Lydus' stance represents the culmination of a long process of marginalization of paganism in Constantinople during the fourth and fifth centuries. First to go at Constantinople had been broad popular support for pagan cults. Paganism remained among professors and court functionaries. Then in 415–16 pagans were forbidden to serve in the militia or in the administration of justice.[73] Dagron has shown that the paganism in the capital city was not the age-old worship of local deities prevalent in the rural areas that Christianity had not yet completely captured.[74] Nor was it the sophisticated, urban-centered cults of the great hellenic metropoleis of the east like Antioch; such phenomena had never developed in the new Rome. Constantinopolitan paganism lacked the deliberate association with ancient philosophy characteristic of the university town, Athens. Paganism at Constantinople produced no parties of political opposition as in late-fifth-century Rome. Paganism, like Christianity, at Constantinople found its inspiration in the imperial traditions of Roman antiquity.[75] Constantine's city was as much heir to the Roman imperial legacy of power and rule as it was to Christianity, and from the fourth century we see already a mixture of beliefs.[76] Their mutual accommodation was in fact the creative principle in the emergence of the Byzantine identity. Paganism at Constantinople reflected an attitude toward the past and classical culture as well as a belief in the efficacy of cultic sacrifice.[77]

These trends continued into the mid-sixth century to provide a proper context for Lydus' books, whose treatment of antiquity represents a final phase of accommodation of the non-Christian past with the Christian world. Antiquarianism starts to take on a new force here because it was neither incompatible with Christianity nor associated directly with cultic sacrifice. In Lydus' hands, however, as we will see, the antiquarianism resisted Justinian's version of Christian imperium.

PHOCAS

We turn now to evidence of Lydus' political allegiances and their relation to Justinian's purges. *De Magistratibus* reveals Lydus' special devotion to the patrician Phocas, the son of Craterus,[78] who served as the Praetorian Prefect for less than a year in 532 in the aftermath of the Nika revolt. Lydus' treatment of Phocas illuminates the difficulties in understanding paganism discussed above. The last surviving chapters of de Magistratibus are a paean to this man. They emphasize not only his merits, accomplishments, and his patronage of Latin studies,[79] but also his close personal relationship to Lydus. Even if Lydus exaggerates the degree of their association, the fact that he chooses to do so is telling, because Phocas is one of the handful of victims known by name to have been persecuted in the anti-pagan purges of the 520s and the 540s.

Phocas' career was extremely distinguished. At court he held the position of silentiarius;[80] he was sent to Antioch after the earthquake in May 526, with funds to aid in the rebuilding;[81] in 532 he became Praetorian Prefect. Lydus explains that Phocas joined with the emperor to build St Sophia,[82] full of joy in furthering the purposes of God. As Prefect he could scarcely have done anything other than execute the emperor's command. On the other hand, Lydus carefully avoided mentioning that Phocas would have overseen the undoubtedly unpopular requisitions and exactions of cash to pay for the cathedral.[83]

Phocas' removal from that office and his replacement by John the Cappadocian shows that public uproar after the Nika revolt had died down and that Justinian needed a more effective gatherer of revenues with which to pay for his Persian wars. Then, due to his experience in the Praetorian Prefecture and his familiarity with the law, Phocas was made a iudex pedaneus by Justinian in 539;[84] he was sent to investigate the murder of Bishop Eusebius of Cyzicus in 542-3 and find out to what degree his nemesis John the Cappadocian was responsible for the cleric's death.[85] De Magistratibus breaks off before we learn of the end of Phocas' career, but we know from Theophanes that Phocas was accused of paganism in the first great purge of Justinian in 529, but that he survived the inquiry without harm.[86] The purges began again with new vigor in 545-6, and we know that rather than face the charges and the probable execution for backsliding, Phocas took his own life.[87]

Lydus gave Phocas a central role in the thematic development of de Magistratibus as the foil to John the Cappadocian, who was totally evil:

God, however, bestowed upon the calamities a kindness which

compensated for the evil. It was Phocas, a patrician gentleman, grandson of the most righteous Salvius and son of the most pious of all men, Craterus.[88]

He cast Phocas as the very exemplar of an altruistic patrician, a gentleman-scholar of the old school, an anomaly in the changing environment of Justinianic Constantinople. His moderation and abstemiousness made him a model of balance and decorum in contrast to the Cappadocian's excesses. Lydus explained that during his brief tenure of the Praetorian Prefecture in 532 "the political order regained its brilliance, precisely as one, when a flame is about to go out, abundantly pours oil on it and revives it." Phocas brought back light to the government; under his administration the "Temple of Justice" opened again – that is, the observance of law and order in the courts resumed.[89] Rhetoric came back into vogue, learning flourished, and books were produced. And not least of all, "competition for glory returned over the whole complexion of government." [90]

Lydus praises the Prefect Gabriel, the man to whom he dedicated his earlier works, in the same way:

> Since Gabriel is a gentleman he respects those who vie with him in lineage, mode of life, and munificence.[91]

Lydus' appreciation of aristocratic competition points to a political problem. Justinian's autocracy threatened this venerable form of behavior that Lydus prized so highly. Insecure on the throne in the early years of his reign and especially vulnerable immediately after the Nika revolt of 532, Justinian would tolerate aristocratic competition only if it was firmly subordinated to his own pre-eminence. At the same time, however, once his dominance had been clearly demonstrated, to allow such forms of aristocratic social behavior to continue served as a clever sop to this influential group. Justinian had to control an ambitious and restless aristocracy whose eyes were on his throne, but he also needed their help to administer the empire. This tension found grandiose expression in Justinian's response to the construction in 524–7 of the monumental St Polyeuktos by Anicia Juliana, last representative of the previous ruling house.[92] At least partly in response to the challenge posed by this edifice Justinian declared that churches might be built only with public funds or at imperial direction,[93] and he went on to construct St Sophia after the Nika riots. His church was bigger and better than that of his rival, a clear statement of his superiority. Competitive building was the cornerstone of public activity of aristocrats in the urban centers of the Roman empire, a tangible measure of their civic responsibility, wealth, and status. Lydus made a virtue of necessity by praising Justinian for allowing such activity to continue. That the emperor should have to be described as "permitting" such traditional activity shows the degree to which it was at risk. Lydus himself said that the Roman custom of public display and public generosity was not continued in his day since "the illustrious men among us display the superiority of their fortune only towards themselves." [94]

Phocas' generosity so enhanced his prestige that he received the further honorific "Father of the Empire." [95] Like other great lords at Constantinople, Belisarius, Peter the Patrician, Flavius Bassus (Praetorian Prefect in 547), and many others, [96] Phocas made benefices in the religious sphere. He endowed a church in Galatia with an annual subsidy of 80 solidi to pay for those who were "performing priestly functions and offering hospitality." [97] Though pronounced with some fanfare, this contribution was rather modest in comparison with those made by his peers. [98] Phocas spent far greater sums on the ransoming of hostages, an act perhaps with political motives, since the emperor and bishops were also active in this task. [99] Lydus noted Phocas' "liberality of spirit" [100] and suggests he was generous to a fault. He explains away Phocas' study of Latin (difficult to understand in an experienced judge) by suggesting that he feigned ignorance of Latin in order to employ as tutor an indigent Libyan rhetorician. Phocas, mindful of the man's pride, did not wish to seem that he was doing him a favor. [101] Phocas' condition as a "man of Providence" was demonstrated to Lydus' satisfaction when God brushed aside an assassin's arrow aimed at him. [102]

Lydus' paean to Phocas follows upon a lurid description of John the Cappadocian's first tenure of the Praetorian Prefecture. That Lydus specifically notes that it was the Cappadocian's first tenure of office (before 531–2) makes it certain that he had Phocas' dismissal and the Cappadocian's second term (531–41) in mind as he wrote these paragraphs. Most unfortunately, the manuscript breaks off before the matter of virtue unrewarded can be seen by modern readers. We have lost his treatment of Phocas' removal from office and his suicide to avoid the punishment for backsliding. More than a little criticism of Justinian must rest just beyond our grasp in these lost paragraphs. [103] Lydus remembered Phocas' months in the Prefecture as a period of favor for literati. During this period Lydus received his important commissions. The years after Phocas' dismissal were disillusioned ones for Lydus: John the Cappadocian came back to the Prefecture until 542; intellectuals were purged in 546; and most significantly, Lydus' career seems to have been bogged down. He mentions no more imperial commissions or dramatic leaps in his career. There is no evidence that by the mid-540s Justinian was interested in promoting learned endeavors as he had been a decade earlier when he was still actively involved in generating propaganda.

When we remember that this period of good fortune for the empire lasted less than a year and that it occurred about twenty years before the composition of *de Magistratibus*, we can be certain of Lydus' condemnation of the intervening decades. Even from what does remain in the manuscript we see that Lydus chose to associate himself in his book with a man who had fallen from power and died in a most suspect and ignominious fashion. Thus Lydus revealed a political stance at odds with Justinian's policies.

I would suggest that Lydus paid homage to the very aspects of Phocas' character and career that were most problematic in Constantinople. Lydus describes his idol in terms that are redolent of antique philosophy and evoke an aristocratic system of values. In Phocas, Lydus idealized aristocratic competition, learning, public generosity, and the independent performance of such services as ransoming captives – an activity most often described in the period as the prerogative of emperors or churchmen. Did he sacrifice in secret? To Lydus he was a hero, but to Justinian he became a pagan enemy of the state.

With this political background in mind, we can now turn to Lydus' most important book, *de Magistratibus*, to see how he combined philosophical knowledge, antiquarian lore, and bureaucratic history to produce a political response to Justinian's reign.

6

DE MAGISTRATIBUS AND THE THEORY OF IMPERIAL RESTORATION

If the origin of a public office is worthy of praise, and if a good beginning can commend subsequent developments, then the Praetorian Prefecture can take pride in its distinguished founder, most sagacious among men and greatly esteemed by God. For when Pharaoh, the King of Egypt, was beset by unfathomable dreams concerning the danger of impending famines, and no human counsel could unravel their meaning, Joseph, a blessed man, was found, who could speak the truth about the future and help the threatened populace most farsightedly. This very man was the first to dedicate himself to the sacred responsibilities of the office [of Praetorian Prefect]. Inspiring awe, he mounted the carriage [of office] and was taken to such a height of glory that through wisdom he might bring to the people what the power of his master had not been able to provide.

Cassiodorus, "Formulae Praefecturae Praetorio", *Variae*, VI.3
(AD 511)[1]

With this tale, Cassiodorus, the aristocratic chamberlain of Theoderic the Ostrogothic king of Italy in the early sixth century, sought to establish a pedigree for the Praetorian Prefecture. Lydus was equally concerned to glorify the Prefecture in which he served, but though he and Cassiodorus were near-contemporaries, their choices of a past to legitimize their present could scarcely have been more different. Cassiodorus, more devoutly Christian than Lydus and with fewer immediate ties to functioning Roman institutions, made Joseph the first Prefect – at Pharaoh's court. To show the importance of his bureau throughout the entire span of Roman history, Lydus explained that the first Prefect had been Romulus' lieutenant.

83

Roman legend, not the Bible, took priority in his historical imagination. So it was in the Roman past that he found the answers to pressing problems. The setbacks of his career and the political and social disorder around him left Lydus disappointed but not without hope. In his fond imaginings, the emperor would restore the Praetorian Prefecture by drawing lessons from the past, for

> One can comprehend by sufficient signs the magistracy's celebrated character and cedence to the scepter alone even from the faint shadow itself which alone it seems to preserve, for great things are naturally prone to be grasped even from their reduction itself. Time, however, is clever at both eating away and undermining whatever has been allotted generation and corruption. But the emperor's excellence is so great that whatever has utterly perished in the past awaits regeneration through him.[2]

This chapter examines how Lydus created a theory of imperial restoration based on the Prefecture and how he evaluated Justinian in terms of this theory.

De Magistratibus, Lydus' third and most important book, discusses the growth and decay of the administrative offices of the Roman state. Its primary concern is the Praetorian Prefecture, which Lydus considered to be superior to all other offices and indispensable to the proper direction of the government. For Lydus the Prefecture was "an ocean of the affairs of state from which flow all the rivers and every sea . . . [It is] truly the magistracy of magistracies." [3] He wrote *de Magistratibus* certain that the Prefecture had declined in its competence and honor, and he wished to record and save its history and procedures from oblivion so that it might be restored – and the state improved – by the emperor.[4] *De Magistratibus*, he believed, contained the information necessary to complete that restoration. In each of its three books, loosely but logically connected as they are, the Prefecture comes into clearer focus. Although each book contains a wealth of other information, it is the history of the Praetorian Prefecture that gives shape and purpose to the work.

Book I lists and describes, not without error, the magistracies of the Roman state as they came into existence as the problems of the state grew more complex. According to Lydus, when the Roman citizens began to fear that the rivalry of certain magistrates might result in the re-establishment of kingship, for example, they created the dictatorship.[5] When warfare became complicated and expensive, the censorship was invented to make sure that citizens' wealth was recorded properly,[6] while the tribunate in turn came about in response to abuses of the censors.[7] These explanations are more than mere aetiologies; they reveal Lydus' conviction that magistracies, and especially the Praetorian Prefecture, were inextricably linked to the health and development of the state. He asserted that the first office to be created, the Tribune of the Cavalry, became the Master of Horse and, in time, the Praetorian Prefecture. Thus Lydus made the history of the bureau span the entire history of Rome from Romulus to Justinian. In this way he created a bureaucrat's overview of Rome's history.

The first book of de Magistratibus starts out on a note of contemporary politics, while drawing comparisons to antiquity. In the course of a set-piece about Romulus and Remus and the differences between a *tyrannos*, *basileus*, and *autokrator*,[8] Justinian enters the picture as a monarch who obeys the law and acts as a father to his people. No tyrant, he is "a father and leader such as God and the felicity of circumstance have granted us." [9] Even as this panegyrical note is sounded in the development of his ideas about the Prefecture and restoration, Lydus' great ambivalence about Justinian becomes apparent, for the emperor had so far failed to enact the changes that Lydus believed to be necessary. Justinian's presence will be felt throughout the treatise.

Book II starts with a rapid sketch of the end of the republic, beginning with the tyranny of Marius[10] and including Augustus' transformation of the office of Master of Horse into the Praetorian Prefecture. Thirteen chapters follow on the organization of the officium of the Prefecture, its regalia, the courts under its jurisdiction, its official buildings, and other aspects of its organization. Lydus does not limit himself to the Praetorian Prefecture. He discusses the Master of Offices as well as the Prefect of Scythia, the Justinianic Praetor, the Master of the Rolls, and the Quaesitor, which he describes as "not novel contrivances but . . . offices revived after a period of neglect." [11] As successfully restored offices they stand as models for the improvement of the Praetorian Prefecture.

The Prefecture becomes the focus of Book III, as Lydus describes "the splendid, disciplined system which prevailed in the Prefecture long ago" [12] but with its administrative procedures now in a state of utter collapse.[13] He traces in some detail the decline of the Prefecture from Constantine's reign to his own day, devoting particular attention to the malign influence of Justinian's Prefect, John the Cappadocian. Lydus puts the best face possible on Justinian's failure to restore the Prefecture completely, saying that the emperor did not let the bureau's glory and good order fade away completely.[14] He goes on to praise Justinian's reconquests in the west, legal reforms, and general preservation of ancient grandeur.[15]

There follows a recapitulation of the creation of the Praetorian Prefecture under Augustus, a long description of the Prefecture's staff,[16] then an account of the post of *cornicularius*, which serves as a starting-point for a description of Lydus' life and career. Chapters 31–8 describe further minor offices within the Prefecture. With Chapter 39, the contradiction between his praise of Justinian and his expectations of imperial action and what the emperor has actually accomplished becomes more evident as he resumes his main concern:

> to explain the causes of [the Prefecture's] reduction and of so great a change in its circumstances. Even if perchance it is possible to perceive even to this day the magistracy itself both greater than itself and more renowned by reason of the emperor's vigilance . . . it is clear that time, because it is destructive by nature, either has completely extinguished the many at once useful and seemly features of the staff obedient to the magistracy or has altered them so much as to preserve henceforward only a faint trace of what was once admired.[17]

THE HUMILIATION OF THE PREFECTURE

To outward appearances, Lydus says, the Prefecture currently seems more distinguished than it really is, and he will reveal the reasons for the decline in its authority. First he explains that time, the arch-destroyer, has wiped out the institutions once subordinate to the Prefecture. Then he blames inefficient or evil magistrates for bringing about the decline.[18] He does not assert that flaws in the internal structure of magistracies could have caused the decline. This venerable principle of distinguishing between the office-holder and the office which he held[19] allowed Lydus both to criticize Justinian for failure to make reforms and to invest the imperial office with the responsibility to enact reforms. From this emerges the tension between Lydus' idealized portrait of his emperor (as we will see below), beneficent restorer of great institutions, and that of another Justinian, a wishy-washy temporizer on the matter of the Praetorian Prefecture, one of those offices "eagerly awaiting rebirth." [20]

First, Lydus faults Constantine (and Fortune) for abandoning Rome. He explains that during Constantine's reign barbarians crossed the unguarded Danube and took Scythia and Moesia. The loss of these provinces increased the tax burden of the eastern provinces. The Prefect was relieved of his military responsibilities and his paramount position at court and given the title of Praetorian Prefect of the East with responsibility for tax revenues.[21]

Rufinus, Arcadius' Praetorian Prefect, next is singled out as a true villain who "hurled the Prefecture down into a vast pit."[22] When Rufinus attempted to seize power, Arcadius responded by stripping the Prefecture of its authority over arms manufacture and the public post.[23] In Theodosius II's reign, the Prefect lost all but his financial responsibilities because he was constrained to stay at court by a law of Arcadius.[24] At this point in Book III, Lydus recalls an oracle that Fortune would desert the Romans when they forgot their ancestral language.[25] He blames Theodosius II's Prefect Cyrus, who knew no Latin, for violating ancient custom and issuing his decrees in Greek.[26] Subsequently the emperor stripped the Prefecture of even further responsibilities.[27] (The parallel with the contemporary switch from drafting laws in Latin to doing so in Greek – a brain-child of John the Cappadocian – would have been obvious to Lydus' readers.)

The sad saga continues with a description of Emperor Leo's ill-fated expedition against the Vandals which cost 65,000 pounds of gold and 700,000 pounds of silver. Meeting the enormous expenses of this fiasco fell to the Prefect, and the Prefecture was brought into the most dire straits.[28] The wreck of the entire state soon followed. Financial ruin was matched by domestic disaster, yet God did not permit the empire to fall.[29] Zeno further degraded the Prefecture by forcing it to provide the gold with which to purchase ignominious peace treaties from the barbarians. Then Anastasius was put on the throne.[30] Lydus praises his canny financial policies;[31] unfortunately, Anastasius made the unscrupulous Marinus Prefect, and Lydus catalogues this scoundrel's crimes with gusto.[32] Lydus has here the same difficulty in describing the relationship of a good emperor to a villainous Prefect that he will have in his treatment of Justinian and John the Cappadocian.

Lydus loathed John the Cappadocian without reservation and angrily chronicled the Prefect's disgusting personal habits and administrative abuses.[33] Lydus resented the Cappadocian's rapid rise from a humble position in the office of a Master of Soldiers to the Praetorian Prefecture and friendship with Justinian.[34] Not only did the Cappadocian come to the Prefecture as an "outsider" from another bureau, in Lydus' eyes he deserved scorn simply because he was a

Cappadocian. While taking pains to emphasize the Prefect's crafti-
ness, dishonesty, cruelty, greed, and sexual excesses, Lydus particularly dwelt on his extortionate methods of tax-collection, which were
so destructive to Lydus' native Philadelphia,[35] and several administrative changes. He accuses the Cappadocian of hampering justice and
persecuting respectable men through his indifference to legal procedure. Legal business ceased at the usual court, the *Secretum*, and the
legal staff diminished accordingly. Lydus' discussion is confused but
none the less heartfelt.[36] Lydus also hates the Cappadocian for not
using Latin, "the language of the Italians," in his transactions and for
his innovations in issuing documents and keeping official records.
Again, his discussion is rather sketchy, and he affects to be too upset
to discuss the matter at any length.[37]

Before examining where Lydus placed Justinian in this continuum
of decline, we must turn to the theory that Lydus devised to
rationalize his plea for reform.

THEORY OF DECLINE AND RESTORATION

Lydus explained the history of the Prefecture from Romulus to John
the Cappadocian with a carefully considered, though eccentric, theory
of decline and restoration. This theory, which provides the working
premise of *de Magistratibus*, brought together his professional experience, his learning, and some philosophical terminology[38] that he did
not understand very well. The use of this philosophical language
emphasizes the fact that he avoided the language of restoration seen
in inscriptions, coins, and panegyric.[39] Lydus states the operating
principles of his theory at *de Magistratibus*, II.23:

> In accordance with the nature of the Good, all that exists is of
> two sorts: that which comes into being and that which is. That
> which exists simply exists, but that which comes into being does
> not always exist nor is it always the same, for it passes from
> generation to decay and then turns back from that state to
> coming-into-being again. In respect of existence it is immortal,
> but in so far as it changes it is mutable. A returning to itself is in
> its very essence; decay generates the return since Nature of her
> own accord watches over it and leads it forth again to the light
> of existence according to the laws established by the Demiurge.
> *This is the meaning of the story concerning the original form of*
> *the constitution which we have now, in the case of which we*

know that the power of the Master of Horse came into being, as has been said, before any other office did; and next, that when that magistracy was wiped out by time, it was transformed into the office of the [Praetorian] Prefect. After this office had taken over the commonwealth, once again the imperial power came around to the need for the Master of Horse, and forth there came into public life, or rather there was brought forward by the nature of events, the office which had been wiped out through the use of another designation, in no way falling short of its own fundamental essence, but strengthened by greater power and by the addition of prerogatives which formerly it did not have.

Here, using Aristotelian terms, Lydus describes a cyclical process of "coming-into-being" (*genesis*), "decay" (*phthora*), and "coming-into-being again" (*eita . . . genesis*; at II.5, *palingenesia*), that conforms with the most basic principle in the neoplatonic cosmology, the nature of the Good. He suggests that, despite changes undergone in the course of this cycle, especially superficial alterations of name, the material that is changing retains its basic identity. The Demiurge intends an object to return again to its original state after it decays.

Lydus takes this cyclical pattern quite deliberately from the field of pure abstraction to everyday life where it becomes a principle active in history that can give meaning to observable phenomena. Human activity in compliance with the cyclical theory can be discussed. Thus *de Magistratibus* spells out a vital role for the emperor as restorer and for many individuals as agents of decay. The cyclical periods represent historical time – that is, the coming-into-being of an office may mean its development and accumulation of power over centuries. Nature, as the agent of the Demiurge, deliberately brings this about.[40] Lydus does not say how quickly or when one state will replace another, though he is prepared to set the cyclical pattern within the entire course of Roman history. The theory justifies Lydus' hope for the renewal of the Praetorian Prefecture.

THE DEVELOPMENT OF THE PREFECTURE

It was Lydus' original intention to organize *de Magistratibus* around the development of the Praetorian Prefecture, and his account of the growth of the Praetorian Prefecture begins with a description of the Master of Horse, the first magistracy he claims to have been created.

Romulus handed over the . . . cavalry to Celerius,[41] who

previously had been leader of the entire army, and enjoined him to assume responsibility for all of its resources, vicissitudes, and administrative tasks; consequently, the king withheld from the cavalry commanders nothing other than the crown alone as a power over which they could not exercise ownership. Both the kings and the dictators all had this magistracy, and afterwards so did the Caesars, though they had changed the name of the cavalry commander (*hipparchos*) to Prefect (*eparchos*).[42]

He elaborates upon the change in name (at II.6):

Only to the Master of Horse . . . did Caesar leave power with a greater sphere of authority. After him, Caesar Octavianus . . . appointed this official as his Prefect, not merely controlling the court but also an entire army and staff of civilians which he had not disposed of before. In a short time the title became perverted as a result of careless usage, and he came to be called *hyparch* instead of *hipparch*.

We note his concern to establish the antiquity of the office:

It is clear that since the Praetorian Prefecture is considered to be older and greater than all the magistracies, it is both needful and fitting to discuss all its staff and power. But, then, since it was not instituted from the beginning but from the time of Augustus in place of the *hipparch*, as I said, it will suffice at this point to speak about its antiquity and whence the Prefecture gets its origins.[43]

He deliberately stretched the facts in order to give the Master of Horse the distinction of being the first. Ancient sources agreed that the Master of Horse came into being at the time when dictators orginated,[44] that is, long after Romulus, and Lydus knew this received opinion perfectly well.[45] He persisted none the less in connecting the office with Romulus:

As first Master of the Horse (*hipparchos*), he [the first dictator] appointed Spurius Cassius as his lieutenant, just as Romulus had created Celerius Tribune of the Cavalry.[46]

This awkward equation illustrates the lengths to which Lydus would go to establish a chain of continuity. In accordance with his theory, the process of coming-into-being of the Prefecture entailed a change of name and the accumulation of powers, a process of many years. Quite clearly Lydus distinguished between the first Master of Horse, Spurius Cassius, and the first Tribune of the Cavalry, Celerius, yet he wanted the two to be considered essentially the same. This conforms to his general theory of "coming-into-being and passing-away" that we have seen above. No contradiction arose for him, since in his theory a changing of names did not alter the fundamental character of the changing magistracy.

He describes in similar fashion how the Master of Offices came into being when the Praetorian Prefect lost his military responsibilities and became head of the civil government:[47]

> And let no one recoil at the new designation; for if one should carefully look into the facts, one will find that not even the name itself of the magistracy is inconsistent with it. For the *hipparch* always was in attendance with the king or the sole ruler, commanding the equestrian force and heading the entire court; consequently, he who is called by the newer designation, magister [Master of Offices] is nothing else than *hipparch*. . . . As for the name Master of Offices, it signifies, as I already said, nothing but "head of the court registers," in which both the equestrian and the infantry forces of the emperor are seen to have ten thousand warriors.[48]

Lydus' source for the history of the Prefecture was an excerpt of Aurelius Arcadius Charisius found in the *Digest*.[49] This jurist, however, had not used philosophical theories to explain the changes in the office: that was Lydus' work.

Some serious inconsistencies in paragraph II.23, however, illustrate both Lydus' clumsiness in argument and, more important, the vigor with which he presses his theory. The first half of the passage spells out the theory of cyclical change, which follows his mention of how the Master of Horse was renamed and replaced by the Praetorian Prefecture. This transformation conforms to the theory of cyclical change as presented in the first half of the passage.

Yet the example which Lydus gives in the second part of the passage to illustrate his theory is that of the Master of Horse being called back into service after the creation of the Prefecture. Lydus fails to explain satisfactorily the coexistence of these two offices, the

Prefecture and the Master of Horse, once the latter has been reintroduced.

Lydus never completely resolved this problem, but he does provide some parts of an answer. Elsewhere in the book he remarks that the decline of the Praetorian Prefecture began with Constantine.[50] The rebirth of the Master of Horse to which he alludes[51] took place at the same time in Constantine's reign.[52] Lydus thus suggested indirectly that the reintroduction of the Master of Horse was effected to the detriment of the Prefecture. It is no wonder that the role of the Master of Horse between Constantine and Justinian is never discussed any further; the whole matter is permitted to slip away quietly.

Another example of an office treated in this fashion is the *cornicularius*. Lydus describes its responsibilities:

> Since [the *cornicularius*] is the unifying element behind the whole establishment, he ought to illustrate both its beginning and its end as well. Mere considerations of time alone are sufficient to win credence for the case of the *cornicularius*: for over 1003 years he has been the leader of his section, and it was at the actual building of Holy Rome that he appeared upon the scene. . . . Thus from the very beginning of the Roman State one can find evidence for the *cornicularius*, even if nothing but his styling has been left to tell us about him, for from the time of Domitian . . . everything underwent change.[53]

The *cornicularius*, like the emperor, was "leader of his section." Lydus here presents the *cornicularius* as the kind of emperor-imitating, hard-working bureaucrat so important in Justinian's pyramidal view of the world.

THE EMPEROR'S ROLE IN THE THEORY OF CHANGE AND RESTORATION

For the most part, Lydus presents Justinian in laudatory terms. He describes the emperor as a good bureaucrat at the top of the administrative hierarchy, whose activity was to be reflected throughout the empire.

> [Justinian] used to think that something was somehow lost from his own life unless everyone was like him, working without respite and doing battle on the state's behalf.[54]

He approves of Justinian's intent to recall the lofty authority of the past form of the state,[55] and he praises in the most grandiloquent terms the emperor's achievements as a restorer:

> Although the splendor and good order of [the Praetorian Prefecture] had almost vanished, our noble emperor did not allow it to be completely extinguished. He holds together, as it were, and strengthens ancient institutions which are flowing away in the course of time. Through him the state is larger than it had been not long ago,[56] because Libya has been restored to us ... and Rome herself, the mother of our empire, has been liberated by the sweat of the emperor from the bonds and power of barbarians. All the institutions of distinction which once belonged to the state are being presented with greater exercise of power; the laws, too, have been liberated from disorders and burdensome confusion. Justice is clearly visible, and the litigious regret their former vigilance over contentious points, since no dispute is left unresolved. . . . The Emperor's virtue is altogether too great to be praised.[57]

In Lydus' view only the emperor could end the period of *phthora* and restore an office to its original form. *De Magistratibus'* theory of cyclical change suggested that the essence or the proper condition of an office could be comprehended from its very ruins[58] and so provides a precedent upon which restoration might be undertaken. Lydus states that many institutions currently in decline eagerly await rebirth through Justinian's efforts.[59] He presents the emperor as a great force, tirelessly laboring to preserve for Rome those things lost through the indolence of previous generations.[60] Lydus poses Justinian's task quite clearly, but how should the emperor go about it? Lydus credited earlier Roman emperors with outstanding education.[61] Knowledge of literature was "the greatest of all virtues"[62] to Constantius; for Julian it was "the second ornament of peace."[63] Themistius praised learning as an imperial virtue,[64] and Plutarch's suggestion that wisdom came from God and was a peculiar attribute of the ruler gained wide popularity.[65] Lydus employed the cliché, but gave it new force by specifying the kind of learning the emperor should have and how he should put it to use. He gave it a specific function in a theory of restoration that had not been previously put forth.

Justinian, a lover of learning[66] according to Lydus, was aided in his great effort to restore the empire by specific historical knowledge. It was impossible to call back the past without having knowledge of that past. For example,

[Justinian], in his eagerness to preserve everything that was of use for the commonwealth and aiming to summon back all the lofty authority of the form it had possessed of old, first of all hit upon the so-called Prefect of Scythia. Being a wise man and having discovered from books how materially prosperous and strong in arms the country Scythia is now and has long been . . . he thought fit, as he personally was in no way inferior to Trajan, to preserve the North . . . for Rome.[67]

In another instance Lydus shows the emperor putting his historical knowledge to gracious use. Lydus explains that Justinian permits himself to be called *dominus* although it causes him some embarrassment, for he knows that in the time of Augustus or Tiberius the term had a negative connotation. But Justinian is wise and understands that in popular usage it now had come to mean "good father" (*de Mag.* 1.6). Thus Lydus gives us an alert and historically knowledgeable Justinian who is not misled by the outward form suggested by a name. In order to illustrate his sovereign's extreme mildness of character, Lydus has conveniently forgotten that "dominus noster" was an established epithet, found regularly on coins, including those of Justinian, and in its Greek form *Kyrios*, emphasized with renewed vigor by Justinian.[68]

With knowledge of the past the key to restoration, the history of the Prefecture took on a special urgency. Lydus described the third book of *de Magistratibus* as a mirror of the vanished glory and discipline of the Prefecture.[69] Would Justinian take the hint and restore the Prefecture? Here we must confront the problem of the real and the idealized Justinian.

Lydus dared not – and perhaps did not wish to – blame the emperor overly for the ills of the empire. In fact, Lydus took pains to absolve him. He acknowledged that Justinian had not allowed the Prefecture to be "completely obliterated." [70] Lydus showed that the decline of the Prefecture had occurred over many years since the time of Constantine, and he described a succession of corrupt or inefficient Prefects, the last of whom, John the Cappadocian, was virtually an agent of the devil. Nevertheless, we must suppose that not very far behind his careful treatment of Justinian there lay considerable disappointment and frustration. Lydus cannot explain his emperor's failure to deal with the excesses of John the Cappadocian and his restoration of the minister after the fall of Phocas in 532. Lydus knew

94

that the emperor's energy and care had not touched the Praetorian Prefecture, which was one of those institutions waiting to be restored.

Lydus did not develop this criticism in a forceful or thematic way, and there is no reason to assume that *de Magistratibus* should be understood as a clumsily written "Secret History"; Lydus did not intend to make a venomous attack on Justinian. He was torn between his idealization of a "good emperor," trained in history and eager to restore the state, and a more practical Justinian who could overlook his Prefect's excesses as long as he produced hard cash. As we have seen, Lydus was blind to the value of the reforms enacted by Justinian and his Prefect. Lydus' equivocation is best illustrated in his description of the Nika revolt and the causes that led to it – primarily the Cappadocian's criminal activity.[71]

> Our emperor, gentlest of men, knew nothing of these affairs because everyone, though abused by the Cappadocian's unrestricted exercise of power, spoke in defense of that wicked man. Their praises of him were most lavish when in the emperor's presence. Who would have dared to utter even the Cappadocian's name without fawning? Only the emperor's wife and helpmeet, who was most vigilant in her sympathy towards those suffering injustice, found it intolerable to ignore the destruction of the state. She armed herself with grievances that were of the utmost severity and approached the emperor and informed him of everything that had up to this time escaped his notice. She said that there was a risk that not only would the citizenry be destroyed by such evil machinations, but that even the empire itself was on the verge of collapse. Naturally, then, the emperor, being a good man though slow to requite evil, was in the grip of a baffling situation. He was not able to dislodge the wrecker of the government. Since the Cappadocian had badly deranged the affairs of state and had benighted the taxes with perplexity and indissoluble confusion, he succeeded in muddling up the so-called assessments in such a way that there might never be an end to his magistracy nor might any member of the senate or anyone at all vigilant about justice venture to assume the administration. Nevertheless, the Emperor tried to help his subjects so far as was humanly possible.[72]

Lydus was compelled to present Justinian as a well-meaning but ill-informed monarch dependent upon the good offices of his wife. This characterization of Justinian is ludicrous, and not in keeping with anything else Lydus has to say about the emperor. Yet what else might Lydus have done? Prudence, perhaps even genuine confusion, must be assumed.

There is one other hint of Lydus' disapproval of the emperor to be found in his discussion of tyranny. Tyrannical behavior, according to Lydus, is irrational, arbitrary, illegal, destructive to the state, and a source of ruin for posterity. Tyrants destroyed the wisdom of the ancients. With Domitian, who "rejoiced in innovations," everything underwent change.[73] This archetypal tyrant nearly destroyed even the memory of the Master of Horse by "not leaving axes, standards, or even the so-called rods to the office." [74] Rufinus "the Insatiable," Prefect of Theodosius II, "brought the magistracy catastrophically to ruin" (II.10) in his pursuit of tyrannical power. Lydus never accuses Justinian of tyranny; indeed he took pains to point out that the emperor's reforms were restorations, not innovations.[75] When we consider the procedural changes in the Prefecture to which Lydus objected, however, and when we recall how Lydus intended *de Magistratibus* to preserve threatened knowledge about the Prefecture, it is fair to conclude that Lydus to some degree felt that Justinian had acted like a tyrant in his failure to restore the Prefecture properly.

In sum, Lydus' serious reservations about Justinian only found open expression regarding the emperor's peculiar indifference to the decline of the Praetorian Prefecture. Though the manuscript breaks off with the dismissal of John the Cappadocian, we know, as did Lydus, that he was soon to be reappointed.[76] Justinian must bear that responsibility.

With Lydus' vision of imperial restoration and the disappointing reality that confronted it in mind, we now turn to the source of some of the theory's main ideas. We will see in the next chapter how Lydus' theory drew from philosophy and participated in a debate between pagan and Christian centered on those ideas.

7

LYDUS AND THE
PHILOSOPHERS

Throughout his books Lydus maintained a consistent view of the
physical universe and the forces that motivate and determine human
action within it. As with most other educated men, his knowledge of the
cosmos was based on Plato, Aristotle, and their followers, whose
doctrines had become standard currency. Lydus had a first-hand
knowledge of some of their writings (he often quoted directly from
Plato's *Timaeus* and Aristotle's *de Generatione et Corruptione*, for
example), and he used secondary handbooks as well.[1] He was familiar
with a wide range of philosophical texts.[2] Quoting the masters lent
authority to his discussion, and through them he displayed his own
learning and wide reading. This is not to imply that he lacked
intellectual integrity. He simply was not interested in rigorous
empirical investigation. Lydus had something of a "handbook mental-
ity" that gave credence to the pronouncements of recognized authorities. The resultant farrago of quotations might seem at times to be
confused, but Lydus was not indiscriminate in his selection of material.

What set Lydus apart from his peers was not his education but its
application. In his books he combined his studies in philosophy (as a
young man in Constantinople he read Plato and Aristotle with the
neoplatonist Agapius, a student of Proclus[3]) with his observations of
the natural and political worlds. In *de Magistratibus*, for example, he
turned to Aristotle when he needed a vocabulary and conceptual
model to explain the contemporary decline in offices of state and in
society. Lydus thus becomes important as someone who tried to apply
a formal understanding of philosophy to everyday experience. This
may be said without over-intellectualizing him, for his understanding
was limited and his discussion sometimes confusing. His books,
despite their shortcomings, or because of them, show how a traditional education could be put to use.

Lydus is even more valuable, however, as a witness to the embattled status of these canonical beliefs, for during the period in which he wrote, new and vigorous attacks were being mounted against the doctrines of Plato, Aristotle, and Ptolemy by certain writers who felt them to be incompatible with Christianity. Philosophers who thought of themselves as upholders of the old beliefs, and whom Christians called "pagans," argued in their support. Lydus, in his modest way, involved himself in this debate. While it is difficult to tie him directly to any of the contemporary pagan spokesmen or their Christian counterparts, he does demonstrate how far the discussion had reached into the intelligentsia. The arguments reflected in Lydus' books help us understand the differences between Christians and pagans more clearly than do imperial laws about cultic practice.

Two controversial ideas about the physical universe underlie Lydus' works. He held to the belief that matter existed before creation, and he distinguished between the celestial and the sub-lunar realms.[4] This distinction between celestial and sub-lunar originated with Plato,[5] for whom the celestial was the unchanging realm of the sun, the planets, and the stars, while the sub-lunar was characterized by constant change and uncertainty. Into this latter realm, of course, fell human affairs. Writers following Plato, including Lydus,[6] might variously call these two realms the "intelligible" and the "sensible," or the "ungenerated" and the "generated," but the distinction remained the same: in a zone superior to that of earthly matter, there operated eternal and immutable laws that directly affected the inhabitants of Earth. This realm was not simply an abstraction, but might be seen by the naked eye in the heavens above. The predictable complexities of planetary or stellar motion proved the operation of these laws in the heavens. Ptolemy's astrological work presupposes this distinction between the intelligible and the sensible. Numerology, too, sought to discover unchanging principles in the motions of the denizens of the celestial realm. By accepting these ideas, Lydus joined most late-antique philosophers who espoused a non-literal interpretation of Plato's *Timaeus*, arguing that the universe had neither beginning nor end.

Lydus thought that the world was created not *de novo* but from pre-existent "amorphous matter"[7] and that the original stage of creation from pre-existing matter ("that which is") was flux.[8] Later God (or the Demiurge[9]) brought harmony to the universe.[10] He created the five planets, as well as the sun, moon, and the earth, and he placed all of earthly creation under the governance of the moon, which affects all generation.[11] Ideas and the other non-generated participants in the perceptible realm were placed under the control of the sun.

De Magistratibus II.23 shows how Lydus joined his interpretation of Plato with some terms taken from Aristotle's de Generatione et Corruptione. This treatise was undoubtedly among "the most important of the teachings of Aristotle" that Lydus studied in his youth.[12] References to the treatise appear throughout his books, and de Magistratibus in particular was based upon what Lydus thought to be an Aristotelian foundation.

Aristotle argued that matter and the universe were eternal and could have no beginning or end,[13] with genesis occurring only in the sub-lunar realm of earth, air, fire, and water, where substantial change might take place. De Generatione et Corruptione presupposes that things come into being as a kind of change of material already in existence.[14] The supra-lunar sphere, the realm of the heavens, is made of a fifth element, eternal, ungenerated, and unchanging in quantity or quality – the "ether." [15] All generation in the sub-lunar realm is motivated by the eternal movement of the sun,[16] and the process of coming-to-be and passing-away is always cyclical.[17] Although Lydus describes the phases of being in terms derived from this treatise[18] and although he quoted Aristotle many times,[19] it is certain that he did not understand the philosopher. Basic to Lydus' theory is the idea that an office maintains its essence despite outward change in form or nomenclature. Aristotle, on the contrary, intended to show that real "coming-into-being" meant the creation of a new substance.[20] What Lydus describes comes closer to Aristotle's notion of *alloiosis* or qualitative change – that is, the mere alteration of the incidental properties of a substance that does not lose its basic essence in the process of change.[21] Lydus further differs from Aristotle when he introduces human institutions into the discussion of states of being. To Aristotle, a magistracy could not qualify as a substance. We must conclude that although Lydus was familiar with *de Generatione et Corruptione* and sought to apply its ideas to his theory of magistracies, his debt does not exceed a few key terms.

Though his comprehension was not great, his interest in *de Generatione et Corruptione* was characteristic of the day. Ammonius, professor of Aristotelian philosophy in Alexandria, lectured on the text in the late fifth century.[22] His student, and Lydus' contemporary, the Alexandrian Monophysite John Philoponus[23] (see below), collected Ammonius' lectures and added a commentary of his own.[24] There were as well other contemporary discussions of Aristotle's treatise that are no longer extant.[25] Aristotle's discussion of creation stirred much debate.[26]

There was controversy in the ancient world about how to interpret Plato's account of the creation of the universe.[27] Did matter exist prior to the orderly arrangement of the cosmos? Did the world have a beginning in time? To interpret Plato as saying that the world did not have a beginning in time was more compatible with the doctrines of Aristotle, and this was the approach taken by many writers since Porphyry, concerned as they were to show the unity of the two philosophers.[28] A minority, however, insisted that Plato meant the universe to have a beginning in time. Christians who interpreted the account of creation in Genesis literally could also accept the *Timaeus* on these terms.[29] In Lydus' day, however, most neoplatonists, in the face of Christian insistence upon a creation in time, espoused a non-literal interpretation of the *Timaeus*, arguing that the universe had neither beginning nor end, though they might accept a beginning of the present organization of matter.[30] Most Christians, on the other hand, accepted the primacy of God over all creation.[31] "In the beginning God created the heavens and the earth," implied that God made everything out of nothing and that no matter existed before creation. There could be no eternal fifth element for them.

This argument with Platonists hardened the Christian belief in divine creation *ex nihilo*. In general, the position one took on creation distinguished Christians from pagans. Sorabji explains that, "With only a very few possible exceptions, such a view [sc. that the universe had a beginning] was denied by everybody in European antiquity outside the Judaeo-Christian tradition. That tradition's belief that God could have given a beginning to the material universe would have seemed to most Greeks an absurdity." [32] This distinction was not absolute, however. Platonism did influence a few Christian thinkers such as Synesius of Cyrene, the fourth-century bishop;[33] Elias, a head of the Alexandrian neoplatonist school in the sixth century; and perhaps Boethius in the *Consolation of Philosophy*, to the extent that they seem to have accepted a universe without beginning or end.[34] Such individuals, however, are most rare in the record and atypical.

Several pagan philosophers (including Simplicius and Damascius, who influenced Lydus) left the Roman empire when Justinian forbade non-Christians to teach philosophy at Athens in 529. They sought patronage and safety at the Persian court[35] where, among other matters, one of the topics important enough to be discussed was the creation of the world.[36] Michel Tardieu has proposed that a new pagan

Academy was established at Harrān in Syria by Simplicius, who grew disillusioned in Persia and left after a short stay.[37] The effect of their work was felt mainly in later years in the Islamic world.

CHRISTIAN ATTACKS

In Lydus' day, Christians for different reasons and with different arguments attacked the physical theories of Plato, Aristotle, and Ptolemy.[38] These arguments came from two directions: from Philoponus and from the Nestorians, such as Cosmas Indicopleustes, Mar Aba, and Junillus, all of whom drew at some remove from Theodore of Mopsuestia.[39] These men represent the debate as we know it, but they were not the only participants. A travelling bishop, a court official, and an Alexandrian merchant illustrate the wide scope of interest in these issues. That Lydus refers to none of these figures by name, and could not have known Cosmas' work when he wrote *de Ostentis*, does not mean that he was unaware of their ideas or those of others like them whose work does not survive.

In the sixth century the most articulate opponent of the Aristotelian system was an Alexandrian Monophysite, John Philoponus. He wrote in an intellectual environment different from Proclus' Athens or Lydus' Constantinople. In Alexandria the neoplatonists and Christians had reached an accommodation of sorts;[40] Christians had even held the chair of philosophy there.[41] Philoponus' teacher, Ammonius, for example, had tried to interpret Aristotle in a way that made him seem as consistent as possible with Christianity. Philoponus, however, rejected Aristotle's teachings on the separation of heaven and Earth, the eternity of the cosmos, and other matters as well.[42] To Philoponus the ancient cosmologies were false.[43] He denied the distinction between the celestial and sub-lunar realms and attributed the rotation of the heavens to a superior and immaterial power. He argued that God made the world, movement, and time not by any process of generation and decay but solely by his own will, from non-being. Philoponus' attacks appeared in a variety of books,[44] in particular in *de Aeternitate Mundi Contra Proclum*,[45] which appeared in 529 – coincidentally the year that Justinian prohibited pagan neoplatonists from teaching philosophy at Athens – and in the *contra Aristotelem*.[46] The first of these works was intended as a rebuttal to the pagan Proclus' *de Aeternitate Mundi contra Christianos*. Proclus had been the leader of the neoplatonic School in Athens in the late fifth century and was one of the teachers of Lydus' teacher,

Agapius. Philoponus argued against Proclus' ideas, maintaining that the world had a beginning and an end and that it was corruptible and subject to decay.[47]

On the other side of the aisle was Simplicius who, as a leader of the Athenian neoplatonic school, spoke for pagans. He had been among the philosophers who travelled to Persia in 529 when Justinian closed the Academy in Athens.[48] Simplicius responded forcefully to Philoponus' attacks on Aristotle. He charged that Philoponus' Christianity was a dangerous innovation,[49] his philosophical method inadequate, and his writings an Augean stable of filth.[50]

Simplicius defended Aristotle in several ways. In his commentary on Aristotle's *Physics*, Simplicius sought to support Aristotle's teaching on the eternity of the world.[51] He attacked Philoponus' belief that God created the world through an act beyond movement and time. Instead, Simplicius repeated the Aristotelian view that coming-to-be and passing-away is a cyclical process without beginning or end, each stage always referring to an earlier movement.[52]

In his commentary on Aristotle's *de Caelo*, Simplicius reaffirmed that the eternal celestial and the sub-lunar worlds were separate.[53] Where Philoponus exploited inconsistencies between the *Timaeus* and the *de Caelo*, Simplicius emphasized the unity of Plato's and Aristotle's works in defence of the fifth element, the existence of which Philoponus denied. Simplicius reconciled contradictions noted by Philoponus from the *Timaeus* by saying that Plato meant that the world comes from a higher cause while Aristotle meant that the world did not have a temporal beginning.[54]

Lydus echoes some ideas of Simplicius. *De Magistratibus* II.23 discusses offices in a fashion evocative of Simplicius' distinction of generation, being, and non-being in his essay *On Aristotle's Physics*.[55] Such resemblances suggest that Lydus knew of Simplicius' ideas about Aristotle, but Lydus does not cite Simplicius in his works and direct ties cannot be established.[56] Without doubt, however, we may say that Lydus kept informed of developments in philosophy.

The debate over creation also influenced contemporary discussion of the generation and fate of the soul: was the soul a creation of God or was it pre-existent and immortal in the Creator's mind?[57] Generation, destruction, and rebirth were central to the discussion. One could not discuss *genesis* and *phthora* without thinking of the soul, or think of the soul without encountering the weight of neoplatonic formulations. The ideas of Damascius, one of the leading neoplatonist philosophers of the day, on this issue may have influenced Lydus.

Damascius was head of the Academy in Athens and led the exodus of the neoplatonic philosophers to Persia in 529.[58] He had studied in Alexandria under Ammonius and later in Athens under Marinus, one of the teachers of Lydus' mentor, Agapius. After he returned from Persia he wrote several treatises, the chief being *On First Principles* and a commentary on the *Parmenides* in which he discussed the nature of the soul, developing the innovative notion that the human soul maintained its identity when it descended into the body even though it changed substantially.[59] In Damascius' theory the formal structure of the soul's being is permanent even though the soul itself continually changes in quality. The soul may become something other (*alloion*) but not another thing (*allo*). The soul's essence remains the same throughout its different dispositions at different points in its career, each disposition being a form of the same. Though the soul might fall and become entwined with material life, it could return to itself. It would maintain its identity in change.[60] These ideas about the soul clearly parallel Lydus' ideas about magistracies.

If we follow this analogy a bit further, another similarity emerges. Damascius maintained that the essence of the soul could be seen in its activities.[61] This idea parallels the "archaeological" aspects of Lydus' theory – that is, his belief that institutions can be perceived from their ruined state.[62] Despite these correspondences, the precise nature of the relationship between Lydus and Damascius must remain an open question, for Lydus never cites Damascius' works.

A final word on a different aspect of philosophical thought – theurgy. Plotinus, like Plato, believed that the soul could be purified through philosophy and moral self-discipline. His disciple Porphyry suggested that philosophy was too difficult for the man on the street and recommended the practice of theurgy, a sort of magical system of ritual purification. For Iamblichus and his followers theurgy alone could provide full salvation. Their beliefs stressed the importance of maintaining traditional ritual.[63] There is more than a whiff of theurgy in Lydus' conception of the role of the emperor. Through specialized knowledge (in Lydus' system this would be historical information) and understanding of traditional ritual (that is, proper appreciation of the regalia of magisterial office and the proper functions of magistracies), the emperor could perform his restorative acts. Lydus seems to assume there is some *arcanum imperii*, almost an occult science of state, that depends on knowledge about the past. The emperor, with his special relationship to God and with law as his instrument, by virtue of sheer hard work could effect dramatic change in a magistracy. Imperial intervention would save not merely a man or even a community, but the entire empire, through the restoration of the proper offices.

In this chapter we have seen the philosophical underpinnings of Lydus' theories in terms of sixth-century debate. We will see in the next a different range of scientific information, astrology, and portents, and find Lydus again reacting to contemporary argument.

8

DE OSTENTIS: PORTENTS AND THE ENEMIES OF PTOLEMY

LYDUS AND PTOLEMY

In *de Ostentis*, Lydus combatively asserted his allegiance to the astrological teachings of Ptolemy, the great second-century scientist whose writings on the heavens dominated astronomy until the Copernican revolution. "These few examples," Lydus announced in *de Ostentis*,[1] "[are] in reply to those who object to signs and dare to speak against Ptolemy." Although Justinian, like emperors before him, persecuted astrologers,[2] the sort of material in *de Ostentis* was not problematical from an official point of view; Lydus dedicated the work to the City Prefect, Gabriel.[3] While Lydus does not elaborate upon the identity of Ptolemy's opponents, it is possible to situate *de Ostentis* within the context of contemporary discussion about the heavens. This chapter will help us understand Lydus' defensive attitudes by considering the uncertainty at Constantinople about the status of traditional cosmologies.

Establishing the precise relationship between Lydus and Ptolemy is complicated for several reasons. Ptolemy's book of applied mathematics, the so-called *Almagest*, which shows how to derive a theory of planetary motion to predict the location of celestial bodies, was far too technical for Lydus to have employed in *de Ostentis*.[4] The *Tetrabiblos*, however, which discusses astrological influences on human affairs,[5] was useful to Lydus, though only in a limited way. On close examination of Lydus' work it becomes clear that he possessed no sure understanding of Ptolemy's work, despite his claims to be defending him.

One difficulty lies in Lydus' own attitude. He explained:

> We are not concerned to explain the physical causes of these [celestial] phenomena or to discuss theories about them – that is

for the philosophers to worry about – but rather to see if anything is to be gained from these signs to predict the possible outcome of future events.[6]

That it was not Ptolemy's purpose, either, seems to have escaped him. At a stroke, however, Lydus distanced himself from the precise scientific character of Ptolemy's studies, in particular the *Almagest*, as well as from the formal discussion of astrology as represented by the *Tetrabiblos*, while maintaining the authority of association with his illustrious predecessor. The reader of *de Ostentis* is warned not to expect a scientific treatise on the structure of the heavens or even an organized defense of astrological investigation. Instead, Lydus only presents proofs of astrological assumptions, leaving their premises unexamined.

Ptolemy considered astrology inferior to astronomy.[7] Through astronomy, he believed, unvarying principles of motion could be demonstrated to operate among the heavenly bodies. His *Almagest* provided such material. Astrology, on the other hand, he considered to be weaker because it was less predictable and less certain.[8] Yet Ptolemy did not reject astrology since "it is so evident that most events of a general nature [sc. on earth] draw their causes from the enveloping heavens."[9] He believed all heavenly bodies to have a physical effect on earthly things. The influence of the heavenly bodies was for Ptolemy only one of the determinants of earthly events, but none the less, through careful observation of the effects of these celestial bodies on human affairs he thought it possible to make predictions.[10] Ptolemy thought that a properly read horoscope could reveal an individual's character, physical appearance, and destiny. This could be achieved through precise knowledge of celestial movements and understanding of "potential effects of the sun's heating and the moon's moistening."[11]

Ptolemy's distinction between astronomy and astrology is Aristotelian, for he associated astrology with material things in the sub-lunar realm, where unpredictable changes occur constantly, and he made the occupants of the heavenly realm, the planets and stars with their regular, unchangeable, and so predictable motions, the subject of astronomy.[12] He accepted the Aristotelian fifth element.[13]

Lydus' avowed interests are at the same time narrower and broader than Ptolemy's. While he limits himself to a consideration of the "outcome of events," he admits a wider range of evidence. In *de Ostentis* Lydus dealt with different categories:

We are eager to speak about the overshadowing of the sun and moon that some call sudden eclipses of light, about comets and about the differences among them, about furrows in the ground and shooting stars, flashes of lightning, thunderbolts, [thunderstorms] and other portents of the heavens, and finally about earthquakes, fires, and their oracular significance.

(proem. 4)

De Ostentis is a straightforward compilation of astrological works. Lydus combines his own introductory remarks (proemion 1–8) with a section on solar and lunar signs (9–9d). There follows a long discussion of comets, including material attributed to Apuleius (10–10b) and Campester (11–15b), observations on the moon (16) and their relation to the lunar calendar (17–20), and a discussion of thunder, including "Egyptian learning" (21–6). Lydus adds his own translation from the Latin of the writings of Tages as preserved by Nigidius Figulus (27–38), and his own translation of the Roman writer Fonteius, whose oracles he is so fond of quoting (39–41). Then Lydus offers his own translation of Labeo on the moon from the summer solstice (42), a discussion of thunderbolts (43–6), with material from Labeo's *Liber Fulguralis* (47–52). He next moves on to earthquakes (53–4), and the observations of Vicellius (55–8), followed by his own translation of Claudius Tuscus' calendar (59–71h). The treatise ends with an astrological ethnography that associates different nations with zodiacal signs (71).[14]

This wide range of material made *de Ostentis* a useful handbook for men of his own day. The book had great value as entertainment as well. The apocalyptic stories are quite lurid[15] and must have been fun to read. For modern scholars, the treatise is an invaluable source for the history of astrology.

Two general assumptions underlie *de Ostentis*: that the learning of the past is still valid and that general celestial principles can be seen to operate through their earthly manifestations. Lydus posits no discontinuity with the scientific tradition of which he understood himself to be a part. When he adds his own observations and conclusions to the extensive excerpts he has culled from the astrological corpus, he affirms their validity, continued utility, and reliability. He is, in effect, deliberately contributing to a long scientific tradition. Lydus does not hope to add any new twists, only to demonstrate that the old principles still hold true. His concern is to show that portents foretell future events. His approach is characteristic of a systematic, astrological explanation of the universe that is recognizably pagan in origin.

107

Lydus' attitude toward the relationship of historical events to celestial phenomena is revealed in his treatment of two episodes: the fall of Antioch in 540 and the revolt of Vitalian (during the reign of Anastasius).[16]

The Persian destruction of the beautiful and wealthy city of Antioch dealt a serious blow to the military prestige and self-confidence of the empire. The event left scars and prompted contemporary writers to speculate on the survival of the empire. Lydus links celestial phenomena to historical event and offers their coincidence as an incentive for his beginning *de Ostentis*. He starts with the catastrophe at Antioch. In his preface he explains that while in his youth he eagerly read books about portents, only direct experience convinced him of their validity:

> because of the coming of the comet and the early rising of the star said to have the shape of a horse, because of the subsequent invasion of the devilish Persians which reached as far as the Orontes, and because of their most rapid retreat made when the victory of our most powerful emperor was evident, from the consequences of these events themselves [i.e., the taking of Antioch] and from the evidence they provide, I was drawn to write about these matters.
>
> *(de Ostentis*, proem. 1)

Lydus did not explain the destruction of Antioch in terms of divine retribution. He extracts no moral truths. In his scheme of causation, impersonal forces are active. Here is the link to *de Magistratibus*, which demonstrates that human affairs and institutions follow a cyclical pattern of generation, decline, and regeneration. The ruin of Antioch was but one more indication of the empire's decline and its need for renovation through imperial initiative. In particular, Lydus connects the catastrophe at Antioch to the problems of the Praetorian Prefecture. In *de Magistratibus* his discussion of the events at Antioch[17] fits precisely into this analytical scheme, when he finally attributes the loss of the city to the weakness of the Prefecture. That Lydus cannot quite bring himself in *de Ostentis* to admit the catastrophe but tries instead to present it as a Roman victory illustrates his ambivalence about Justinian's failure to restore the Prefecture. It also shows that there were constraints upon his freedom to criticize the emperor. Finally, it suggests that *de Ostentis* was written before the explanatory system of *de Magistratibus* had been thought through.

The proemion to *de Ostentis*[18] mentions a second celestial phenomenon and its relationship to contemporary events. Its sixth chapter describes how a solar eclipse and a fiery light in the sky during the reign of Anastasius anticipated the revolt of Vitalian (513–15).[19] Since we have information from other sources about this rebellion, it is possible to see how Lydus presented the sequence of events to suit his own purposes.

Vitalian, an ambitious and well-connected Count of the Federates in Thrace, hoped to seize the throne for himself.[20] As the self-proclaimed champion of orthodoxy, he challenged the regime of Anastasius, a Monophysite. In the course of his protracted struggle with the emperor, Vitalian besieged Constantinople unsuccessfully three times – in 513, 514, and finally 515, when he was decisively defeated by Marinus, the ex-Praetorian Prefect. Lydus tells that in the sixth year before the death of Anastasius – that is, in 512 – a solar eclipse followed by a flaming light in the sky "causing the heavens to seem on fire" prefigured the revolt of Vitalian. Indeed, a total eclipse is known to have occurred on June 29, 512.[21] Lydus continues to explain that these signs occurred "when the people were in revolt against the emperor."[22] This is an allusion to the riots that broke out in Constantinople in 512 when Anastasius ordered a Monophysite phrase to be added to the Trisagion hymn.[23] Lydus fails to note, however, that this imperial command was not issued until November 4.[24] In other words, he compressed the time between the heavenly signs and the consequent riots by four months.

When Lydus explains that Vitalian "got as far as the city walls and came within an inch of seizing power," he is omitting Vitalian's two prior assaults on the city in 512 and 513. His mention of a treacherous barbarian attack at the time of Vitalian's defeat refers to an incursion of the Sabir Huns in 515.[25] It comes as no surprise that Lydus fails to mention the role of Marinus in the defeat of Vitalian; Lydus blamed Marinus for contributing to the decline of the Praetorian Prefecture, as we saw in *de Magistratibus*.[26]

Quite clearly Lydus compressed his time-frame to establish a firm connection between celestial sign and political event. This is done forthrightly, however. Lydus breezily explains that "it would be superfluous to relate all the minor details to my learned readers." There has been no falsification; Lydus intended only to prove the value of signs, not to provide a complete account of the insurrection.

THE ENEMIES OF PTOLEMY

When Lydus talks about "the opponents of Ptolemy," to whom is he referring? There must have been many – even Ptolemy himself had been on the defensive: in the introduction to the *Tetrabiblos* the astronomer confronted his challengers, drawing his arguments largely from the *Tetrabiblos* of the Stoic apologist Posidonius.[27] Though Lydus cites the *Tetrabiblos* several times,[28] he does not identify these detractors. We may be sure, however, that he was doing more than paying homage to his mentor's difficulties. He intended *de Ostentis* to address contemporary critics.

Among the people hostile to the Ptolemaic world-view in the sixth century were Nestorians. The facts that a Nestorian theologian visited Constantinople in the 520s, that a very high court official translated certain Nestorian tracts into Latin, and that the so-called "Three Chapters controversy" involved Nestorian beliefs, testify to a far-reaching Nestorian influence in the eastern empire. If Lydus opposed these ideas, he would have had plenty of people to argue with.

The chief evidence we have that Nestorian beliefs were popular – and that attacks were launched on Aristotelian science – comes through the medium of Cosmas Indicopleustes. Cosmas was an Alexandrian merchant whose name tells us that he had sailed in Indian waters and who wrote a most peculiar book, the *Christian Topography*, full of eccentric observations about the structure of the earth.[29] Cosmas envisaged the cosmos as a cube[30] and the earth as flat. The merchant had a considerable knowledge of ancient philosophy, but was proud of his divergences from Aristotle and other ancient authorities (he was particularly fond of mocking Ptolemy[31]). Despite such hostility, it can be shown that he knew at first hand some of Aristotle's work and followed him closely on some matters of physics, though there were often major points of disagreement.[32] He opposed, for example, the fifth element.[33] Most important, Cosmas popularized Nestorian ideas. He had known the Nestorian bishop Mar Aba who was active in the cities of the eastern Empire in the first decades of the century. The bishop was in Alexandria, probably in the early 520s, and in 523 or 524 visited Constantinople.[34] Mar Aba propagated the ideas of Theodore of Mopsuestia and other Nestorians. He was an advocate of a Nestorian world-view that was taking hold in areas where Syriac was spoken and in the Greek east, too, and therefore certainly in Constantinople. Cosmas wrote in this tradition.[35]

110

Lydus did not know the *Topography*. Cosmas wrote it at some point between the condemnation of the Three Chapters in 543–4 and the Council of 553 – a dangerous period in which to endorse a forbidden doctrine.[36] This is not the place to investigate the complex christological issues and the attendant doctrinal controversies; however, it should be stressed that this Nestorian doctrine contradicted the absolute distinction between lunar and sub-lunar realms. Though an outsider, Cosmas shows himself to be aware of the dispute among Proclus, Simplicius, and Philoponus, whose *de Opificio Mundi* opposed Cosmas' Nestorian cosmology.

Cosmas' chief targets, however, were Monophysites, not pagan polemicists. He was interested in pagans only inasmuch as their theories were used by his Christian opponents. Certain "pagan" ideas about the shape of the universe, for instance, had entered into the Christian world-view, and Cosmas felt these beliefs to be wrong and tried to show that his view of the world was the one described in the Bible. By confuting pagan theory he hoped to persuade Christians who accepted the principal ideas of the Hellenic scientific tradition to follow Nestorian teachings.[37] He opposed the attitude found in some philosophical circles in Alexandria, as represented by Ammonius who tried to accommodate Aristotle and Christian doctrine.[38]

Nestorian ideas had a spokesman high in the imperial bureaucracy. This was Junillus, the *Quaestor Sacri Palatii* of 542–8, who replaced Tribonian.[39] There is no reason to think this man was alone in Constantinople. We may feel confident that Lydus knew him but probably did not like him, if we believe Procopius' criticisms of the Quaestor's poor rhetorical education, bad Greek, and avarice.[40] Sometime between 541 and 548–9[41] Junillus composed the *Instituta Regularia Divinae Legis* [*de Partibus Divinae Legis*], a translation into Latin of some material about portents and prophecy. Junillus claims as his source Paul, a Persian from Nisibis.[42] Junillus' treatise contains certain teachings of the Nestorian School of Nisibis that in turn echo the teaching of Theodore of Mopsuestia.[43] In his introduction,[44] Junillus tells that Paul was educated at the school of Nisibis, "where divine law is correctly and regularly taught by public teachers, just as in our communities grammar and rhetoric are taught in daily classes." This comment contains an implicit criticism of the sort of education that had produced Lydus. The reproach may be taken to represent the sort of attitude about learning and the intellectual traditions of antiquity that Lydus sought to save.

Junillus discussed the significance of portents in a fashion quite different from that used by Lydus in *de Ostentis*. He based his discussion entirely on the Bible and was not concerned with predictions in everyday life. Rather, he wished to show how prediction and prophecy work between the Old and New Testaments. For Junillus, "prophecy is the revelation of hidden things, past, present, or future, through divine inspiration." [45] Junillus has no interest in Ptolemaic science because for him there is no predictability. Only God's will determines whether or not something hidden will be made known. All must be proven by the testimony of divine scripture. [46] God's plan for humankind may reveal a logic as it works out through time, but only the Bible, not the natural world, holds clues to its direction. Junillus wrote "The purpose of prophecy is not to tell a story, but to confirm the outcome of predictions." [47] Thus Junillus differed from Lydus in his objectives and in his understanding of ultimate causes: a god, perhaps arbitrary in his decision-making, had replaced a principle of scientific order. For Junillus a revealed text was an adequate alternative to the tradition of empirical observation to which Lydus subscribed.

John Malalas, a contemporary of Lydus, wrote about portents in a different way. Like Lydus he came from a major provincial city, Antioch, to which he was deeply attached and where he served at a high level in the imperial bureaucracy. [48] He probably moved to Constantinople about 535–40 where he worked until about 570, finishing his *Chronicle* of world history at the death of Justinian. The first edition of this work was probably intended for other imperial officials in Antioch and Constantinople. He seems to have been a loyal supporter of Justinian who generally ignored doctrinal debate. Unlike Lydus, Malalas openly referred to Christian ideas and institutions, although he had little interest in theology. Like Lydus and his audience, Malalas was interested in ancient scientists and scientific achievements, even in the ancient pedigree of current festivals. [49]

Malalas related portents to events just as had Lydus, only (like Junillus) he named God as the prime actor:

> during [Leo's] reign there occurred in Constantinople a fall of ash instead of rain. . . . Everyone was terrified and went on processions of prayer saying "It was fire, but through God's mercy it was quenched and became ash." [50]

Natural disasters in his *Chronicle* always indicate divine wrath. [51] Malalas was ready to report contemporary celestial events:

During this reign there appeared a great and formidable star in the western region, sending a white beam upwards; its surface emitted flashes of lightning. Some people called it the Firebrand. It continued shining for twenty days, and there were droughts and murderous riots in every city as well as many other events full of ill-omen.[52]

CONCLUSIONS

What makes Lydus different from his Christian peers is not his belief in portents nor his identification of the natural phenomena that might be portents, but his system of cosmic explanation in which the portents play a part. Lydus' explanatory system is without recourse to divinity of any sort. It is more scientific, so to speak, predicated on empirical observations demonstrated in historical events. For Lydus the past and the present were filled with manifestations of the link between natural laws and history.

Lydus' interests in portents are neither specifically Christian nor pagan, though his allegiance to Ptolemy would have earned him the disapproval of men who shared Junillus' beliefs. Lydus and Malalas had similar backgrounds and professional lives, while Junillus was of superior rank. The fact that all three were ostensibly Christian illustrates what wide-ranging beliefs and interpretations were possible in sixth-century Constantinople. Lydus believed there to be many ways of describing the truth. His whole encyclopedic approach demonstrates this. He describes his method in *de Ostentis*:

> We, after having gathered opinions from various authors, and similar material from the writings of the ancients, have placed it here, recording data about the shapes of the moon in relation to the zodiac.[53]

> Some [people] prophesy through signs according to the intertwined poles, others according to the rising of the stars or their phases. Some people observe the sun following the zodiac, others pay attention to the rising and setting of the moon, while others study other natural phenomena. Nature is the herald of what is concealed from us, so that it is not without folly that people cast aspersions on the methods through which we are led to conjecture about the future.[54]

Lydus' works remain faithful to this synthetic and pluralistic approach; in the prevailing court atmosphere of intolerance and insistence on orthodoxy, Lydus' attitude seems almost poignant.

9

CONCLUSION: COLLUSION

We have seen Lydus in many guises: as a bureaucrat and born subordinate wanting very much to be loyal to figures of authority, yet restive at the abuses of his superiors; as a provincial with sentimental attachment to the city of his birth and its ancestral customs; as a "Sunday philosopher" who in his writings tried to integrate the formal studies of his youth with his own professional experience; as a scholar, especially a Latinist, with a professional concern for Roman antiquity and a vested interest in the survival of Latin in the imperial administration; as a Christian with ambiguous ties to Christianity; and perhaps most important of all, as someone who saw his world in crisis. This list is varied, but a coherent portrait emerges if we understand him to be the product of two developments that were for him, if not for all his contemporaries, irreconcilable.

First, the cities' loss of status in the imperial hierarchy and the accompanying decline in influence of the curial elite and the classically educated intelligentsia (especially in the bureaucracy) created uncertainty about the status of traditions of education, urban life, and government that had been fundamental to late-antique culture. Part of the identity of the urban upper class that constituted an administrative cadre in the government depended upon an education that included classical philosophy and literature and a knowledge of Latin. Lydus exemplifies a bureaucrat trained in this tradition. His works are the best source we have concerning sixth-century beliefs about the role of proper education and the status of classical antiquity in imperial government. Lydus resented Justinian's policies, which altered bureaucratic procedures and the balance of urban life. In his eyes, this equilibrium represented the heritage of Roman civilization, and when it was shaken his loyalties became confused. Though his perception of crisis was not ours, and though he could not share our

114

long view of the decline and fall of the empire, he felt threatened, and rightly so.

The second development that heightened Lydus' anxiety – and so shaped his view of crisis – was the renewed and intensified emphasis on imperial power at the center of society. The reign of Justinian was characterized by centralization and regimentation. These were part of a developing myth of Constantinopolitan cosmopolitanism that diminished the role of provincial cities but recognized (and perhaps even encouraged) provincial identity – even while subordinating it to the imperial center. Uniformity of Christian culture was actively pursued. The imperial bureaucracy (and particularly the Praetorian Prefecture) was obviously an agent of this centralization. At the same time, imperial autocracy was expressed in Christian terms to a greater extent than ever before, evincing the inexorable Christianization of the state. The emperor pursued a unitary view of society that excluded the possibility of disagreement and linked religious orthodoxy with proper administration. His totalitarianism put new pressures on society and exacerbated some old ones. Lydus' books reflect some of these pressures.

Lydus found himself on a fault-line produced by these developments. In his story about the silver bowl, his plea for a strong autocrat suggests that he accepted the highly centralized, autocratic status of the emperor. He expected the emperor to improve society, to restore social cohesion and stability. We have seen this played out in detail in his theory of restoration developed in *de Magistratibus*. On the other hand, it was Justinian's autocratic policies and hand-picked administrators that Lydus felt to be eroding the Praetorian Prefecture and the foundations of the society he so loved. As schools closed and uneducated men reached the highest positions in the government, as intellectuals were persecuted and the provincial elite fell victim to ruthless revenue collection, an unsolvable problem emerged for Lydus. The imperial power that he hoped might restore his society seemed to him in fact to be destroying what he wished to save. Yet, Lydus himself had benefitted greatly from imperial patronage. No wonder he had such difficulty articulating his allegiances beyond the Praetorian Prefecture. His divided loyalty was one expression of the price of life under Justinian. Of course, Lydus produced such a distorted and ambiguous evaluation of Justinian in *de Magistratibus*.

Yet it is unfair to present Lydus simply as a champion of an old order against the new, just as it is wrong to cast the argument as one between Christian and pagan. In the centuries before Justinian, paganism in Constantinople had developed a custodial attitude toward the past and the traditions of imperial rule that came to be more important than a devotion to cultic sacrifice. In Lydus' day "paganism" represented a threat to the Christian establishment only in the presumptions of Justinian's propaganda, for the imperial view of empire could not tolerate divergence from the imperially determined norm. One result was the forced conversion in the countryside of thousands of peasants who still worshipped the old gods. In Constantinople the situation was somewhat different. The charge of paganism there was in part a political accusation made all the more convenient by the fact that among the elite most unhappy about the emperor's policies, the habits of education and private life made allegiance to antique traditions of philosophy and science a likelihood if not a certainty. But not only "pagans" held allegiance to the past, and so at Constantinople there was a struggle for control of the legitimizing aspects of antiquity between the emperor, who understood the need to bring Christian and Roman together in his theory and practice of monarchy, and an educated class put on the defensive by his agressive policies. These men were Christian, perhaps in the way that Lydus was Christian, and they were by no means uninterested in participating in the governing of the state.

Justinianic society defined itself in historical terms, and the Roman, non-Christian past had much to contribute. What knowledge from the past was still useful? What vehicles would carry the "new" cosmopolitanism? Lydus shows some ways in which the past might be hitched to the regime. What makes him so interesting is the way he resorted to philosophy and antiquarian knowledge to discuss change. *De Ostentis* offers itself as a defense of Ptolemy and so in rather obscure fashion points to contemporary attacks upon the traditional cosmology made by Christians of different stripes. This treatise presumes that old science is still timely. It offers scientific principles, not divine fiat, as the ultimate cause of natural phenomena. *De Mensibus* offers data so obviously not Christian that it probably was intended simply as a collection of arcana to be enjoyed for its own sake. Virtually all its calendrical data are far removed from contemporary practice – not at all risky. It does contain some hints, however, that Lydus sought to prod the sensibilities of the Church.

De Magistratibus suggests that the past could supply models of a properly run empire. Lydus subtly transformed the general attribute of imperial wisdom to a specific kind of knowledge, awareness of the past, making it the criterion of successful government. By knowing what the past was like, the emperor would be able to restore his empire properly. While *de Magistratibus* presents the emperor as a restorer, as do Justinian's reform laws (which, curiously, Lydus never praised), Lydus' perception of the nature of change is different from that expressed in the Novels of Justinian. Lydus describes cycles of generation and decay along Aristotelian lines, not random and unpredictable manifestations of change. Perhaps most important of all, *de Magistratibus* confidently presents a secular past whose value is not lessened by the absence of Christianity. In this way he provided an historical guide to the Praetorian Prefecture that was entirely appropriate to his day. By integrating philosophy with the history of the office, he brought the bureau's character into the realm of the educated elite. His choice of the Prefecture itself as a topic for his monograph reflects his pride in its status. Since the foundation of Constantinople young men had left their provincial cities for careers in the imperial offices at the capital as new routes to prestige gradually replaced the urban curial offices. As the character of city life altered in the sixth and seventh centuries, Lydus represents one of the last generations of these young men. It was to the Prefecture, not his home town, that Lydus felt most loyal. He would rather be in the New Rome than in Philadelphia.

At the same time, the treatises are handbooks that collect interesting and useful data in order to preserve it. Their custodial function carries an edge of political criticism; it is implied that in a properly run empire such material would not be at risk. There is also the implication that discontinuity results in disaster. Lydus posits a society in decline. As a defense of ancient knowledge for its own sake, Lydus' writings illuminate one aspect of Justinian's effort against "paganism."

In intellectual circles at Constantinople, debate about the nature of the world and political power was lively and shaped by reaction to imperial policies of coercion. We have noted the originality and sometimes the idiosyncrasy with which Lydus manipulated the data at his disposal. A first reading of Lydus' books might lead us to think that he lived in an earlier century when the degree of Christianization of everyday life was less complete, but such was not the case. Given the background of Justinianic policy, Lydus' silence on Christian matters speaks loudly against a confidently Christian view of history and society. Unfortunately for Lydus, there was at Constantinople no future for such a willful denial of reality. At least in terms of political analysis without Christianity, he represents a dead end.

Lydus' attitude toward Christianity points to a deep-seated area of personal conflict as well. As a Christian himself, his refusal to accept the new idiom is most peculiar and goes somewhat beyond literary style. For him it was a necessary artifice. Because he was so insecure, he created an illusion of a lovely past. He pined for a restoration of the old order – against all reasonable hope. The perfect emperor he dreamt of was not the emperor on the throne, and the functioning bureaucracy he mourned was in fact less efficient than the one Justinian and John the Cappadocian tried to implement. Certainly Lydus confronted the present. We can see in his reluctance to accept Justinian's message, however, a more disturbing truth, one that he was unwilling or unable to admit: Lydus was part and parcel of the new society that he deplored.

Lydus lived in Constantinople, not Philadelphia. He made a career in the Praetorian Prefecture that implemented reforms to the detriment of his class. Particularly in his views of the offices of state he reveals the extent to which he had bought the imperial line. A vision of a hierarchical, autocratic state is basic to his treatment of the magistracies. He reveals no understanding of magistracies once having been elective offices, but can conceive of them only as extensions in miniature of the emperor's power and office. Not even a dim memory of the *cursus honorum* lingers in his mind. Lydus studied philosophy, but he expressed no sympathy openly for the pagan philosophers who made their ill-fated expedition to Ctesiphon, even though he may have been familiar with their work. He was not purged, but kept a teaching position in the capital. He went further than any contemporary in associating the literary tradition in which he was trained with the emperor, the purger of rhetors. These few examples show that in many outward ways he conformed – but at what cost? Much was regrettable about the reign of Justinian, and we may wonder if Lydus felt some guilt about conforming. Unable to admit to himself the extent to which he participated in the Justinianic system, he hid from his own collusion. Others, whose reliance on the past was less problematic than Lydus', would be the ones to carry Rome into Byzantium.

APPENDIX: AUTHORITIES
CITED BY LYDUS

If there is no bibliography given, Lydus is our only source.
[Title] = Lydus does not give title, but it is known.
Title in English = translation from the Greek.
English + title in Latin = Lydus gives the title in Latin, transliterated.
Citations from known works precede those that are unidentifiable.

All references to *de Magistratibus* are from the edition of Bandy (Philadelphia, 1983); to *de Mensibus* from that of Wuensch (Leipzig, 1898, repr. 1967); to *de Ostentis* from that of Wachsmuth (Leipzig, 1897). They are abbreviated as *de Mag.*, *de Mens.*, and *de Ost.* respectively.

Recurrent abbreviations are as follows:
Bandy: *On Powers or the Magistracies of the Roman State*, ed. A.C. Bandy (Philadelphia, 1893);
Diels, *DG*: H. Diels, *Doxographici Graeci* (Berlin 1879, repr. 1958);
Diels and Kranz: H. Diels, *Die Fragmente der Vorsokratiker*, 6th edn, ed. W. Kranz, 3 vols (Berlin, 1952);
Jacoby, *FGrH*: F. Jacoby, *Die Fragmente der griechischen Historiker*, 3 parts in 12 vols (Berlin and Leiden, 1924–58);
Müller, *FHG*: C. Müller, *Fragmenta Historicorum Graecorum*, 5 vols (Paris, 1885–8);
Müller, *GGM*: C. Müller, *Geographi Graeci Minores*, 3 vols (Paris, 1855–61);
Peter, *HRR*: H. Peter, *Historicorum Romanorum Reliquae*, 2 vols (Leipzig, 1883).

Book and chapter numbers are listed first, followed by page and line numbers. Bibliographic material follows citations.

ACUSILAUS OF ARGOS
V BC
(via Josephus, *Antiquitates Judaicae*   *de Mens.* III.5 (39,19)
I, par. 108, ed. B. Niese (Berlin,   Jacoby, *FGrH* #2, IA, 49–58 =
1987) 25)   Müller, *FHG* I.102, fr.15

AEMILIUS ASPER
AD II
[*Commentary on the Histories of Sallust*]
de Mag. III.8 (142,11–13)
B. Maurenbrecher, *Sallustii Crispi Historiarum Reliquiae* (Leipzig, 1891–3) vol.I, fr. 48
perhaps the same as:
de Mens. IV.85 (135,3)
de Mens. IV.71 (123,5)

AESCHYLUS
VI–V BC
Aetna
de Mens. IV.154 (170,12)
H.J. Mette, *Die Fragmente der Tragoedien des Aischylos* (Berlin, 1959) fr. 29
de Mens. IV.107 (144,14)
(via Seneca, *de Nilo* 17)
Mette, fr. 193

AMMONIUS
AD V
de Mens. IV.159 (176,13)

ANAXAGORAS
VI–V BC
de Mens. III.12 (53,10)
de Mens. IV.107 (144,12)
D. Sider, *Beiträge zur Klass. Philol.* 118 (1981)

ANAXARSIS THE SCYTHIAN
?
de Mens. III.1 (36,17)

ANAXIMANDER
VI BC
de Mens. III.12 (53,14)
de Mens. IV.40 (97,26)
Diels and Kranz, 358a

Anaximenes
VI BC
de Mens. III.12 (53,6)
Diels and Kranz, 355a
(Anaximander is the true source)

"ANCIENTS"
de Mens. I.11 (32,7)
de Ost. 1 (5,23)
de Ost. 1 (6,7)

de Ost. 8 (17,12)
de Ost. 16 (46,14)
de Ost. 16a (47,24)
de Ost. 16a (47,25)
de Ost. 22 (56,13)
de Ost. 27 (62,9)
de Ost. 43 (95,11)
de Ost. 43 (95,12)
de Ost. 44 (97,20)
de Ost. 46 (101,3)
de Ost. 46 (101,5)
de Ost. 46 (100,7)
de Ost. 47 (102,11)

ANTIGONUS
III BC
de Mens. II.10 (30,22)
de Mens. III.11 (50,11)
A. Giannini, *Paradoxographorum Graecorum reliquiae* (Milan, 1965)

ANTIGONUS [= NICAENUS?]
AD II
de Ost. 2 (6,18)
W. Kroll, *Codices Vindobonenses* [*Catalogum codicum astrologorum graecorum*] 6 (Brussels, 1900) 67–71

ANTIPHON
V BC
de Mens. III.12 (53,16)
Diels and Kranz, II,339

[Antonius] DIOGENES
AD I–II
[*Concerning the Wonders beyond Thule*]
de Mens. III.5 (40,1)
de Mens. IV.42 (99,24) (Bk 13)
R. Hercher, *Scriptores Erotici Graeci* vol.I (Leipzig, 1858) 233–8

ANYSIUS
AD ?V
On Months
de Mens. IV.25 (83,5)

APOLLODORUS
AD I–II
On Siegecraft
de Mag. I.47 (74,21–2)

R. Schneider, *Griechische*
Poliorketiker (Berlin, 1908) 8–50
(*Abh. Königl. Gesellschaft d.*
Wiss. zu Göttingen. Phil-Hist.
Kl. 10 (1908) 8–50)

APOLLODORUS OF ATHENS
II BC
[*Concerning the Gods*]
de Mens. IV.34 (93,2)
Müller, *FHG* IV.649 = Jacoby,
FGrH #244, IIB, 1079 (fr.131)
de Mens. IV. 51 (107,2)
FHG, I.433, fr.29 = *FGrH* #244,
IIB, 1076 (fr.117)

APOLLONIUS
?
de Mens. IV.11 (76,18)
de Mens. IV.74 (126,8)
de Mens. IV.125 (159,20)

APULEIUS
AD II
Erotic Tales
de Mag. III.64 (234,9)
de Mens. IV.116 (154,10)
de Ost. 3 (8)
[*On the Art of Divination*]
de Ost. 54 (110)

AQUILINUS
?
Explanation of Numbers
de Mens. IV.76 (128,11)

ARCHELAUS OF CAPPADOCIA
I BC–AD I
(via Pseudo-Plutarch, *De Fluviis*
I,9)
[*History?*]
de Mens. III.11 (50.14)
de Mens. III.11 (52.7)
Παραδοξογράφοι. *Scriptores*
Rerum Mirabilium Graeci, ed. A.
Westermann (Brunswick, 1839)
160, fr.10
(Jacoby omits references to Lydus:
FGrH #123, IIB, 630–1)

ARCHYTAS
IV BC
de Mens. II.9 (29,4)

Diels and Kranz, 431–9, frs 1–9
de Mens. II.9 (29,4)
Diels and Kranz, 47B (I,439,28)

ARETAS THE PHYLARCH OF THE ARABS
AD I
Letter to Claudius Caesar
de Mens. IV.104 (143.14)

ARISTEAS
III–I BC
[*Letter to Philocrates*]
de Mag. I.31 (48,7–8)
ed. A. Pelletier, *Lettre d'Aristée à*
Philocrate (Paris, 1962)

ARISTIDES [OF MILETUS]
?
Persian History
de Mens. Fr. incert. sed. 5
(179,20)
Müller, *FHG* IV, 321, fr.21 = *FGrH*
#286, IIIA, 167
(= Plutarch, *Parall. Min.* 4A, in
Jacoby, *Plutarchi Moralia*, 2.2 ed.
W. Nachstädt, Leipzig, 1935,
repr. 1971)

ARISTODEMUS [Lydus calls him
Aristides]
I BC
Mythology III
de Mens. IV.147 (165.21)
Jacoby, *FGrH* # 22, IA, 186 =
Müller, *FHG* III.311, fr.12
(= Plutarch, *Parall. Min.* 35 B, in
Plutarchi Moralia, 2.2, ed. W.
Nachstädt, Leipzig, 1935, repr.
1971)
(n.b. Jacoby includes this ref. on
page 165 under Aristides of
Miletus)

ARISTOPHANES OF ATHENS
V–IV BC
Acharnians 180–1
de Mag. I.10 (20,22–3)
V. Coulon and M. van Daele,
Aristophane I (Paris, 1967) 12–
66

ARISTOPHANES OF BYZANTIUM
III–II BC
Epitome of the Physical Properties

of Fishes
de Mag. III.63 (232,12–13)
(W.J. Slater, *Aristophanis Byzantii Fragmenta* (Berlin/New York, 1986) does not include this reference)

ARISTOTLE
IV BC
[*History of Animals*]
de Mag. III.63 (232,11) (II.13; 505ᵃ15)
de Mens. IV.89 (137,9) (VII.4)
P. Louis (Paris, 1964–9)
de Mens. I.34 (16,4)
de Mens. II.8 (26,6) Diels, *DG* 392b, 3

[*Meteorology*]
de Mens. III.10 (44,12) (Bk 5)
de Mens. IV.116 (154,9)
de Mens. IV.79 (131,22) (Bk 3.7)
F.H. Fobes, *Meteorologica* (Cambridge, Mass., 1919, repr. 1967)

[*On Generation and Corruption*]
de Mag. II.5 (90,6–7)
de Mens. III.18 (58,10) (Bk II)
de Ost. 16a (46,18)
C. Mugler (Paris, 1966)

[*On the Heavens* I]
de Mens. II.10 (31,2)
P. Moraux (Paris, 1965)

On the Peplos
de Mens. fr. incert. sed. 4 (179,15)

de Mens. IV.100 (140,11)
Bekker, Rose, *Arist. Pseudep.*, fr.79
de Mens. IV.7 (72,7)
de Mens. IV.77 (131,8)
de Mens. IV.83 (134,8)
Diels, *DG* 382a, 16
de Ost. 2 (6,23)
de Ost. 10b (32,15)
de Ost. 10b (33,5)

ARRIAN
AD I–II
History of Parthia
de Mag. III.53 (214, 22–3)
de Mens. III.1 (37,14)

A.G. Roos and G. Wirth (Leipzig, 1967) II.224–52
History of the Alans
de Mag. III.53 (214,21–2)
Roos and Wirth, II.177–85
On Alexander
de Mag. I.47 (76,1–3)

ASCLATION
?
de Ost. 2 (6,24)

ATHENAEUS
AD II–III
[*The Learned Banquet*, Bk VII.294E]
de Mag. III.63 (232,9–10)
G. Kaibel (Leipzig, 1887–90, repr. 1965–6) II.149

AURELIUS [ARCADIUS CHARISIUS]
AD IV
[*On the Office of the Praetorian Prefect*]
(= *Digest* I, tit.XI)
de Mag. I.14 (26,12–28,3)
O. Lenel and L. Sierl, *Palingenesia Iuris Civilis* (Graz, 1889, repr. 1960) vol.I, col.59

AURELIUS VICTOR
AD IV
History of the Civil Wars
de Mag. III.7 (140,13)
P. Dufraigne, *Livre des Césars* (Paris, 1975)

CAESAR (G. JULIUS CAESAR)
I BC
Gallic War I.1
de Mag. III.32 (182,20–1)
W. Hering (Leipzig, 1987) I.1
CAESAR [?CLAUDIUS]
AD I
On the Stars
de Ost. 70 (158,2)

de Mens. IV.18 (79,14)
de Mens. IV.128 (160,13)

CALLIMACHUS
IV–III BC
Causes, I

de Mens. IV.1 (64,9)
R. Pfeiffer (Oxford, 1949) vol.I,
  fr.33, pp.39–40

CALLIPUS
?
  de Mens. IV.18 (79,8)
  de Mens. IV.141 (164,4)
Jacoby, *FGrH* #385; IIIB, 263 (=
  Pausanias 9.29; Jacoby omits this
  reference to Lydus)

CALLISTHENES THE PERIPATETIC
IV BC
Greek History, IV
  de Mens. IV.107 (146,20)
Jacoby, *FGrH* #124, IIB, fr.12
  de Mens. IV.77 (131,8–10)
Jacoby, *FGrH* #124, IIB, fr.5

CALLISTHENES THE SYBARITE
?
(via Ps.-Plutarch, *de Fluviis* 6.1 =
  Müller, *GGM* II.128)
  de Mens. III.11 (52,6)
Jacoby, *FGrH* #291, IIIA 175

CAMPESTER
IV–III BC
On Comets
  de Ost. 11–15b (35.11–45)
  de Ost. 9c (24,5)

[CANDIDUS]
AD V
[*History*]
  de Mag. III.43 (200,20–2)
Müller, *FHG* IV.135–7
see Bandy 323, note 200.20–2

CAPITO [GAIUS ATEIUS CAPITO]
AD I
  de Mens. I.37 (16,27) = proem.
  de Mag. (2,11)
  de Mens. fr. incert. sed. 6 (180,9)
  de Ost. 2 (7,8)
  de Ost. 3 (8,24)
W. Strzlecki, *C. Atei Capitonis
  Fragmenta* (Leipzig, 1967) frs 29,
  30 and 35

CASTOR
?
  de Mag. I.2 (10,11)

see Bandy 263, note 10.8–12

CATO
II BC
On Roman Antiquity
  de Mag. I.5 (14,20–1)
Peter, *HRR* 57

"CHALDEANS"
  de Mens. I.11 (3,4 and 12)
  de Mens. I.12 (6,11 and 14)
  de Mens. II.4 (21,1)
  de Mens. II.8 (26,16)
  de Mens. II.8 (28,4 and 6)
  de Mens. II.10 (31,18)
  de Mens. II.11 (32,4)
  de Mens. II.12 (33,2)
  de Mens. III.8 (41,9)
  de Mens. III.19 (58,22)
  de Mens. IV.8 (41,21)
  de Mens. IV.22 (80,20)
  de Mens. IV.53 (110,21)
  de Mens. IV.1 (111,1)
  de Mens. IV.107 (147,5)
  de Mens. IV.159 (175,9)
  de Ost. 21 (55.5)
W. Kroll, *De Oraculis Chaldaicis*
  (Breslau, 1894) [= *Breslau philol.
  Abh.* vii. 1]

CHARAX
II BC
  de Mens. IV.154 (170,10)
Jacoby, *FGrH* #103; IIA, 489 and
  IIIB, 741–2

CHARES
IV–III BC
  de Mens. IV.113 (152,8)
G.A. Gerhard, *Veröffentlichungen
  aus der Heidelberger Papy-
  russammlung IV: griechische
  literarische Papyri (P.
  Heidelberg, 434)* (Heidelberg,
  1911)

CHRESTUS THE ROMAN
?
  de Mens. IV.107 (147,7)
  de Mens. IV.107 (148,23)

CHRISTODORUS OF COPTUS
AD V–VI
On the Pupils of the Great Proclus

de Mag. III.26 (172,19–21)
Jacoby, *FGrH* #283, IIIA, 161
(Jacoby does not mention Lydus)
E. Heitsch, *Die griechischen Dichterfragmente der römischen Kaiserzeit* II (Göttingen, 1964) 48

CHRYSIPPUS
III BC
de Mens. IV.64 (116,13)
de Mens. IV.71 (122,18)
J. von Arnim, *Stoicorum Veterum Fragmenta* II (Leipzig, 1903) fr.1098
de Mens. IV.81 (133,22)

CICERO
I BC
Against Verres 1.71; 2, 69, 74; 3,154 etc.
de Mag. I.13 (24,28–25,1)
W. Peterson (Oxford, 1917, repr. 1965)

CINCIUS [L. CINCIUS ALIMENTUS] THE ROMAN
III–II BC (? or eponym, I BC–AD I)
de Mens. IV.22 (80,12)
de Mens. IV.64 (118,1)
de Mens. IV.86 (135,18)

On Festivals
de Mens. IV.144 (164,17)
Jacoby, *FGrH* #810, IIIC, 876ff.
(Jacoby omits this reference)

CLAUDIAN
AD IV–V
On the Consulate of Stilicho
de Mag. I.47 (74,25)
M. Platnauer (Cambridge, Mass., 1922); see Bandy 282, note 74.22–5

CLODIUS TUSCUS
?
de Ost. 59–70 (117–58)

CONSTANTINE I [EMPEROR]
AD IV
Tractate
de Mag. II.30 (128,14–15)
H. Peter, *Historicorum Roma-*

norum Fragmenta (Leipzig, 1883), 364

CORNELIUS NEPOS
I BC
[?*Exempla*]
de Mag. III.63 (232,14)
K.F. von Halm, *Cornelii Nepotis Quae Supersunt* (Leipzig, 1871) 121, fr. 19

"COSMOGRAPHERS"
de Mens. II.2 (19,11)

CRATES
II BC
de Mens. I.28 (14,15)
de Mens. IV.71 (122,15)
de Mens. IV.71 (123,7)
H.J. Mette, *Sphairopoiia* (Munich, 1936) testimonia 7, frs 4a and 4b

[T. STATILIUS] CRITO
AD II
[*Gothic History*]
de Mag. II.28 (126,7)
Jacoby, *FGrH* #200, IIB, 31–2 = Müller, *FHG* IV.373–4

CTESIAS THE CNIDIAN
V–IV BC
de Mens. IV.14 (77,10)
Jacoby, *FGrH* #688, IIIC, 420–517 = Müller, *GGM* I.1–97

DARDANUS [DARDANIUS]
?
On Weights
de Mens. IV.9 (74,11)

DEMOCRITUS
V–IV BC
de Mens. III.12 (53,10)
de Mens. IV.16 (78,15)
de Mens. IV.18 (79,5)
de Mens. IV.18 (79,16)
de Mens. IV.51 (109,3)
de Mens. IV.81 (133,11)
de Mens. IV.124 (159,17)
de Mens. IV.135 (162,6)
de Mens. IV.139 (163,10)
de Mens. IV.152 (169,3)
de Ost. 70 (157,20)
Diels and Kranz, 130–207

DEMOPHILUS
? AD II–III
de Mens. IV.2 (66,8)
E. Elter, *Gnomica homoemata* pt 5
(Bonn, 1905) 1–36

[DEMOSTHENES]
IV BC
[*Olynthian*, 1.20]
de Mag. III.564 (216,3–4)
S.H. Butcher vol.I (Oxford, 1903,
repr. 1966) 20

DERCYLLUS
?
de Mens. III.11 (51,17)
Jacoby, *FGrH* #288, IIIA, 170–2

DICAEARCHUS
IV BC
On the Compass of the World
de Mens. IV.107 (147,1)
F. Wehrli, *Dikaiarchos* (Basle,
1967) 13–37

DIO CASSIUS COCCEIUS
AD II–III
[*Roman History*]
de Mag. I.7 (18,2–3)
U.P. Boissevain, I (Berlin, 1895) 10,
fr.6,1a
de Mens. IV (66,12)
Boissevain, frs 6,7, vol.I, 14

DIODORUS SICULUS
I BC
Historical Library
de Mag. I.47 (76,8–9) (cf.
Diodorus I.28,98)
de Mag. III.30 (180,2–3) (cf.
Diodorus I.13.1)
F. Vogel and K.T. Fischer, 5 vols
(Stuttgart, 1888–1906, repr.
1964)

DIOGENES APOLLONIATES
V BC
de Mens. IV.107 (145,20)
Diels and Kranz, 59–66

DIOGENIANUS
AD II
[*Lexicon*]
de Mag. I.5 (14,17)

see Bandy 266, note 14.17–18
de Mag. I.17 (30,20)

DIONYSIUS OF CHALCEDON
?IV BC
On the Foundation of Cities
de Mens. II.12 (36,7)
Müller, *FHG* IV, 393–6, fr.8

[DOROTHEUS THE CHALDEAN]
[*Italian History*]
de Mens. IV.147 (165,11–15)
Jacoby, *FGrH* #289, IIIA, 172

DOSITHEUS [?OF ALEXANDRIA]
III BC
de Mens. IV.128 (160,11)
G. Keil, *Grammatici Latini* (Leipzig,
1880) 363–436

"EGYPTIANS"
de Mens. II.4 (21,2)
de Mens. II.9 (28,18)
de Ost. 23–6 (57,11–62,2)

ELPIDIANUS
?
On Festivals
de Mens. IV.4 (68,16)

EMPEDOCLES
V BC
de Mens. IV.81 (133,9)
de Mens. IV.84 (135,1)
de Mens. IV.159 (176,24)
Diels and Kranz, 308–74

EPHORUS OF CUMAE
IV BC
(via Josephus, *Ant.Jud.* I.108)
Histories, I
de Mens. III.5 (39,19)
de Mens. IV.107 (146,11)
Jacoby, *FGrH* #70, IIA, 43–109 =
Müller *FHG* I, 329, fr.24

EPICURUS
III–II BC
de Ost. 21 (55,5)
H. Usener, *Epicurea* (Rome, 1887,
repr. 1963)

EPIMENIDES (the followers of)
de Mens. IV.17 (78,20)
Diels and Kranz, 3B.26 (I.37, 26)

ERATOSTHENES
III–II BC
[*Catasterismus* 30]
  de Mens. IV.71 (123,12)
A. Olivieri, *Pseudo-Aratosthenes
Catasterismi [Mythographi
Graeci]* 3.1 (Leipzig, 1897) 1–52
  de Mens. III.12 (54,8)
Diels, *DG* 5.358a and 5
  de Mens. IV.47 (103,8)

"ETRUSCAN SACRED BOOKS", "ETRUSCANS"
  de Ost. 3 (7,17–18)
  de Ost. 3 (8,23)
  de Ost. 27 (62,16)
  de Ost. 43 (95,16)
  de Ost. 70 (157,18–19)

EUCTEMO
V BC
  de Mens. IV.18 (79,8)
  de Mens. IV.54 (111,16)
  de Mens. IV.141 (164,1)
  de Mens. IV.156 (173,8)

EUDEMOS
?
  de Mens. IV.98 (139,22)

EUDOXUS [OF CNIDOS]
IV BC
  de Mens. IV.18 (79,11)
  de Mens. IV.18 (79,14)
  de Mens. IV.44 (101,7)
  de Mens. IV.50 (106,14)
  de Mens. IV.126 (160,1)
  de Mens. IV.136 (162,12)
  de Mens. IV.139 (163,12)
  de Mens. IV.149 (168,9)
  de Mens. IV.155 (172,19)
  de Ost. 71 (157,20)
F. Lasserre, *Die Fragmente des
Eudoxos von Knidos* (Berlin,
1966) 39–127

EUHEMERUS
III–II BC
[*Sacred Scripture*]
  de Mens. IV.154 (170,13)
Jacoby, *FGrH* #63, IA, 310, fr.16

EUMELUS THE CORINTHIAN
VIII–VII BC

  de Mens. IV.71 (123,14)
D.L. Page, *Poetae Melici Graeci*
(Oxford, 1967) fr.696, p.361

EUPHORION
III BC
  de Mens. IV.140 (163,16)
J.V. Powell, *Collectanea Alexan-
drina* (Oxford, 1925) 43, no.68

EURIPIDES
V BC
[*Bacchae* 13]
  de Mag. III.58 (224,5)
E.R. Dodds (Oxford, 1962)
[*Hecabe* 570]
  de Mag III.64 (232,22–23)
G. Murray, 3 vols (Oxford, 1901–
13)
Helen 167ff.
  de Mens. fr.incert. sed. (179,10–
13)
Hypsipyle
  de Mens. IV.7 (72,15) (fr.942,
Nauck = *P.Oxy.* VI.852 fr.60)
W. Cockle, *Euripides' Hypsipyle*
(Rome, 1987) 100 and 164
[*Inus*]
  de Mens. IV.7 (73,1) (fr,420,ff.,
Nauck)
[*Iphigenia in Aulis* 787]
  de Mag. III.58 (224,5)
G. Murray, 3 vols (Oxford, 1901–13)
Peleus
  de Mens. IV.7 (71,21) fr.1025,
Nauck
  de Mag. III.25 (170,18–19) fr.
628, Nauck
A. Nauck, *Tragicorum Graecorum
Fragmenta*, 2nd edn (Leipzig,
1889)
[*Scyriorum*]
  de Mens. IV.7 (71,23–5)
(fr.684,1–3, Nauck)
  de Mens. IV.100 (140,7)
(fr.684,1–3, Nauck)
[*Troades*]
  de Mens. IV.64 (116,11)

de Mens. IV.100 (140,18) (fr.942,
Nauck)
de Mens. IV.107 (144,15) (frs
and 288, Nauck)

EURYTUS OF SPARTA
?
de Mens. IV.154 (172,10)
T. Bergk, *Poetae Lyrici Graeci* III
(Leipzig, 1882) 639

[EUSEBIUS]
AD III–IV
[*Chronicle*]
de Mag. I.2 (8,13)
de Ost. 10a (31,10)
A. Schöne (Berlin, 1866–75, repr.
1967)

EUTHYMENES OF MARSEILLES
?II BC
[*Chronicle*]
de Mens. IV.107 (145,5)
Jacoby, *FGrH* #243, IIB, 1021–2

EUTROPIUS
AD IV
[*Breviarium ab Urbe Condita*
IX.26]
de Mens. I.26 (12,25)
C. Santini (Leipzig, 1979)

FENESTELLA
I BC–AD I
[*Histories*]
de Mag. III.74 (252,5)
Peter, *HRR*, II 80, fr.8

[FESTUS]
AD II
[*On the Meaning of Words*]
de Mag. III.37 (190,4)
W. M. Lindsay, *Sexti Pompeii Festi
de Verborum Significatu Quae
Supersunt cum Pauli Epitome*
(Leipzig, 1913) 46

FONTEIUS
?
[*On Statues*]
de Mens. I.37 (17,1)
de Mens. IV.2 (65,3)
de Mens. IV.80 (132,16)
de Mens. fr. incert. sed. 7

(180,10)
de Ost. 3 (8,24)
de Ost. 39–41 (88.10–92)
S. Weinstock, "Fonteius of the Libri
Tagetici", *Papers of the British
School at Rome* 18 (1950) 44ff.

FRONTINUS
AD I–II
(via Vegetius?)
de Officio Militari
de Mag. I.47 (74,23)

FULVIUS
?
de Ost. 16a (47,22)

GAIUS
AD II
(via Pomponius, cf. *Digest* I,
tit.II,23)
*On the Law of the Twelve Tables/
ad Legem XII Tabularum*
de Mag. I.26 (42,10)

GAVIUS BASSUS
I BC
Concerning the Gods
de Mens. IV.2 (65-7)
H. Funaioli, *Grammaticae Romanae
fragmenta* (Stuttgart, 1907, repr.
1969) 486ff.

"GEOGRAPHERS"
de Mens. III.1 (37,6)

GRACCHANUS
ante AD I
(via Ulpian, cf. *Digest* I.13)
On Powers
de Mag. proem.
de Mag. I.24 (38,21–40,8)

"GRAMMARIANS"
de Mens. IV.34 (91,21)
de Mens. IV.107 (144,10)

HEBREW BIBLE AND HEBREWS: *see*
Septuaginta

HECATAEUS
VI–V BC
(via Josephus, *Antiquitates Judaicae*
I, par.108, ed. B. Niese (Berlin,
1887) 25)
de Mens. III.5 (39,18)

Müller, *FHG* I.30 fr.265 = Jacoby,
  FGrH #1, IA, 16, fr.35; H.J.
  Mette, "Die kleinen griechischen
  Historiker heute", *Lustrum* 221
  (1978) 6

HELIODORUS
?
  de Ost. 2 (6,23)

HELLANICUS
V BC
(via Josephus *Antiquitates Judaicae*
  I, par.108, ed. B. Niese (Berlin,
  1887) 25)
  de Mens. III.5 (39,19)
Müller, *FHG* I.57, fr. 89 = Jacoby,
  FGrH #4, IIIB, 40–50, IIIB suppl.
  1–57

HERACLIDES OF PONTUS
IV BC
  de Mens. IV.83 (134,8)
  de Mens. IV.89 (137,11)
  de Mens. IV.42 (99,18)
F. Wehrli, *Herakleides Pontikos*
  (Basle, 1969) 13–54

HERACLITUS
VI–V BC
  de Mens. III.12 (53,12)
  de Mens. III.12 (54,3)
  de Mens. III.14 (55,14)
  de Mens. IV.81 (133,14)
  de Mens. IV.81 (133,20)
Diels and Kranz, 150–82

HERENNIUS PHILO OF BYBLOS
AD I–II
[*Phoenician History*]
  de Mag. I.12 (24,2)
  de Mens. IV,53 (111,13) [cited as
  "Herennius"]
  de Mens. IV.154 (170,6) [cited as
  "Herennius Philo"]
Jacoby, *FGrH* #790, IIIC, 802–24 [=
  Müller, *FHG* III.560ff.]

HERMES
Cosmopoiia
  de Mens. IV.64 (116,18)
A.D. Nock, A.-J. Festugière (Paris,
  1954)

Teleios Logos
  de Mens. IV.7 (70,22)
  de Mens. IV.32 (90,24)
  de Mens. IV.149 (167,15 and 21)
  de Mens. IV.7 (71,7)
  de Mens. IV.53 (109,15)

[HERODIAN]
AD III
[*History after the Death of the
  Emperor Marcus*]
  de Mag. III.70 (246,1)
C.R. Whittaker (Cambridge, Mass.,
  1969–70)

HERODOTUS
V BC
[*Histories*]
  de Mens. IV.107 (146,3) (Herodotus, II.24)
  de Mens. IV.118 (156,13) (Herodotus, III.154)
C. Hude (Oxford, 1927)

HESIOD
VIII–VII BC
Catalog
  de Mens. I.13 (7,26)
R. Merkelbach and M.L. West,
  Fragmenta Hesiodea (Oxford,
  1967)
[*Theogony*]
  de Mens. IV.7 (70,18)
M.L. West (Oxford, 1966)
[*Works and Days*, 109–10]
  de Mag. III.67 (236,27)
  de Mens. IV.76 (127,5) 802
(via Josephus, *Antiquitates Judaicae*
  I.108)
  de Mens. III.5 (39,18)
F. Solmsen (Oxford, repr. 1970)

HIPPARCHUS
II BC
[*Commentary on the Phenomena of
  Aratus*]
  de Ost. 7 (15,2)
C. Manitius (Leipzig, 1894)
  de Mens. IV.18 (79,9)
(S. Weinstock, *Codices Britannici*

APPENDIX

[Catalogus Codicum Astrologorum Graecorum] 9.1
(Brussels, 1951) 189–90 lacks this reference)

HIPPOCRATES
IV BC
[On Birth in the Seventh Month]
de Mens. II.12 (35,12)
E. Littré (Paris, 1839, repr. Amsterdam, 1973) 7.436–52

"HISTORIANS"
de Mens. IV.102 (142,13)
de Mens. IV.105 (143,21)
de Ost. 10b (34,13)
de Ost. 5 (11,18)
de Ost. 25 (60,10)

HOMER
VII–VI BC
[Iliad]
de Mag. I.36 (54,8–9) (*Iliad* 2.204)
de Mens. II.8 (25,16) (*Iliad* 15,189)
de Mens. IV.7 (70,17)
de Mens. IV.54 (111,21) (*Iliad* 1.197)
de Mens. IV.60 (113,21–4) (*Iliad* 5.428,430)
de Mens. IV.72 (124,18–19) (*Iliad* 5.860)
W.T. Allen (Oxford, 1931)

"HYMNS"
de Mens. IV.64 (118,16)

IAMBLICHUS
AD III–IV
Chaldeans, I
de Mens. IV.159 (175,10)

On the Journey of the Soul, I
de Mens. IV.149 (167,23)

Roman Priests
de Mens. IV.94 (139,5)

de Mens. IV.6 (69,23)
de Mens. IV.25 (83,14)
de Mens. IV.35 (93,10)
de Mens. IV.53 (110,22)

ISIGONUS
III BC–AD I

Concerning the Palician Gods
de Mens. IV.154 (170,12)
Müller, *FHG* IV.437 (A. Giannini, *Paradoxographorum Graecorum Reliquiae* (Milan, 1967) 147–8 lacks this reference)

[ISOCRATES THE RHETOR]
V–IV BC
[For Demonicus, 11]
de Mag. III.44 (202,3)
de Mens. IV.7 (73,12)
de Mens. IV.100 (140,21)
G. Mathieu and E. Brémond (Paris, 1929, repr. 1963) I.122–35

JULIAN
AD IV
? *On Military Engines*
de Mag. I.47 (74,22)
see Bandy 282, note 74.22–5

[Letter to the Jews]
de Mens. IV.53 (110,4)
J. Bidez (Paris, 1932)

JUVENAL
AD I–II
[Satires, 5.110–1]
de Mag. I.20 (32,29)
W.V. Clausen (Oxford, 1959)

[CORNELIUS] LABEO
?AD III
Book of Lightning
de Ost. 3 (8,24)
de Ost. 42–52 (93–107.6)

de Mens. I.21 (11.16)
de Mens. III.10 (47,18)
de Mens. IV.1 (63,8)
de Mens. IV.25 (83,8)
de Ost. 3 (8,25)
W. Kahl, *Philol. suppl.* V. 730ff.

LEPIDUS
I BC?
On Priesthoods
de Mag. I.17 (32,4–6)

[LIVY]
I BC
[History]
de Mag. I.34 (50,26–7)

129

R.S. Conway, C.F. Walters and S.K.
Johnson (Oxford, 1914–65)
(*History* III.31)
de Mens. IV.53 (109,23) (*History*,
Bk 102?)

[PS.-]LONGINUS
AD I
[*On the Sublime*]
de Mens. IV.1 (64,6)
D.A. Russell, *"Longinus" On the
Sublime* (Oxford, 1964)

LUCAN
AD I
On the Civil War
de Mag. III.46 (204,12–13) (cf.
Civil War, 2.610)
de Mens. IV.53 (109,25) (*Civil
War* 2.592)
A.E. Housman (Oxford, 1927)

LUTATIUS [Q. LUTATIUS CATULUS]
II–I BC
de Mens. IV.2 (65,16)
Peter, *HRR* 194, fr. 13

LYCOPHRON
IV–III BC
Alexandra
de Mag. III.60 (226,27–228,1)
(*Alexandra* V.38)
de Mens. IV.67 (121,1) (*Alexan-
dra* V.33–4)
L. Mascialino (Leipzig, 1964)

LYDUS, JOHN
AD VI
de Mag. I.7 (2.7) (*de Mens.* "book
I")
de Mag. I.8 (18,27) (incert.)
de Mag. I.9 (20,18–19) (incert.)
de Mag. II.4 (88,8) (*de Mens.*
I.20)
de Mag. II.12 (102,5) (*de Mens.*
fr. incert. sed.7)
de Mag. II.13 (104,10–11) (*de
Mens.* I.39)
de Mag. II.19 (112,17–19) (*de
Mens.* I.40)
de Mag. III.42 (198,6–7) (incert.)
de Mag. III.61 (228,7–8) (*de
Mens.* I.32)

de Ost. 7 (16,8) (*de Mens.* III.8)
de Ost. 25 (59,24) (*de Mens.*
IV.63)

[MACROBIUS]
AD IV–V
[*Saturnalia*, 3.16]
de Mag. III.63 (232,5)
J. Willis (Leipzig, 1963)

MANETHO
III BC
Commentary on Egyptian History
III
de Mens. IV.86 (136,1)
Müller, *FHG* II.526, fr.1 [= Jacoby,
FGrH #609, IIIC, 98]
On Festivals
de Mens. IV.87 (136,7)
Müller *FHG* II.615, fr.82 = Jacoby,
FGrH #609, IIIC, 98–9, fr.15

"MATHEMATICIANS"
de Mens. I.17 (10,4)
de Mens. II.12 (34,3)

MAXIMUS
?
de Mens. IV.14 (77,17)

MELIAS: *see* Aemilius Asper

MENANDER [OF EPHESUS]
ante II BC
[*Phoenician History*]
de Mens. IV.154 (171,4)
Jacoby, *FGrH* #783, IIC, 789–95,
fr.6

MESOMEDES
AD II
[*Hymn to Nemesis*]
de Mens. fr. fals. attrib. 6
(184,13)
E. Heitsch, *Die griechischen
Dichterfragmente der römischen
Kaiserzeit* I, fr.3, lines 7–8 (Gött-
ingen, 1963) 26

MESSALA
I BC?
de Mens. IV.1 (64,12)
Peter, *HRR* ii, lxxviiiff. and 65ff.
(cf. Macrobius, *Saturnalia* 1.9.14)

METRODORUS
?
  de Mens. IV.49 (106,12)
  de Mens. IV.61 (114,3)
  de Mens. IV.123 (159,9)
  de Mens. IV.141 (164,5)
  de Mens. IV.148 (166,19)
  de Ost. 70 (158)

MOSES
  de Mens. IV.54 (172,15)

"MYSTIKOS LOGOS": see "Chaldeans"

"MYTHOLOGERS"
  de Mens. I.1 (1,1)
  de Mens. II.2 (19,12)
  de Mens. II.8 (25,9)
  de Mens. IV.3 (67,7)
  de Mens. IV.34 (91,18)
  de Mens. IV.64 (116,6)
  de Mens. IV.154 (171,12)
  de Mens. IV.154 (172,8)
  de Mens. IV.15 (175,26)

"NATURAL SCIENTISTS"
  de Mens. II.7 (23,20)
  de Mens. III.10 (47,7)
  de Mens. IV.21 (80,3 and 10)
  de Mens. IV.34 (92,8)
  de Mens. IV.64 (115,23)
  de Mens. IV.66 (120,1)
  de Mens. IV.71 (123,22)
  de Mens. IV.94 (138,19)
  de Mens. IV.116 (155,8)
  de Mens. IV.159 (175,1)
  de Mens. IV.26 (84,14)
  de Ost. 9c (24,22)
  de Ost. 21 (54,23)

NICANOR
ante II BC
Life of Alexander
  de Mens. IV.47 (102,13)
Jacoby, FGrH #146, IIB, 814–15, 532

NICOLAUS
I BC
(via Josephus, Ant. Jud. 1,108)
  de Mens. III.5 (39,19)
Jacoby, FGrH #90, IIA, 328–430,
    fr.97 [= Müller, FHG III.418,
    fr.87]

NICOMACHUS
ante AD II
[?On the Festivals of the
  Egyptians]
  de Mens. IV.67 (120,7)
  de Mens. IV.162 (177,22)
Jacoby, FGrH #662, IIIC, 213–14,
  p.213 fr.1

NIGIDIUS FIGULUS
I BC
  de Ost. 3 (8,26)
  de Ost. 10b (35,7)
  de Ost. 27–38 (62,3–88,9)
A. Swoboda (Graz, 1889)

NUMA
  de Ost. 16a (47,23)

NUMENIUS
? AD II
  de Mens. IV.53 (110,2)
  de Mens. IV.86 (135,13)
  de Mens. IV.80 (132,12)
  de Mens. fr. fals. attrib. 6
  (184,12)

OCELLUS THE PYTHAGOREAN
ante I BC
  de Mens. II.8 (27,7)
Diels and Kranz, 48,8 (I,441,5)

ODAPSUS OF THEBES
?
  de Ost. 2 (6,24)

"ORACLES"
  de Mens. II.5 (22,2)
  de Mens. III.10 (44,6)
  de Mens. IV.8 (73,17)
  de Mens. IV.42 (98,23)
  de Mens. IV.67 (120,5)
  de Mens. IV.80, 132,3)
  de Mens. IV.89 (137,3)
  de Mens. IV.101 (141,1)
  de Mens. IV.106 (144,3)
  de Mens. IV.120 (158,10)
  de Mens. IV.134 (161,18)
  de Mens. IV.135 (162,1 and 9)
  de Mens. IV.154 (172,4)
  de Mens. fr. incert. 7 (180,11)

ORIGEN
AD II–III
[*Philocalia* 33]
 de Mens. IV.53 (110,15)
J.A. Robinson (Cambridge, 1893)

ORPHEUS
 de Mens. I.15 (9,6) (fr. 151)
 de Mens. II.6 (22,21) (fr. 144)
 de Mens. II.8 (26,2) (fr. 145)
 de Mens. II.11 (32,21) (fr. 147)
 de Mens. II.12 (33,11) (fr. 148)
 de Mens. IV.42 (99,22) (fr. 263)
E. Abel (Prague, 1885)

OVID
I BC–AD I
[*Fasti* I.103]
 de Mens. IV.2 (66,11)
E.H. Alton *et al.* (Leipzig, 1985)

PANAETIUS
II BC
 de Mens. IV.115 (153,25)
M. van Straaten (Leiden, 1962)

PATERNUS THE ROMAN
AD II
Tactics
 de Mag. I.9 (21,1-29)

PEISANDER [OF LARANDA?]
AD III
[*Heroic Offspring of Divine
   Marriages*]
 de Mag. III.64 (232,28)
see Bandy 336, note 232.28; R.
   Keydell, "Die Dichter mit
   Namen Peisandros", *Hermes* 70
   (1935) 301-11

PERSIUS
AD I
[*Satires*, 1.20]
 de Mag. I.1 (32,21-4)
W.V. Clausen (Oxford, 1956)

PETER THE PATRICIAN
AD VI
[*On the Magister Officiorum*]
 de Mag. II.25 (120,27-30)
see A. Cameron, *Procopius and the
   Sixth Century* (Berkeley, 1985)
   251

PETOSIRIS
ante II BC
 de Ost. 2 (6,14)

 de Ost. 9c (24,5)
E. Reiss, "Nechepsonis et Petosir-
   idis fragmenta magica",
   Philologus suppl.6 (1891-3) 332-
   87

PHERECYDES
VI BC
 de Mens. II.7 (24,13)
Diels and Kranz, 7 B14 (I,51,11)
 de Mens. IV.3 (67,3)
Diels and Kranz, 7 A9 (I,46,20)

PHILIPPUS
?
 de Mens. IV.17 (79,3)
 de Mens. IV.61 (114,1)

PHILO: *see* Herennius

PHILO JUDAEUS
I BC–AD I
[*Life of Moses*]
 de Mens. IV,47 (103,17) (*Life* I.2)
 de Mens. IV.47 (103,22) (*Life* II.
   5.6)
L. Cohn (Berlin, 1896, repr. Berlin/
   New York, 1962) vol.IV, 119ff.

PHILOLAUS
V BC
 de Mens. I.15 (9,5)
 de Mens. II.12 (33,14)
 de Mens. II.12 (34,1)
 de Mens. IV.64 (114,20)
Diels and Kranz 406-19

"PHILOSOPHERS"
 de Mens. II.9 (28,22)
 de Mens. II.10 (31,10)
 de Mens. IV.64 (117,24)
 de Mens. IV.67 (121,24)
 de Mens. IV.82 (134,6)
 de Mens. IV.83 (134,16)
 de Mens. IV.149 (168,2)
 de Mens. IV.159 (175,3)
 de Mens. fr. falsa.1 (181,6)
 de Ost. 4 (9,10)
 de Ost. 53 (107,8)

PHILOXENUS
BC ?I
[*On the Roman Language*]
 de Mag. I.42 (64,8)
 de Mens. IV.34 (92,3)
C. Theodorides (Berlin, 1976) frs
 328 and 327

PHLEGO [PUBLIUS AELIUS PHLEGO]
AD II
On Festivals
 de Mens. I.21 (11,14)
Müller, *FHG* III,602ff. = Jacoby, *FGrH*
 #257, IIB, 1159ff.; #257, IIB, 744
 add. (omits references to Lydus)

PHYLARCHUS
III BC
[*History*, Bk 16]
 de Mens. IV.154 (171,4)
Jacoby, *FGrH* #81, IIA, 171, fr.33 =
 Müller, *FHG* I.343, fr.34

PINDAR
V–IV BC
[*Pythian Ode*, IV,194]
 de Mens. IV.100 (140,5)
B.K. Braswell, *A Commentary on
 the Fourth Pythian Ode of Pindar*
 (Berlin/New York, 1988)

PISO
AD II
[*On Constellations?*]
 de Mens. fr. incert. sed. 6 (180,9)

PLATO
V–IV BC
[*Cratylus*]
 de Mens. IV.94 (138,21) (cf.
 401C)

[*Laws*]
 de Mens. IV.154 (171,21) (III
 701C)

Phaedo
 de Mens. IV.32 (91,7) (113B)

Phaedrus
 de Mens. I.17 (9,17) (247A)
 de Mens. I.17 (9,20) (cf. 247A;
 Timaeus 55C)
 de Mens. II.8 (27,12) (246A)
 de Mens. II.8 (27,19) (246A)

 de Mens. IV.54 (112,6) (245C).
 de Mens. I.11 (3,2) (253ff.; n.b.
 text says it is in *Phaedo* but
 Wuensch suggests *Phaedrus*)

[*Republic*]
 de Mens. IV.38 (96,6) (X.617ff.)

Symposium
 de Mens. IV.64 (116,24) (180D)
 de Mens. IV.154 (172,11) (203B)

Timaeus
 de Mens. II.8 (27,18)
 de Mens. II.12 (35,17) (36D)
 de Mens. III.3 (38,13) (cf. 26C)
 de Mens. IV.35 (93,9 and 23)
 (29ff.)
 de Mens. IV.38 (96,11) (30B)
 de Mens. IV.51 (108,4) (55D)
 de Mens. IV.53 (109,16) (27D)
 de Mens. IV.76 (126,25) (cf. 55A)
 de Mens. IV.159 (175,23) (30A)

J. Burnet (Oxford, 1900, repr. 1967)

 de Mens. 11.8 (28,1)
 de Mens. III.12 (53,9)
Diels, *DG* 324
 de Mens. IV.7 (72,5)
 de Mens. IV.7 (73,13)
 de Mens. IV.81 (133,12 and 16)
Diels, *DG* 19,18,5
 de Mens. IV.81 (134,1)
 de Mens. IV.83 (134,17)
Diels, *DG* 5
 de Mens. IV.100 (140,21)

[PLINY]
AD I
[*Natural History*]
 de Mag. I.23 (38,10) (cf. *NH*
 18.3)
 de Mag. I.42 (64,21) (cf. *NH*
 7.17)
 de Mag. III.63 (232,4–5) (cf. *NH*
 9.27)
 de Mag. III.63 (232,15–16) (cf.
 NH 9.29)
 de Ost. 3 (8,26)
 de Ost. 7 (15,4) (*NH*, II.53)
L. Jan and C. Mayhoff (Leipzig,
 1909)

PLOTINUS
AD III
[*Enneades*]
  de Mens. IV.37 (95,19) (II.3)
  de Mens. IV.37 (95,27) (II.3.8)
  de Mens. IV.38 (96,6) (II.3.9)
P. Henry and H.R. Schwyzer, vol.1
  (Leiden, 1951)

PLUTARCH
AD I–II
[*de Aud. Poet.* 6]
  de Mens. IV.86 (135,19)
W.R. Paton and I. Wegehaupt,
  Moralia I (Leipzig, 1974) 46
[*Isis and Osiris* 32]
  de Mens. IV.45 (101,19)
W. Sieveking, *Moralia* II (Leipzig,
  1935) 503
[*Marcellus* 22]
  de Mens. I.2 (1,8)
K. Ziegler, *Vitae* (Leipzig, 1969)
[*Pompey* 40]
  de Mag. II.21 (116,19)
R. Flacelière and E. Chambry
  (Paris, 1973)

[*Quaestiones Conviviales* IX.6]
  de Mens. II.7 (25,1)
C. Hubert, *Moralia* IV (Leipzig,
  1938) 315
  de Mens. IV.4 (68,6)
  de Mens. IV.148 (166,24)

"POETS"
  de Mens. III.10 (44,5)
  de Mens. IV.32 (91,6)
  de Mens. IV.51 (107,6)
  de Mens. IV.64 (177,1)
  de Mens. IV.99 (140,3)
(cf. Solon, fr. 42.4, ed. T. Bergk,
  Poetae Lyrici Graeci III, Leipzig,
  1882)
  de Mens. IV.149 (167,20)

POLEMON
III–II BC
  de Mens. IV.154 (170,12)
Müller, *FHG* III, p.148, fr.102; *P.
  Oxy.* XVIII,2176

POLEMON
AD IV
Commentary on Lucan's Civil War
  de Mag. III.46 (206,4)

POLLES
?
  de Ost. 2 (6,25)
  de Ost. 8 (17,12)

[? POLYCHARMUS]
About Dionysus (? MSS corrupt)
  de Mens. IV.154 (170,17)

POMPONIUS
AD II
[*Enchiridion*]
[= *Digest*, I.2.2.34]
  de Mag. I.48

"PONTIFICAL BOOKS"
  de Mens. IV.25 (83,12)

PORPHYRY
AD III
[*On Abstinence* II.5]
  de Mens. IV.149 (168,4)
A. Nauck (Leipzig, 1886, repr.
  Hildesheim, 1962)

[*On Philosophy from Oracles*]
  de Mens. IV.53 (110,18)
G. Wolff (Berlin, 1856, repr.
  Hildesheim, 1962)
  de Mens. IV.7 (71,7)
  de Mens. IV.94 (138,24)
  de Mens. IV.122 (159,7)

POSIDONIUS
?AD II
  de Mens. IV.71 (122,17)
  de Mens. IV.81 (133,23)
Diels, *DG* 324a,4 and Plutarch,
  Epitomes I,29,30

PRAETEXTATUS THE HIEROPHANT
?
  de Mens. IV.2 (65,20)

PROCLUS
AD V
Hymnal
  de Mens. II.6 (23,11)
  de Mens. II.8 (27,19)
de Mens. IV.7 (71,14)

de Mens. IV.35 (93,15)
de Mens. IV.53 (110,23)
de Mens. IV.58 (113,16)
de Mens. IV.76 (128,3) *Commentary on the First Alcibiades of Plato,* ed. L.G. Westerink, (Amsterdam, 1954)
de Mens. IV.154 (171,8)
de Ost. 3 (8,6)

PTOLEMY [CLAUDIUS PTOLEMAEUS]
AD II
Geography VII.5,3
   de Mens. III.1 (37,7)
C.F.A. Nobbe, vol.11 (Leipzig, 1845, repr. 1966)
Harmonics [?]
   de Mens. IV.36 (94,14) cf.
   Harmonica II.9
I. Duering (Göteborg, 1930)
Tetrabiblos II.8 fr.23
   de Mens. IV.116 (155,5)
   de Ost. 10a (32,6)
S. Feraboli (Rome, 1985)
   de Ost. 2 (6,25)
   de Ost. 8 (17,15)

"PYTHAGORAS" and "PYTHAGOREANS"
   de Mens. I.35 (16,7)
   de Mens. II.4 (21,5)
   de Mens. II.6 (22,5)
   de Mens. II.8 (28,8)
   de Mens. II.9 (29,3)
   de Mens. II.10 (31,14)
   de Mens. II.12 (33,8)
   de Mens. III.4 (39,14)
   de Mens. III.9 (43,4)
   de Mens. III.12 (53,13)
   de Mens. IV.1 (64,11)
   de Mens. IV.42 (99,14)
   de Mens. IV.42 (100,13)
   de Mens. IV.51 (108,5)
   de Mens. IV.88 (136,21)
   de Mens. IV.97 (139,19)
   de Mens. IV.111 (150,11)
   de Ost. 21 (55,12)
PYTHIAS OF MARSEILLES
IV BC
   de Mens. IV.83 (134,14)
Diels, *DG* 383a, 1

SALLUST
I BC
History, I
   de Mag. I.1 (2,13)
B. Maurenbrecher, 2 vols (Leipzig, 1891-3)

SAMMONICUS
On Various Questions
   de Mag. III.32 (184,12)
see Bandy 318

SENECA
AD I
[*Natural Questions* 4a,2]
   de Mens. IV.107 (144,16)
   de Mens. IV.107 (145,13)
A. Gercke (Leipzig, 1907)

[SEPTUAGINTA]
Daniel
   de Mag. I.31 (48,5)
Isaiah I:11-14
   de Mens. IV.24 (82,12)
Psalms 80:3
   de Mens. III.11 (50,5)
Leviticus 10:9
   de Mens. IV.53 (111,11)
   de Ost. 22 (56,7)

SIBYLLINE ORACLES
   de Mens. IV.8 (73,17)
   de Mens. IV.47 (104,13ff.)
A. Rzach, IV.140-4 and VI.26

SISENNA
I BC
[*History*]
   de Mag. III.74 (252,5)
Peter, *HRR* 296, no.133

SOPHOCLES
V BC
Ajax, 135
   de Mag. I.3 (12,6)
A. Dain and P. Mazon (Paris, 1968)
   de Mens. IV.107 (144,14)
Radt, *Tragicorum Graecorum Fragmenta* IV (Göttingen, 1977) fr.882

STOICS
   de Mens. III.12 (53,9) = Diels,

DG 356a, adn.5
de Mens. III.16 (57,12) = Diels,
DG 468a, 8ff
de Mens. IV.40 (98,3) = Diels,
DG 468a, 8ff
de Mens. IV.63 (114,10) = Diels,
DG 376a, 22
de Mens. IV.81 (133,17) = Diels,
DG 322a, 9
de Ost. 7 (15,7)

STRATO [text says "Plato"]
de Mens. IV.84 (134,21)
Diels, *DG* 421a,1

[SUETONIUS] TRANQUILLUS
AD I–II
[*Lives of the Caesars*]
de Mag. II.6 (92,6) (proem to
Lives)
de Mag. I.12 (24,19) (*Augustus*
40.5)
J.C. Rolfe (Cambridge, Mass., 1944)
*On Famous Courtesans/De Scortis
Illustribus*
de Mag. III.64 (234,9)
de Mag. I.34 (52,13)
Reifferscheid (Leipzig 1820),
frs 200, 202

SYRIANUS
AD V
de Mens. IV.53 (110,23)

TAGES
ante III BC
On Predicting Earthquakes
de Mens. IV.79 (131,24)
de Mens. frs incert. sed. 2
(178,15) and 6(180,8)
de Ost. 2 (7,2 and 11)
de Ost. 3 (7,24 and 26)
de Ost. 27 (62,103)
de Ost. 54 (110,7)

TARCHON
de Ost. 2-3 (7-8)

TARCUTUS [TARQUITIUS PRISCUS]
? AD I
[*Etruscan Lore*]
de Ost. 2 (7,7)

TARROUTIUS THE MATHEMATICIAN
?
de Mens. I.14 (8,8)

TERPANDER OF LESBOS
?VII BC
de Mens. IV.51 (106,20)
D.L. Page, *Poetae Melici Graeci*
(Oxford, 1967) 362

THALES
VI BC
de Mens. III.12 (54,1)
Diels and Kranz, 80–1

"THEOLOGIANS"
de Mens. II.11 (32,14)
de Mens. IV.53 (109,13)
de Mens. IV.94 (138,20)

THEOPHRASTUS
?IV–III BC
de Mens. II.8 (26,9) (?*On Music*)
de Mens. IV.7 (72,7)
F. Wimmer (1866, repr. Frankfurt,
1964)

THRASYALCES THE THASIAN
V–IV BC
de Mens. IV.107 (146,16)
Diels and Kranz, 337

[THUCYDIDES]
V BC
[*History*]
de Mag. III.46 (204,14)
H.S. Jones, J.E. Powell (Oxford,
1942)

ULPIAN
AD III
*On the Office of Quaestor/de
Officio Quaestoris*
de Mag. I.24 (40,9)
de Mag. I.28 (44,12)

Protribunalia [*de omnibus
tribunalibus*]
de Mag. I.48 (78,2)
O. Lenel, *Palingenesia Iuris Civilis*
(Graz, 1889, repr. 1960)
II.903,962; J. Caimi, *Burocrazia e
diritto nel de Magistratibus di
Giovanni Lido* (Milan, 1984) 177

APPENDIX

VALES [VALENS, THE EMPEROR]
AD IV
  de Mens. IV.102 (142,21)
Peter, *HRR* II. 161

[TERENTIUS] VARRO
II BC

Antiquities, XIV
  de Mens. IV.2 (64,18)

Human Affairs
  de Mag. III.74 (252,6)

Introduction to Pompey
  de Mag. I.5 (14,21)

On the Roman Language, V
  de Mag. II.13 (104,19)

[*On the Stars*]
  de Ost. 10b (35,6)
  de Ost. 70 (158,1)

Portraits
  de Mag. I.12 (24,1-3)
G. Goetz and F. Schoell (Leipzig, 1910)

  de Mens. I.37 (17,1)
  de Mens. IV.16 (78,15)
  de Mens. IV.48 (105,13)
  de Mens. IV.51 (109,4)
  de Mens. IV.53 (110,25)
  de Mens. IV.76 (128,24)
  de Mens. IV.135 (162,8)
  de Mens. IV.139 (163,13)
  de Mens. IV.143 (164,14)
  de Mens. IV.147 (165,20)
  de Mens. IV.154 (172,18)

VERGIL
I BC
Aeneid
  de Mag. I.7 (16,23) (*Aen.* 7.169, 188)
  de Mag. I.12 (34,6) (*Aen.* 1.312)

  de Mag. I.25 (40,21-2) (*Aen.* 6.432-3)
  de Mens. IV.118 (156,14) (*Aen.* 2.79; here called "Vergilianus")

Eclogues I.30
  de Mens. IV.73 (125,7)
R.A.B. Mynors (Oxford, 1969)

VICELLIUS
post AD II
On Earthquakes
  de Ost. 55-8 (110,11-117,4)
  de Ost. 3 (8,25)

XANTHUS
V BC
  de Mens. III.20 (59,6)
Müller, *FHG* IV.629, fr.14 = Jacoby, *FGrH* #765, IIIC, 756, fr.23

XENOCRATES
IV BC
  de Mens. III.10 (48,21)
Jacoby, *FGrH* #248, IIB, 1130 [= Müller, *FHG* IV.530]

XENOPHANES
VI-V BC
  de Mens. III.12 (53,8)
Diels and Kranz, I,126-38

ZOPYRUS THE BYZANTINE
IV-III BC
  de Mens. IV.150 (168,20)
Jacoby, *FGrH* #494, IIIB, 465-6 = Müller, *FHG* IV.532 (Jacoby omits this reference)

ZOROASTER
?
  de Mens. II.6 (23,17)
  de Ost. 2 (6,14)
J. Bidez and F. Cumont, *Les mages hellenisés* (Paris, 1938)

NOTES

Translations are those of the author unless otherwise noted. Translations of *de Magistratibus* are based on those of A.C. Bandy, *On Powers*.

The following works are referred to in abbreviated form only:

de Mag.: John Lydus, *De Magistratibus Populi Romani Libri Tres*;
de Mens.: John Lydus, *Liber de Mensibus*;
de Ost.: John Lydus, *Liber de Ostentis et Calendaria Omnia*;
CIL: *Corpus Inscriptionum Latinarum* I.1, ed. Theodore Mommsen (Berlin, 1862);
CJ: *Codex Justinianus*, in *Corpus Iuris Civilis*, vol. I, ed. Paul Krüger (repr. Berlin, 1915);
CTh.: *Codex Theodosianus cum Constitutionibus Sirmondianis et Leges Novellae Pertinentes*, ed. Theodore Mommsen and Paul M. Meyer (Berlin, 1905);
Jones, *LRE*: A.H.M. Jones, *The Later Roman Empire* (Oxford, 1964);
NJ: *Novellae Justiniani* in *Corpus Iuris Civilis*, vol. III, ed. Rudolf Schoell and William Kroll (repr. Berlin, 1912);
PG: *Patrologiae cursus completus. Series Graeca*, ed. J.P. Migne (Paris, 1857–1936);
PLRE: J. R. Martindale, *The Prosopography of the Later Roman Empire* 2. AD 395–527 (Cambridge, 1980);
RE: A. Pauly, G. Wissowa, W. Kroll *et al.*, eds, *Paulys Real-Encyclopädie der Klassischen Altertumswissenschaft* (Leipzig, 1893–);
Stein: Ernest Stein, *Histoire du Bas-Empire*, ed. Jean-Remy Palanque (Paris/Bruges, 1949; repr. Amsterdam, 1968) vol. II.

Abbreviations of journals and series:

AHR: *American Historical Review*
AJA: *American Journal of Archaeology*
BCH: *Bulletin de Correspondance Hellénique*
ByzF: *Byzantinische Forschungen*
BZ: *Byzantinische Zeitschrift*
CFHB: *Corpus Fontium Historiae Byzantinae*
CHR: *Catholic Historical Review*
CR: *Classical Review*
CSCO: *Corpus scriptorum christianorum orientalium*
CSHB: *Corpus scriptorum historiae byzantinae*
DOP: *Dumbarton Oaks Papers*
GCS: *Griechische Christliche Schriftsteller*
GRBS: *Greek, Roman and Byzantine Studies*
HAW: *Handbuch der Altertumswissenschaft*
HSCP: *Harvard Studies in Classical Philology*
HTR: *Harvard Theological Review*
JAOS: *Journal of the American Oriental Society*
JHS: *Journal of Hellenic Studies*
JRS: *Journal of Roman Studies*
JTS: *Journal of Theological Studies*
PAPS: *Proceedings of the American Philosophical Society*
PCPS: *Proceedings of the Cambridge Philological Society*
REG: *Revue des Études Grecques*
REL: *Revue des Études Latines*
RIDA: *Revue Internationale des Droits de l'Antiquité*
TAPA: *Transactions of the American Philological Association*
ZNW: *Zeitschrift für die neutestamentliche Wissenschaft*
ZSS (*Röm.Abt.*): *Zeitschrift der Savigny-Stiftung für Rechtsgeschichte* (*Römische Abteilung*)

INTRODUCTION

1 To set out the difficulties confronting us and them, it is convenient to use here the modern labels "late-antique" and "Byzantine," with the caveat that Lydus did not know them, nor would he have understood them. I use them only as shorthand to stand for two different attitudes toward society, one relatively pluralistic, the other more tightly focussed upon Christianity. In Lydus' day these overlapped.
2 John Moorhead, "The West and the Roman Past from Theoderic to Charlemagne", in Brian Croke and Alanna Emmett, eds, *History and Historians in Late Antiquity* (Sydney, 1983) 155–69.
3 Franz Dölger, "Rom in die Gedankenwelt der Byzantiner", in *Byzanz und die europäische Staatenwelt* (Ettal, 1953) 70–115, here 70; Julius Jüthner, *Hellenen und Barbaren* (Leipzig, 1923) 103–18; Alexander Kazhdan and

Giles Constable, *People and Power in Byzantium. An Introduction to Modern Byzantine Studies* (Dumbarton Oaks, 1982) 117-39.

4 Dölger, "Rom in die Gedankenwelt" 70.

5 Pierre Chuvin, *A Chronicle of the Last Pagans*, trans. B. A. Archer (Cambridge, Mass., 1990).

6 *PLRE* II "Proclus 4" 915-9.

7 *PLRE* II 633.

8 Chuvin, *Chronicle* 93; *PLRE* II 336-9.

9 I will describe below (Chapter 5) how the emperor's definitions were not adequate to the reality of political and cultural circumstances.

10 Robert Markus, "The Sacred and the Secular: from Augustine to Gregory the Great", *JTS* 36.1 (1985) 84-96, here 96.

11 On this literary affectation see Averil Cameron, *Procopius and the Sixth Century* (Berkeley, 1985) 113-33.

12 Lydus assumes such a problematical stance in his theory of change in *de Mag.*

13 Peter Brown, "Aspects of the Christianization of the Roman Aristocracy", *JRS* 51 (1961) 1-11, here 9 [= *Religion and Society in the Age of St. Augustine* (New York, 1972) 161-82, here 177].

14 Averil Cameron calls this a "simplification of culture": "Images of Authority: Élites and Icons in Late Sixth Century Byzantium", *Past and Present* 84 (1979) 3-35, here 24-9 [= Margaret Mullett and Roger Scott, eds, *Byzantium and the Classical Tradition* (Birmingham, 1981) 205-34, here 224ff.]; Robert Markus raises the issue of "de-secularization" to describe the recasting of secular antiquity within a Christian world view in the west ("The Sacred and the Secular" *passim*).

15 P. Merlan, "Johannos Lydos", *Lexikon der alten Welt* (Zurich/Stuttgart, 1965) 1390.

16 Michael Maas, "Innovation and Restoration in Justinianic Constantinople" (Diss. University of California at Berkeley, 1982), 148.

17 Osvalda Andrei, *A. Claudius Charax di Pergamo. Interessi antiquari e antichità cittadine nell'età degli Antonini* (Bologna, 1984) esp. 121-37; E. L. Bowie, "Greeks and their Past in the Second Sophistic", *Past and Present* 46 (1970) 3-41.

18 Elizabeth Rawson, *Intellectual Life in the Late Roman Republic* (Baltimore, 1985) ch.16, "Antiquarianism" 233-49; Arnaldo Momigliano, "Ancient History and the Antiquarian", *Journal of the Warburg and Courtauld Institutes* 13 (1950) 285-315 [= *Studies in Ancient Historiography* (London, 1966) 1-39; = *Contributo alla storia degli studi classici* (Rome, 1955; repr. 1979) 67-106]; *idem, The Classical Foundations of Modern Historiography* (Berkeley, 1990) 60-2.

19 *de Mag.* II.7; Homer, *Iliad*, 2.204, cited also at *de Mag.* I.36 regarding the creation of the dictatorship.

20 In this case the governor, John, called Maxilloplumbacius, *de Mag.* III.58.

21 *de Mag.* III.59.

22 Berthold Rubin, *Das Zeitalter Iustinians* (Berlin, 1960) 168; see below (Chapter 6) for Lydus' evaluation of Justinian.

23 e.g. *de Mag.* III.70.

24 See Chapter 2.

25 Roger Scott, "John Lydus on Some Procedural Changes", Βυζαντινά 4 (1972) 441-51, discusses his complaints about the simplification of drafting legal documents (de Mag. III.ll); A. H. M. Jones, "The Roman Civil Service (Clerical and Sub-clerical Grades)", JRS 39 (1949) 38-55, here 51-3 [= Studies in Roman Government and Law (Oxford, 1960) 151-75].

26 On change of mood in the empire, see Cameron, Procopius 189.

27 Cameron, Procopius 56-9.

28 Sidney Smith, quoted in Nancy McPhee, ed., The Book of Insults, (London, 1978) 51.

29 e.g. Fridericus Bluhme, De Ioannis Laurentii Lydi Libris Περὶ μηνῶν Observationum Capita Duo (Diss., University of Halle, 1906), notes the nearly unanimous verdict of scholars that Lydus' de Mensibus is an "absurdarum fabularum stultorumque placitorum farraginem" that nevertheless can be used quite profitably as a source for the study of ancient authors (2-3).

30 The one genuine exception is James Caimi, Burocrazia e diritto nel de Magistratibus di Giovanni Lido (Milan, 1984).

31 Wilhelm Christ, W. Schmid and O. Stählin, Geschichte der griechischen Literatur. Die nachklassische Periode von 100 bis 530 nach Christus (HAW 7.2.2, ed. I. Müller, rev. W. Otto et al.; Munich, 1924) 1043.

32 On Powers or the Magistracies of the Roman State, ed. Anastasius C. Bandy (The American Philosophical Society Memoirs 149; Philadelphia, 1982) xxviii in reference to de Ostentis and de Mensibus.

33 H. W. Haussig, A History of Byzantine Civilization, trans. Joan M. Hussey (New York, 1971) 118: "Admittedly his work has no lasting value, but it deserves attention as a valid statement about the literary interests of the general public. . . . John wrote without any real understanding of events . . . he displays great erudition which, however, cannot conceal his inability to understand what he has read and put it across clearly. . . . His whole literary output shows how inadequate the state of education was."

34 Gérard Capdeville, "Jean Lydus, Les Mois", Annuaire 1970-1971 (École Pratique des Hautes Études IVᵉ Section; Paris, 1971) 823-6, here 823.

35 Rawson, Intellectual Life 234 on Gracchanus' de Potestatibus.

36 See Appendix.

37 de Mag. III.27.

38 de Mag. III.28.

39 ibid.

40 de Mag. III.29; On Powers, ed. Bandy xxvi.

41 de Mag. I.15, III.30.

42 Mentioned several times in de Mag.: see Appendix.

43 For a summary, see On Powers, ed. Bandy xxviiff., and for a more detailed examination of de Mag.'s date of composition, Caimi, Burocrazia 111-24. I follow his arguments closely.

44 See On Powers, ed. Bandy xxvii.

45 Stein 838-40; Robert Kaster, Guardians of Language: The Grammarian and Society in Late Antiquity (Berkeley, 1988) 306-9; PLRE II, "Ioannes 75", 612-15; Caimi, Burocrazia 111-24; On Powers, ed. Bandy xxvii-xxviii.

46 *Sudae Lexicon,* ed. Ada Adler, 5 vols (Leipzig, 1928–38) II.465, 649.
47 *de Mag.* III.38; Kaster, *Guardians* 309; Stein 441, note 4.
48 Kaster, *Guardians* 309.
49 Stein 839; Caimi, *Burocrazia* 111–24.
50 Stein 839–40 discussing *de Mag.* III.55.
51 See below, Chapter 5.

1 CHANGES IN THE AGE OF JUSTINIAN

1 Stein 790.
2 Judith Herrin, *The Formation of Christendom* (Princeton, 1987) 155.
3 Jones, *LRE* 986–91; Gilbert Dagron, "Aux origines de la civilisation byzantine: Langue de culture et langue d'État", *Revue Historique* 489 (1969) 23–56, esp. 42–6.
4 Pauline Allen, *Evagrius Scholasticus. The Church Historian* (Louvain, 1981) 98, note 12.
5 Averil Cameron and Judith Herrin, *et al.*, eds, *Constantinople in the Eighth Century: The Parastaseis Syntomoi Chronikai* (Leiden, 1984).
6 ibid., ch. 24.
7 ibid., ch. 28, and Introduction, 28, 31–4 on attitudes toward statuary. See also the comments of Cyril Mango, *Byzantium, the Empire of New Rome* (London, 1980) 80.
8 *de Mens.* I.1; see also *de Mag.* III.39. The notion of combating time is a cliché often found in reference to the restoration of buildings; see Charlotte Roueché, "Theodosius II, the Cities, and the Date of the Church History of Sozomen", *JTS* 37 (1986) 130–2; and note the fourteenth-century synodic act sent to a bishop of Philadelphia: "Time, which alters and changes all things, and causes those which have been well off until now to proceed into oblivion . . ." trans. Clive Foss, *Byzantine and Turkish Sardis* (Cambridge, Mass., 1976) 127. In the post-Justinianic period it will become an important part of imperial activity, e.g. Constantine Porphyrogenitus' *Life of Basil* (Constantine Porphyrogenitus, *Vita Basilii*, ch. V, 211–53, in *Theophanes Continuatus*, ed. Immanuel Bekker (CSHB 33; Bonn, 1838)).
9 Charlotte Roueché, "Cities and Imperial Government in the Early Byzantine Period" (forthcoming). I thank Dr Roueché for discussing this paper with me before publication and permitting me to cite it here.
10 Averil Cameron, "Images of Authority: Élites and Icons in Late Sixth-Century Byzantium", *Past and Present* 84 (1979) 3–25, here 3–5 [= in Margaret Mullett and Roger Scott, eds, *Byzantium and the Classical Tradition* (Birmingham, 1981) 205–34, here 205–8].
11 Sabine MacCormack, *Art and Ceremony in Late Antiquity* (Berkeley, 1981) 245.
12 Herrin, *Formation of Christendom* 42.
13 MacCormack, *Art and Ceremony* 245.
14 John Frederick Haldon, "Ideology and Social Change in the Seventh Century. Military Discontent as a Barometer", *Klio* 68 (1986) 139–90, here 145

15 The term had usually been used for the right to pardon, not legal initiatives. On *nomos empsychos*, see Artur Steinwenter, "Nomos Empsychos. Zur Geschichte einer politischen Theorie", *Anzeiger, Akademie der Wissenschaften, Wien, phil.-hist. Klasse* 83 (1936) 250ff.; Wilhelm Ensslin, "Gottkaiser und Kaiser von Gottes Gnaden", *Sitzungsberichte d. Bayer. Akad. d. Wiss., phil.-hist. Abt.* 6 (Munich, 1943) esp. 98ff., 115ff.; G.J.D. Aalders, "ΝΟΜΟΣ ΕΜΨΥΧΟΣ in Politeia und Res Publica" 315-29 in *Beiträge dem Andenken R. Starks gewidmet* [= *Palingenesia* 4 (1969)]; Gerhard Ladner, "Justinian's Theory of Law and the Renewal Ideology of the *Leges Barbarorum*", *PAPS* 119.3 (1975) 191-200; Mario Amelotti, "Giustiniano tra Teologia e Diritto", in G.G. Archi, ed., *L'imperatore Giustiniano. Storia e Mito.* (Milan, 1978) 133-60, esp. 133-6; G. Lanata, *Legislazione e natura nelle novelle giustinianee* (Naples, 1984) 181; Michael Maas, "Roman History and Christian Ideology in Justinianic Reform Legislation", *DOP* 40 (1986) 17-31, here 29; on emperors as living law in panegyric, see MacCormack, *Art and Ceremony* 264-5.

16 Fritz Pringsheim, "Justinian's Prohibition of Commentaries to the Digest", *RIDA* 5 (1950) 383-415, esp. 414.

17 e.g. *NJ* 25.

18 Gerhard Rösch, *ONOMA BAΣIΛEIAΣ. Studien zum offiziellen Gebrauch der Kaisertitel in spätantiker und frühbyzantinischer Zeit* (*Byzantina Vindobonensia* 10; Vienna, 1978) 40.

19 ibid., 102; for his use of *Victor* on coins, ibid., 130.

20 ibid., 101ff.

21 ibid.

22 ibid., 65, 103; in *Edictum de Recte Fide* of 551.

23 Averil Cameron, "Images of Authority" 206; Alan Cameron, *Circus Factions. Blues and Greens at Rome and Byzantium* (Oxford, 1976) 249-69; on general developments in court ritual see Averil Cameron, "The Construction of Court Ritual: The Byzantine *Book of Ceremonies*" in David Cannadine and Simon Price, eds, *Rituals of Royalty. Power and Ceremonies in Traditional Societies* (Cambridge, 1987) 106-36.

24 e.g. *Menae patricii cum Thoma referendario De scientia politica dialogus*, ed. Carlo Maria Mazzucchi (Milan, 1982) 15ff.; Carlo Maria Mazzucchi and Elisabetta Matelli, "La dottrina dello Stato nel dialogo 'Sulla Scienza Politica' e il suo autore", in G.G. Archi, ed., *Il mondo del diritto nell'epoca giustiniana. Caratteri e problematiche* (Ravenna, 1985) 209-23, esp. 215ff.

25 Agapetus the Deacon, *Expositio Capitum Admonitorium*, in PG 86.1 (Paris, 1867) 1163-86, cap.11, see also capp.13 and 33; Patrick Henry III, "A Mirror for Justinian: The *Ekthesis* of Agapetus Diaconus" *GRBS* 8.4 (1967) 281-308.

26 Wolfgang F. Volbach, *Elfenbeinarbeiten der Spätantike und des frühen Mittelalters* (Mainz, 1952; 2nd edn, 1976) 47-8, no.48; David H. Wright, "Ivories for the Emperor", *Third Annual Byzantine Studies Conference. Abstracts of Papers* (New York, 1977) 6-9; and see his "Justinian and an Archangel", in Otto Feld and Urs Peschlow, eds, *Studien zur spätantiken und byzantinischen Kunst Friedrich Wilhelm*

Deichmann gewidmet, vol. III (Bonn, 1986) 75–80; see *Anthologia Graeca* XVI.62 from a statue of Justinian in the Hippodrome: "O Emperor, slayer of Medes, these gifts does Eustathius [the urban prefect] the father and son of thy Rome bring unto thee: a steed for thy victory, a second victory holding a wreath, and thyself seated on this steed that is as swift as the wind. May thy might, O Justinian, stand high, and may the defenders of the Medes and Scythians remain forever chained to the ground . . ." (trans. Cyril Mango, *The Art of the Byzantine Empire 312-1453. Sources and Documents* (Englewood Cliffs, NJ, 1972) 117–18).

27 Maas, "Roman History and Christian Ideology" *DOP* 40 (1986) 17–31.

28 On the *kontakion* as a new literary form, see Ihor Ševčenko, "A Shadow Outline of Virtue: The Classical Heritage of Greek Christian Literature (Second to Seventh Century)", in K. Weitzmann, ed., *The Age of Spirituality: A Symposium* (New York, 1980) 53–73, here 63; Eva Catafygiotu-Topping, "On Earthquakes and Fires: Romanos' Encomium to Justinian", *BZ* 71 (1978) 22–35.

29 *Sancti Romani Melodi Cantica. Cantica Genuina*, ed. Paul Maas and C.A. Trypanis (Oxford, 1963) 462–71.

30 For example, Justin II placed a mosaic of Christ in his new throne-room directly above his own throne: Averil Cameron, *Procopius and the Sixth Century* (Berkeley, 1985) 259 and *eadem*, "Corippus' Poem on Justin II: A Terminus of Antique Art?", *Annali della Scuola Normale di Pisa*, ser. 3, 51 (1975) 129–65, esp. 132ff.; *eadem*, "The Early Religious Policies of Justin II", in D. Baker, ed., *The Orthodox Churches and the West* (Studies in Church History 13; Oxford, 1976) 51–67.

31 MacCormack, *Art and Ceremony* 265: "In San Vitale, the position of the imperial couple is defined not only from the point of view of past history, brought forward by the intervention and vision of God, as when God intervenes in history at an imperial election, but also from the point of view of the culmination and end of history, the parousia of Christ and the reward of the saints"; Henry Maguire, *Earth and Ocean: The Terrestrial World in Early Byzantine Art* (University Park and London 1987) 75–80; Ernst Kitzinger, *Byzantine Art in the Making* (Cambridge, Mass., 1977) 81ff.; MacCormack, *Art and Ceremony* 259–66; Edmund Leach, "Melchisedech and the Emperor: Icons of Subversion and Orthodoxy", *Proceedings of the Royal Anthropological Institute for 1972* (1973) 5–14.

32 Procopius, *De Aedificiis* (*Opera Omnia*, vol.4, ed. J. Haury and G. Wirth, Leipzig, 1964) II.6.6.

33 Procopius, *Historia Arcana* (*Opera Omnia*, vol.3, ed. J. Haury and G. Wirth, Leipzig, 1963) XXX.30.

34 Procopius, *De Aedificiis* I.1.6ff.

35 ibid., I.1.22ff.

36 MacCormack, *Art and Ceremony* 250.

37 Michael McCormick, *Eternal Victory. Triumphal Rulership in Late Antiquity, Byzantium, and the Early Medieval West* (Cambridge, 1986) 64ff.

38 R.M. Harrison, "The Church of St. Polyeuktos in Istanbul and the

Temple of Solomon", in Cyril Mango and Omeljan Pritsak, eds, *Okeanos. Essays Presented to Ihor Ševčenko on his Sixtieth Birthday*, (*Harvard Ukrainian Studies* 7: 1983) 276-9.

39 Louis Robert, *Epigrammes du Bas-Empire* vol.IV of *Hellenica* (Paris, 1948), esp. 35-110; Peter Brown, "Art and Society in Late Antiquity", in *The Age of Spirituality* 17-29, here 19.

40 Robert, *Hellenica* IV, 63, 70; on imperial restoration, see, e.g., Margherita Guarducci, "Teodosio 'Rinnovatore' di Corinto in una epigrafe greca di Kenchreai", in Jean Bingen *et al.*, eds, *Le Monde grec. Hommages à Claire Préaux* (Brussels, 1975) 527-34, here 528; Justinian figures in a wide variety of inscriptions: Jean Durliat, "Les dédicaces d'ouvrages de défense dans l'Afrique byzantine", *Collection de l'École Française de Rome* 49 (1981) 7-59; Charles Diehl, "Rescrit des Empereurs Justin et Justinien en date du 1ᵉʳ juin 527", *BCH* 17 (1893) 501-20; Suzy Dufrenne, "L'ananeôsis de Quasr el-Lebya", *Antiquités Africaines* 16 (1980) 241-9.

41 e.g. Eusebius, *De Laudibus Constantini Oratio in eius tricennalibus habita* ed. Ivar A. Heikel, *Eusebius Werke* (*GCS* VII; Leipzig, 1902) 1.3; Eusebius, *Vita Constantini* 1.12.2 (*GCS* VII.2, 1975) 215,23-4; Norman Baynes, "Eusebius and the Christian Empire", *Annuaire de l'Institut de Philologie et d'Histoire Orientales et Slaves. Mélanges Bidez* ii (1933-4) 13-18 [= *Byzantine Studies and Other Essays* (London, 1955) 168-72]; F. Edward Cranz, "Kingdom and Polity in Eusebius of Caesarea", *HTR* 45 (1952) 47-56, here 48ff.

42 Glenn Chesnut, *The First Christian Histories. Eusebius, Socrates, Sozomen, Theodoret, and Evagrius* (2nd edn, Macon, Georgia, 1986) 231-51; Pietro de Francisci, *Arcana Imperii* III.2 (Milan, 1948) 131ff.

43 See below, pp.45-8.

44 Note that the favorite word of rebuilding and restoration, *ananeôsis*, employed by Lydus and Procopius and found in contemporary mosaics in reference to Justinian's projects, will be introduced to coins as a legend in the seventh century (Philip Grierson, *Catalogue of the Byzantine Coins in the Dumbarton Oaks Collection and in the Whittemore Collection* II.1: *Phocas to Theodosius III 602-717* (Dumbarton Oaks, 1968) 65ff.).

45 Frank Trombley, "Monastic Foundations in Sixth-Century Anatolia and their Role in the Social and Economic Life of the Countryside", *Greek Orthodox Theological Review* 30.1 (1985) 45-59, here esp. 58-9 [= in N.M. Vaporis, ed., *Byzantine Saints and Monasteries* (Brookline, Mass., 1985)]; also Charlotte Rouché, "A New Inscription from Aphrodisias and the Title πατὴρ τῆς πόλεως", *GRBS* 20 (1979) 173-85, here 184, on secular prosperity in Aphrodisias independent of the generosity of governors.

46 On a reduction in building in the second half of the century see Evelyne Patlagean, *Pauvreté économique et pauvreté sociale à Byzance, 4ᵉ-7ᵉ siècles* (Paris, 1977) 232-3.

47 Pauline Allen, "The 'Justinianic' Plague", *Byzantion* 49 (1979) 5-20; Lawrence Conrad, "The Plague in Bilād al-Shām in Pre-Islamic Times" in Muhammad Adnan Bakhit and Muhammad Asfour, eds, *The IVth*

International Conference on Bilād al-Shām, vol.II (Amman, 1984) 143–63; J.N. Biraben and Jacques le Goff, "The Plague in the Early Middle Ages", trans. Elborg Forster and Patricia Ranum, in Robert Forster and Orest Ranum, eds, *Biology of Man in History* (Baltimore, 1975) [= *Annales ESC* 24 (Nov./Dec. 1969) 1484–510].

48 Hugh Kennedy, "From *Polis* to *Madina*: Urban Change in Late Antique and Early Islamic Syria", *Past and Present* 106 (1985) 3–27, here 5, and bibliographical note on 3 for treatments of continuity and change in this period.

49 *de Mens.* III.23.

50 Jones, *LRE* 762. In an important re-evaluation of the evidence Mark Whittow argues that the decline of the provincial *curiales* was an "institutional rearrangement" that marked successful adaptation to new circumstances: Mark Whittow, "Ruling the Late Roman and Early Byzantine City: A Continuous History", *Past and Present* 129 (1990) 3–29, here 3.

51 Jones, *LRE* 760. Hagiographical sources from the sixth century reveal the increasing role in city affairs taken by churchmen and saints: Dorothy Abrahamse, "Hagiographic Sources for Byzantine Cities, 500–900 AD" (Diss., University of Michigan, 1967) 165, on the life of St Eutychius; Jones, *LRE* 762; see Dietrich Claude, *Die byzantinische Stadt im 6. Jahrhundert* (Byzantinisches Archiv 13; Munich, 1969) 158 for the growing role of bishops in municipal administration; see also Pauline Allen, *Evagrius Scholasticus* 3; André Guillou, 'L'évêque dans la société méditerranéenne des VIe–VIIe siècles. Un modèle", *Bibliothèque de l'École des Chartes* 131 (1973) 5–19 [= *Culture et société en Italie byzantine (VIe-XIe s.)* (London, 1978) art.2]; Garth Fowden, "Bishops and Temples in the Eastern Roman Empire A.D. 320–435", *JTS*, n.s. 29.1 (1978) 53–78.

52 Stein 467.

53 Jones, *LRE* 760; for a different interpretation, E.K. Chrysos, "Die angebliche Abschaffung der städtischen Kurien durch Kaiser Anastasius", Βυζαντινά 3 (1971) 94–102; on evidence for city councils in Egypt in the sixth century, see H. Geremek, "Sur la question des *Boulai* dans les villes Egyptiennes aux Ve–VIIe siècles", *Journal of Juristic Papyrology* 20 (1990) 48–54.

54 Jones, *LRE* 760.

55 *de Mag.* III.49.

56 ibid., I.28.

57 See Chapter 2.

58 Haldon, "Ideology and Social Change" 171–2: "The cities themselves had no economic role in this process. As corporate bodies they had already lost effective control over their lands and had no claim on the surplus wealth produced, which was appropriated either by the state, when it was able, or by private landowners. And thus the formal ties which had previously bound the city as such to its hinterland were dissolved. The inability of the curiales, under pressure from the central government, to cover the demands of the imperial fisc, exacerbated this development. The cities accordingly lost their historic function as the basic – and

essential – component of Roman provincial administration, giving ground instead to the salaried bureaucrats appointed by the central authority. . . . The provincial wealthy sent their sons to Constantinople to be educated, and vied for positions within the sphere of the imperial court and the bureaucracy. By the middle of the seventh century, if not already during the reign of Heraclius, the cities had been superseded in every respect."

59 Leo, Novel 46 (ed. P. Noailles and A. Dain, *Les Nouvelles de Léon le Sage* (Paris, 1944); Abrahamse, *Hagiographic Sources* 142-3.

60 Jones, *LRE* 758.

61 ibid., 757.

62 ibid., 758; Abrahamse, *Hagiographic Sources* 141.

63 This is an exaggeration. Races continued until the twelfth century in many places: Alan Cameron, *Circus Factions* 308.

64 Procopius, *Historia Arcana*, 26 . 6-10.

65 Roueché, "Cities and the Imperial Administration": "The cities were therefore less important vis à vis the imperial government; but they also stood in a fundamentally new relationship to the new class of benefactors. Rich men in the late fifth and sixth centuries . . . probably did not perceive themselves as acting differently from the benefactors of the past. But the titles on which they prided themselves were not civic magistracies, but imperial ranks and offices . . . The cities were not in a position to reward or control the new rich class;" *eadem*, "Acclamations in the later Roman Empire: New Evidence from Aphrodisias", *JRS* 74 (1984) 181-99, here 198; on the background of this process, see Fergus Millar, "Empire and City, Augustus to Julian: Obligations, Excuses, and Status", *JRS* 73 (1983) 76-96; Brown, "Art and Society in Late Antiquity" 19-20; Whittow, "Ruling the Late Roman and Early Byzantine City" 9-12.

66 C. Roueché, *Aphrodisias in Late Antiquity (Journal of Roman Studies Monograph* 5; London, 1989) 89, quoting Zacharias Rhetor, *Vita Severi*, ed. and trans. M.-A. Kugener (Patrologia Orientalis 2; Turnhout, 1907) 17.

67 Roueché, *Aphrodisias* 124, discusses Aristocrates of Aphrodisias, who wrote to Justinian *c*.529 concerning rights to the principal on a civic loan.

68 Roueché, "Cities and the Imperial Government".

69 Jones, *LRE* 280-3, 759.

70 On the prefaces, see Maas, "Roman History and Christian Ideology" passim; Roueché, "Cities and the Imperial Government".

71 Roueché discusses the significance of the provincial councils during Justinian's reign, "Cities and Imperial Government"; Jones, *LRE* 766; Ernst Kornemann, "Concilium" *RE* 4.1 (1900), cols 825-30.

72 Justin II, Novel 5 in *Ius Graecoromanum; Novellae et Aureae Bullae Imperatorium post Justinianum ex editione C.E. Zachariae von Ligenthal*, vol.1, ed. I. and P. Zepos (Athens, 1931) 7-10; this followed a precedent established in Italy in 554 (Justinian, *Novellae Addendum* 7.12); see Roueché, "Cities and the Imperial Government".

73 Roueché, "Cities and Imperial Government".

74 *de Mag.* III.61: "Hence, because the unsold produce was spoiling on the farms, inasmuch as the Asian diocese was almost entirely idle, each land-owner was ruined when gold was exacted from him in place of his produce by those who were collecting the taxes, because he was not able to sell his produce, living as he did so far from the sea, nor was he permitted, as formerly, to give it as payment to the public treasury. This was followed also by the transfer of the military forces stationed in the areas, effected by the state in consequence of necessity, so that as a result of this coincidence, too, the crops remained behind in the field, and whereas the taxes had to be paid in gold, the crops had to be plowed into earth every year"; James Caimi, "Ioannis Lydi *de magistratibus* III.70. Note esegetiche e spunti in tema di fiscalità e legislazione protobizantine", *Rivista di Studi Bizantini e Slavi* I (1981) 317-61. Procopius gives further information: "land-owners in every region, and particularly those who happened to be in inland areas, enjoyed great prosperity because of this system [the public post]: for every year they sold the surplus of their harvest to the state to provide food for the horses and grooms [sc. of the post], and they made a great deal of money. And so, in this way, it happened that the state always received the taxes due from each person and that those who paid [the taxes] received [their money] back immediately. In addition the needs of the state were satisfied" (*Historia Arcana* 30.5-7; translation by Hendy; see Michael Hendy, *Studies in the Byzantine Monetary Economy c.300-1450* (Cambridge, 1985) 294-6, here 295); see also Procopius, *Historia Arcana* 30.11.

75 "The systematic commutation of taxation in kind to taxation in coin, and therefore to precious-metal coin, particularly gold, in the eastern half of the empire, seems to have been the work of Anastasius," Hendy, *Studies* 294. It was the elimination of the cursus publicus in Asiana and elsewhere that precipitated the terrible results described by Procopius and Lydus.

76 Jones, *LRE* 830-4.

77 *de Mag.* III.61.

78 Apparently a law of 412 (*CTh*. 11.1.31) that forbade such occurrences and that had been elaborated by Justinian's prefect Demosthenes in 521 or 529 in an edict (*NJ* 166) sent to the governor of Lydia was deliberately ignored later in the reign when economic circumstances worsened (Jones, *LRE* 814-15). Procopius complains about the ruinous compulsory allocations (*Historia Arcana* 23.15-16).

79 Jones, *LRE* 753; 757-63.

80 For a sketch of conditions in Asia Minor under Justinian, see Clive Foss, *Byzantine and Turkish Sardis* 10-13.

81 *NJ* 145 (AD 553); Jones, *LRE* 294.

82 *Le costituzione giustinianee nei papiri e nelle epigrafi*, ed. Mario Amelotti and Livia Migliardi Zingale, 2nd edn (Legum Iustiniani Imperatoris Vocabularium, Subsidia I; Milan, 1985) 95-100; Foss, *Sardis* 13.

83 Denis Feissel and Ismail Kaygusuz, "Un mandement impérial du VIe siècle dans une inscription d'Hadrianoupolis d'Honoriade", *Travaux et*

Mémoires 9 (1985) 397–419, esp. 410–13.

84 Abrahamse, *Hagiographic Sources* 223, for landowners living in provincial cities.

85 *de Mag.* III.61.

86 ibid., III.58.

87 Marcus Rautman, "Problems of Land Use and Water Supply in Late Antique Lydia", *Abstracts of Papers, Thirteenth Annual Byzantine Studies Conference*, Nov. 5–8, 1987, 6–7.

88 Clive Foss, "Archaeology and the 'Twenty Cities' of Byzantine Asia", *AJA* 81 (1977) 469–86, here 471.

89 See note 47 above.

90 Allen, "Justinianic Plague" 10–11; Mango, *Byzantium* 68, estimates that one-third to one-half of the Constantinopolitan population perished.

91 Allen, "Justinianic Plague" 11.

92 Procopius, *Historia Arcana* 23.19–21; *Bella*, in *Opera Omnia* vols 1 and 2, ed. J. Haury and G. Wirth (Leipzig, 1962–3) II.22–23; John Teall, "Barbarians in Justinian's Armies", *Speculum* 40 (1965) 294–322, esp. 305–10; Anastasius Fotiou, "Recruitment Shortages in Sixth Century Byzantium", *Byzantion* 58 (1988) 65–77.

93 e.g. *NJ* 118 (543 AD), Edict 7, preface (March, 542 AD).

94 Allen, "Justinianic Plague" 19; Patlagean, *Pauvreté économique* 89.

95 Trombley, "Monastic Foundations" 57.

96 Jones, *LRE* 763.

97 ibid., 759–60.

98 Gilbert Dagron, "Le christianisme dans la ville byzantine", *DOP* 31 (1977) 1–25.

99 ibid., 5.

100 ibid.

101 See note 51 above.

102 MacCormack, *Art and Ceremony* 66; E.D. Hunt, review of MacCormack, in *Classical Review* 33 (1983) 83–6, here 85.

103 Herrin, *Formation of Christendom* 85.

104 Dagron, "Le christianisme" 6.

105 John F. Baldovin, *The Urban Character of Christian Worship. The Origins, Development, and Meaning of Stational Liturgy* (Orientalia Christiana Analecta 228, Rome, 1987).

106 *NJ* 59.5 (537 AD); Dagron, "Le christianisme" 14–16. This practice had been going on at least from the time of Anastasius.

107 Dagron, "Le christianisme" 4–8.

108 Clive Foss, *Ephesus after Antiquity: A Late Antique, Byzantine, and Turkish City* (Cambridge, 1979) 87 note 84: "It would seem that a great deal of destruction took place under Justinian, which is not surprising, since his new basilica on Ayasluk would have needed vast quantities of building material"; Trombley, "Monastic Foundations" 55–6.

109 Frank Trombley, "The Survival of Paganism in the Byzantine Empire during the Pre-Iconoclastic Period (540–727)" (Diss., UCLA, 1981) and *idem*, "Paganism in the Greek World at the End of Antiquity: The Case of Rural Anatolia and Greece", *HTR* 78.3–4 (1985) 327–52 for

bibliography, and see below, Chapter 5.

110 Herrin, *Formation of Christendom* 83.

111 Procopius, *Historia Arcana* 26.5; pagans, Jews, and heretics were forbidden to teach: *CJ* 1.5.18.4; 1.1.4; on the state of higher education in the later sixth century, see Mango, *Byzantium*, 133-6; and Cameron, *Procopius* 22, on Zonaras' criticism of Justinian (Zonaras, *Epitomae Historiarum Libri XIII-XVIII*, ed. T. Büttner-Wobst (Bonn, 1897) XIV.6.31-2) for causing the growth of ignorance.

112 Trombley, "Monastic Foundations" 48; Herrin, *Formation of Christendom* 84-7.

113 N.G. Wilson, *Scholars of Byzantium* (Baltimore, 1983) 59.

114 ibid., 58; still useful are: Ludwig Hahn, *Zum Sprachenkampf im römischen Reich bis auf die Zeit Justinians (Philologus suppl.* X.4; 1907) 675-718; B. Hemmerdinger, "Les lettres latines à Constantinople jusqu'à Justinien", *ByzF* 1 (1966) 174-8.

115 *de Mag.* II.12, III.42.

116 Guglielmo Cavallo, "La circolazione libraria nell'età di Giustiniano", in G.G. Archi, ed., *L'imperatore Giustiniano. Storia e mito* (Milan, 1978) 201-36.

117 Guglielmo Cavallo, "Libri e pubblico alla fine del mondo antico", in G. Cavallo, ed., *Libri, editori e pubblico nel mondo antico. Guida storica e critica* (Rome/Bari, 1975) 83-162, here 131-2; Cameron, *Procopius* 21.

118 Evelyne Patlagean, "La pauvreté à Byzance au VIe siècle et la législation de Justinien: les origines d'un modèle politique" in M. Mollat, ed., *Études sur l'histoire de la pauvreté (Moyen Age-XVIe siècle)* (Paris, 1974) vol. 1, 59-81, here 68-70.

119 Jones, *LRE* 692; cf. *de Mag.* II.29 on the responsibilities of the urban prefect assumed by the quaesitor "because of discord among the populace".

120 Procopius criticizes this officer: (*Historia Arcana* 20.9.11).

121 Patlagean, "La pauvreté" 59-81 for further background, see *eadem*, *Pauvreté économique* 11-35.

122 Patlagean, "La pauvreté" 68.

123 ibid.

124 ibid., 70-1. Patlagean mentions the new institutions for dealing with the poor (hospices, etc.) and their presence in various hagiographical texts of the same period.

125 MacCormack, *Art and Ceremony* 250; Roueché, "Acclamations" 181-99.

126 MacCormack, *Art and Ceremony* 255.

127 On the routine association of emperor and Constantinople in eulogies of the capital city, see Erwin Fenster, *Laudes Constantinopolitanae* (Miscellanea Byzantina Monacensia 9; Munich, 1968); Paul J. Alexander, "The Strength of Empire and Capital as Seen through Byzantine Eyes", *Speculum* 37 (1962) 339-57, esp. 343ff [= *Religious and Political History and Thought in the Byzantine Empire* (London, 1978), art. 3]; Ihor Ševčenko, "Constantinople Viewed from the Eastern Provinces in the Middle Byzantine Period", in I. Ševčenko and F. Sysyn, eds, *Eucharisterion: Essays Presented to Omeljan Pritsak on his Sixtieth*

Birthday by his Colleagues and Students (Harvard Ukrainian Studies III/
IV; 1979-80) part 2, 712-41, here 713; MacCormack, *Art and Ceremony*
250.

128 For an overview of the structure of the Prefecture in the sixth century,
see Roberto Morosi, "L'*officium* del prefetto del pretorio nel VI secolo",
Romanobarbarica 2 (1977) 103-48; for detailed analysis of the
Prefecture based on *de Magistratibus*, see James Caimi, *Burocrazia e
diritto nel de Magistratibus di Giovanni Lido* (Milan, 1984) esp. 381ff.;
William Turpin, "The Late Roman Law Codes: Forms and Procedures
for Legislation from the Classical Age to Justinian" (Diss., University of
Cambridge, 1981) discusses changes in the legal competence of the
Prefecture.

129 *de Mag.* II.17-18; III.15; III.66; Caimi, *Burocrazia* 320-2; Stein 438-9.

130 *de Mag.* II.l0; III.40; Arthur E.R. Boak, *The Master of the Offices in the
Later Roman and Byzantine Empires* (University of Michigan Studies,
Humanistic Series 14; New York, 1924) 30-1, 36-7; Manfred Clauss, *Der
magister officiorum in der Spätantike (4.-6. Jahrhundert): Das Amt und
sein Einfluss auf die kaiserliche Politik (Vestigia* 32; Munich, 1981) 32-
40; Caimi, *Burocrazia* 31-2.

131 That of princeps, *de Mag,* III.40; A.H.M. Jones, "The Roman Civil
Service (Clerical and Sub-clerical Grades)", *JRS* 39 (1949) 38-55, here 52
[= *Studies in Roman Government and Law* (Oxford, 1960) 153-75, here
173].

132 *de Mag.* II.12; III.42 and 68.

133 Jones, *LRE* 284-5.

134 Robert Browning, *Justinian and Theodora*, 2nd edn (London, 1987) 51;
Stein, 483.

2 PORTRAIT OF A BUREAUCRAT

1 *Sudae Lexicon*, ed. J.P. Migne, ed. Ada Adler, 5 vols (Leipzig, 1928-38)
II.465, p.649; Leo, *Tactica. Epilog* 67, ed. J.P. Migne, *PG* 107.1092B;
Constantine Porphyrogenitus, *de Thematibus*, ed. A. Pertusi (Vatican
City, 1952) I, 63 (quotes *de Mag.* I.46); anonymous, in *Anecdota Graeca
Codicibus Manuscriptis Bibliothecarum*, ed. J.A. Cramer, 4 vols (Oxford,
1835-7) III.187ff.; Theophylactus Simocatta, *History*, ed. C. de Boor
(Leipzig, 1887) 7.l6.12; Photius, *Bibliotheca*, ed. R. Henry (Paris, 1959-
77) Cod.180; Cod. Vat.1202 chartac. [= excerpt of *de Ost.*].

2 *de Mag.* III.30; Stein, 838-9; *On Powers or the Magistracies of the Roman
State*, ed. Anastasius C. Bandy (American Philosophical Society Memoirs
149; Philadelphia, 1982) xxiii; Robert Kaster, *Guardians of Language:
The Grammarian and Society in Late Antiquity* (Berkeley, 1988) 306-9.

3 *de Mag.* III.47.

4 See Chapter 6.

5 *de Mag.* III.47.

6 Cf.: Andrew Wallace-Hadrill, *Suetonius: The Scholar and his Caesars*
(London, 1983).

7 *de Mag.* III.68.

8 *CTh.* 14.1.1. trans. and discussion, N.G. Wilson, *Scholars of Byzantium* (Baltimore, 1983) 2.

9 Fritz Saaby Pedersen, *Late Roman Public Professionalism* (Odense, 1976) *passim*; Wilson, *Scholars* 2ff.

10 Cf. the career of Suetonius: Wallace-Hadrill, *Suetonius*, ch.4 "The Scholar at Court", 96: "There is no gulf between Suetonius the secretary and Tranquillus the philologist."

11 Kaster, *Guardians* 233–440, 266 no.42, and 272 no.48.

12 On instruction in Latin in the region (Adamantius, teacher of Latin grammar, possibly at Sardis, before 580), see ibid., 238, no.2; on Lydus' Latin, see *On Powers*, ed. Bandy, xxxiii, and Joannes Fridericus Schultze, *Quaestionum Lydianarum Particula Prior* (Diss., University of Greifswald, 1862) 6–11.

13 Kaster, *Guardians* 14.

14 *On Powers*, ed. Bandy ix–x; Kaster 306.

15 Kaster, *Guardians* 17–20.

16 *de Mag.* 3.26, 58ff.; *de Mens.* 4.58; *de Ost.* 53.

17 *de Mens.* IV.58.

18 ibid., III.20: "sardis" = "a year"; Strabo (*Geography*, ed. H.L. Jones, (Cambridge, Mass., 1929) XIII.4.17) reports that Lydian was no longer spoken in his day.

19 *de Mens.* III. 20–1.

20 Annie Pralong, "Les remparts de Philadelphie", in *Philadelphie et autres études* (Byzantina Sorbonensia 4; Paris, 1984) 101–25; G.M.A. Hanfmann and Jane C. Waldbaum, *A Survey of Sardis and the Major Monuments outside the City Walls* (Cambridge, Mass., 1975) 42; A.H.M. Jones, *The Cities of the Eastern Roman Provinces* (2nd edn, Oxford, 1971) 80.

21 Earthquakes: Strabo, *Geography*, XIII.4.10; anti-earthquake festival: *de Mens.* IV.76.

22 David Magie, *Roman Imperial Rule in Asia Minor to the End of the Third Century after Christ* (Princeton, 1950) 693.

23 Magie, *Roman Rule* 637; A.M. Woodward, "The Neocorate at Aegeae and Anazarbus in Cilicia", *Numismatic Chronicle* (ser.7) 3 (1963) 5–10, esp. 8; Kaster, *Guardians* 4.

24 *de Mens.* IV.2.

25 ibid., IV.58; Magie, *Roman Rule* 125; *PLRE* II "Proclus 4" 917; Proclus, *Hypotyposis Astronomicarum Positionum*, ed. Carolus Manitius (Leipzig, 1909, repr. 1974) ch.I, proem. para.4.

26 Mistreatment of Lydians, *de Mag.* III.58–61; *On Powers*, ed. Bandy xviii.

27 *de Mag.* III.70; Evelyne Patlagean, *Pauvreté économique et pauvreté sociale à Byzance, 4ᵉ-7ᵉ siècles* (Paris, 1977) 300ff.; Paul Lemerle, *The Agrarian History of Byzantium from its Origins to the Twelfth Century* (Galway, 1979) 20–6; Gilbert Dagron, *Naissance d'une capitale. Constantinople et ses institutions de 330 à 451* (Paris, 1974) 518–41.

28 *de Mag.* III. 26; on the duties of the memoriales, James Caimi, *Bùrocrazia e diritto nel de Magistratibus di Giovanni Lido* (Milan, 1984) 430–42.

29 *de Mag.* III.26.

30 For Lydus' knowledge of Proclus, see Herman Grabowski, *De Joannis Lydi*

theologumenis arithmeticae (Diss. University of Königsberg, 1921) 33–48; see Appendix for Lydus' references to Proclus.

31 See Chapter 7.

32 *de Mag.* III.26; *PLRE*, II "Zoticus" 1206.

33 *de Mag.* III.26.

34 ibid., III.27.

35 ibid., III.27; Stein 730; not an unusual fee: see Alan Cameron, "Wandering Poets: a Literary Movement in Byzantine Egypt", *Historia* 14 (1965) 470–509, here 477–8 [= *Literature and Society in the Early Byzantine World* (London, 1985) art. I].

36 Ammianus was a prominent "speedwriter" in the magistracy, as well as his cousin (*de Mag.*, III.26).

37 *de Mag.* III.28.

38 Jones, *LRE* II 587; Roberto Morosi, "L'*officium* del prefetto del pretorio nel VI secolo" *Romanobarbarica* 2 (1977) 103–48 on the internal divisions of the prefecture.

39 *de Mag.* III.27; *On Powers*, ed. Bandy xiii: Caimi, *Burocrazia* 50ff.

40 *de Mag.* III.27.

41 ibid.

42 Jones, *LRE* II 988ff.; see note 114 in Chapter 1.

43 Jones, *LRE* II 989; *On Powers*, ed. Bandy xix.

44 *de Mag.* II.12.

45 ibid; *de Mag.* III.42; *de Mens.* fragmenta incertae sedis 7 (p.180, Wuensch).

46 Bandy is more generous: *On Powers* xxxiii.

47 Caimi suggests that the imperial consistorium was enlarged by the participation of senators, *Burocrazia* 55.

48 *PLRE* II, "Ioannes 75" 613; Jones, *LRE* 587; Caimi, *Burocrazia* 51ff.

49 *de Mag.* III.27; *On Powers*, ed. Bandy xiii and 315, note on 176.7; Kaster, *Guardians* 307.

50 Caimi, *Burocrazia* 56-7 and note 174.

51 ibid. II 56.

52 *de Mag.* III.17; Caimi, *Burocrazia* 56; *PLRE*, II "Ioannes 75" 613; Stein 838; Kaster, *Guardians* 307.

53 *de Mag.* III.17.

54 *de Mag.* III.59; Theophanes A.M. 6022 (p.180, ed. C. de Boor).

55 *de Mag.* III.28.

56 Various suggestions: the position of *chartularius* was an annual post (Jones, *LRE* 588); *PLRE* II "Ioannes 75", suggests that Lydus lost his connection with the imperial scrinium when Zoticus was no longer Prefect (after 512) and able to help his protégé; see also *On Powers*, Bandy xiv.

57 *CJ* 12.33.5; Caimi, *Burocrazia* 57.

58 To accept Caimi's answer we must assume that Lydus was not fully forthcoming at *de Mag.* III.28 where he gives no hint of such an enforced choice and in fact suggests that his decision was voluntary. It also requires the assumption that his palatine service lasted from 512 to 524, which is not indicated at III.27-8.

59 *de Mag.* III.28.

60 ibid., trans. Kaster, *Guardians* 307.

61 *de Mag.* III.28.

62 Brian Croke and James Crow, "Procopius and Dara", *JRS* 73 (1983) 143–59; Procopius, *De Bello Persico* (*Opera omnia*, vol. 1, ed. J. Haury and G. Wirth, Leipzig, 1962) I.13.9ff.; *PLRE* II, "Ioannes 75"; Kaster, *Guardians* 308; Thomas F. Carney, *Bureaucracy in Traditional Society: Romano-Byzantine Bureaucracies Viewed from Within* II. *Byzantine Bureaucracy from Within* (Lawrence, Kansas, 1971) 10 note 13.

63 Procopious, *De Bello Persico* I.22.17.

64 If it was composed at all, see Avril Cameron, *Procopius and the Sixth Century* (Berkeley, 1985) 242 note 1.

65 See Chapter 5.

66 Caimi, *Burocrazia* 60–1: either March 530–Feb. 531 or Jan.–Oct. 532.

67 *de Mag.* III.28, trans. and discussed by Kaster, *Guardians* 307.

68 Caimi, *Burocrazia* 57–9, esp. 58 note 182, for different conjectures.

69 *de Ost.* 1.

70 *de Mens.* IV.47.

71 *de Mag.* II.28–9.

72 *On Powers*, ed. Bandy xiv.

73 *NJ* 82 (AD539); Caimi, *Burocrazia* 386–91.

74 Caimi, *Burocrazia* 386–7; Procopius, *Historia Arcana* (*Opera Omnia*, vol. 3 ed. J. Haury and G. Wirth, Leipzig, 1963) 26.1–4 describes John the Cappadocian's hostility to rhetors, in an apparent allusion to the circumstances of *NJ* 82. Note that at *de Mag.* III.76 Lydus praises the prefect Photius for permitting rhetors again to flourish. This need not presume any alteration in judicial procedure. For bibliography and discussion of *NJ* 82, see U. Zilletti, *Studi sul processo civile giustiniano* (Milan, 1965) 259 and R.D. Scott, "John Lydus on Some Procedural Changes" Βυζαντινά 4 (1972) 441–51.

75 *de Mag.* III.66.

76 ibid.

77 *de Mag.* III.66–7.

78 Caimi, *Burocrazia* 57–8; *PLRE* II "Ioannes 75" 613; *On Powers*, ed. Bandy xiv–xv.

79 *PLRE* II "Ioannes 75" 613.

80 Caimi, *Burocrazia* 61ff.

81 *Suda*, II.465.

82 PLRE II "Ioannes 75" 614.

83 *de Mag.* III.29.

84 ibid.

85 Kaster, *Guardians* 308; Jones, *LRE* 605.

86 Kaster, *Guardians* 282, no.56.

87 Stein 838–9.

88 *de Mag.* III.30.

89 ibid.

90 *de Mag.* III.3, 4, 6, 9, 12, 22–5; *PLRE* II "Ioannes 75" 614 supposes he held the rank of *cornicularius*.

91 *PLRE* II "Ioannes 75" 614.

92 ibid.; *CJ* XII 49.2; Stein 731 and note 6. Lydus refers to these titles

obliquely as "the dignity customarily bestowed by the emperor upon those who complete the service", *de Mag.*, III.30.

93 *de Mag.* III.30.

94 See the comments of Carney, *Bureaucracy* 1-2; Walter E. Kaegi, Jr, "Some Perspectives on Byzantine Bureaucracy", in McGuire Gibson and Robert D. Briggs, eds, *The Organization of Power. Aspects of Bureaucracy in the Ancient Near East* (*Oriental Institute Studies in Ancient Oriental Civilization* 46; Chicago, 1987) 151-9.

95 See Chapter 7.

3 THE IDEOLOGICAL TRANSFORMATION OF TRADITION

1 Symmachus, *Relatio III* (in *Libri Quae Supersunt*, ed. Otto Seeck; Berlin, 1883, repr. 1961) 280-3; Brian Croke and Jill Harries, *Religious Conflict in Fourth Century Rome* (Sydney, 1982) 28-51.

2 "But Rome does not adhere to the way she was long ago but changes with time and alters her holy rites, ornaments, laws and weapons of war. She observes many practices she did not observe in Quirinus' reign: some of her enactments are better, some she has abandoned and she does not hesitate to change her custom and entirely reverses laws she formerly laid down. Why, Senator of Rome, do you bring up established usage against me when often a resolution of senate and people has not stood but has been altered by a switch in sentiment? Even in our own day, whenever it is to our advantage to depart from habit and forfeit the usages of the past in favor of a fresh way of life, we rejoice at the discovery of something at last revealed. By constant slow changes does human life grow and increase, and profits from long experience." (Prudentius, *Contra Symmachum II* 303-4; trans. Croke and Harries, *Religious Conflict* 75.)

3 Prudentius, *Contra Symmachum* II 270-5.

4 For example, W.H.C. Frend: "Such concern for the rights and wrongs of the remote past tended to ossify thought and action. Whether one turns to the art of war, to political thought or historical writing, the evidence for the backward-looking tendency in Byzantium is clear. It must be accepted as one of the factors that led to the extinction of its empire and itself." ("Old and New Rome in the Age of Justinian", in Derek Baker, ed., *The Relations between East and West in the Middle Ages* (Edinburgh, 1973) 11-28, here 11.

5 Edward Shils, "Tradition and Liberty: Antinomy and Interdependence", *Ethics* 68.3 (April 1958) 155; 160ff.; see review of Shils, *Tradition* (Chicago, 1981) by A. Momigliano in *Storia della Storiografia* 9 (1986) 159-62 [= *Ottavo contributo* (Rome, 1987) 419-24]; Eric Hobsbawm, "Introduction: Inventing Traditions", in Eric Hobsbawm and Terence Ranger, eds, *The Invention of Tradition* (Cambridge, 1983) 1-14.

6 Some sociologists see "traditionalism" in opposition to new trends such as modernization or Westernization (e.g. S.N. Eisenstadt, "Post-Traditional Societies and the Continuity and Reconstruction of Tradition", *Daedalus*

(Winter, 1973) 1–27, here 22–7). In the sixth century, however, such alternatives did not exist.

7 On the adaptation of the classical historiographical tradition to Christian culture, see the remarks of Brian Croke and Alanna Emmett, "Historiography in Late Antiquity: an Overview", in Brian Croke and Alanna Emmett, eds, *History and Historians in Late Antiquity* (Sydney/New York, 1983) 1–12, esp. 5ff.; Brian Croke, "The Origins of the Christian World Chronicle", ibid., 116–31. John Malalas stood in this tradition (*The Chronicle of John Malalas*, ed. and trans. Elizabeth Jeffreys, Michael Jeffreys, Roger Scott *et al.* (Melbourne, 1986) xxi); Paul Alexander, "The Strength of Empire and Capital as Seen through Byzantine Eyes" *Speculum* 37 (1962) 339–57, here 340 [= *Religious and Political History and Thought in the Byzantine Empire* (London 1978) art. 3].

8 Alexander, "Strength" 340.

9 See Chapter 6.

10 Christian Gizewski, *Zur Normativität und Struktur der Verfassungsverhältnisse in der späteren römischen Kaiserzeit* (Münchener Beiträge zur Papyrusforschung und Antiken Rechtsgeschichte 81; Munich, 1988) 1–65; Hans-Georg Beck, *Senat und Volk von Konstantinopel, Probleme der byzantinischen Verfassungsgeschichte* (Sitzungsberichte der Bayerische Akademie der Wissenschaften, Phil.-Hist. Klasse 6 (1966) 1–75; Dietrich Claude, *Die byzantinische Stadt im 6. Jahrhundert* (Byzantinisches Archiv 13; Munich, 1969) ch.II ("Die Verfassung der frühbyzantinischen Stadt") 107–61; Johannes Karayannopulos, "Der frühbyzantinische Kaiser", *BZ* 49.2 (1956) 369–84; Carmelo Capizzi, "Potere e ideologia imperiale da Zenone a Giustiniano", in G.G. Archi, ed., *L'Imperatore Giustiniano. Storia e mito* (Milan, 1978) 3–35, here 18.

11 Gilbert Dagron, *L'Empire romain d'orient au IVe siècle et les traditions politiques de l'hellénisme. Le témoinage de Thémistios* (Travaux et Mémoires 3; Paris, 1968) esp. 121–46.

12 Capizzi, "Potere e ideologia" 18–19 for convenient references.

13 Dagron, *L'Empire romain* 121–46.

14 Dagron has shown for the fourth century the tension between the guises of the emperor as the chief magistrate and the incarnate law. (This tension will be reconciled in Justinian's posture.) In the conventional constitutional terms the argument about the nature of imperial power and the legitimization of imperial power has been well worked out (see *L'Empire romain* 135–44; Gizewski, *Normativität* 36–65 for historical components of late-antique constitutional theory.

15 *de Mag.* I.15, III.30.

16 John R. Crawford, "De Bruma et Brumalibus Festis", *BZ* 23 (1914–19) 365–96, here 379–82.

17 Averil Cameron, *Procopius and the Sixth Century* (Berkeley, 1985) 23.

18 Gizewski, *Normativität* 148–210; Alan Cameron, *Circus Factions: Blues and Greens at Rome and Byzantium* (Oxford, 1976) 278–80; J.B. Bury, "The Nika Riot", *JHS* 17 (1897) 92–119.

19 Tony Honoré, *Tribonian* (London, 1978), 54 and note 118 for a detailed list of the new restrictions. His discussion of the revolt is on 53–6.

20 The palace viewed the affair as a consequence of Hypatius' plot only: see Bury, "The Nika Riot" 92-119.

21 It is also worth noting that a few years later, in 539, Justinian created the office of the quaesitor (*NJ* 80), one of whose functions was to prevent the city's filling up with crowds of unemployed provincials who might become a volatile and threatening mob.

22 *de Mag.* 1.12. and proem. e; R.I. Frank, *Scholae Palatinae. The Palace Guards of the Later Roman Empire* (Papers and Monographs of the American Academy in Rome 23; 1969) 24ff., and the review of this book by Alan Cameron, *CR* 22 (1972) 136-8. See also Cameron's *Circus Factions* 116-17, and O. Fiebiger, "Excubitorium", *RE* 6.2, cols 1577-8.

23 *de Mag.* 1.16; Frank, *Scholae* 204-5; Alexander A. Vasiliev, *Justin the First. An Introduction to the Epoch of Justinian the Great* (Dumbarton Oaks Studies I; Cambridge, Mass., 1950) 64-5, discusses the formation of the Corps of Excubitores by Leo I and discounts the reference to an excubitor in a letter of Saint Nilus, written before Leo's reign (*PG* 79, col. 357).

24 Michael Maas, "Roman History and Christian Ideology in Justinianic Reform Legislation", *DOP* 40 (1986) 17-31, here 26-7; *NJ* 30.11.2, written after the conquest of Sicily in 536 ("We are inspired with the hope that God will grant us rule over the rest of what, subject to the ancient Romans to the limits of both seas, they later lost by their negligence.").

25 *NJ* 78.4.1.

26 Michael McCormick, *Eternal Victory. Triumphal Rulership in Late Antiquity, Byzantium, and the Early Medieval West* (Cambridge, 1986) 129.

27 ibid., 65-6; 125-7.

28 *de Mag.* III.55.

29 Constantine Porphyrogenitus, *De ceremoniis aulae Byzantinae*, ed. J.J. Reiske (Bonn, 1830) Appendix ad librum primum, I, 497-8; Averil Cameron, "Images of Authority: Élites and Icons in Late Sixth Century Byzantium", *Past and Present* 84 (1979) 3-35, here 8-9 [= Margaret Mullett and Roger Scott, eds, *Byzantium and the Classical Tradition* (Birmingham, 1981) 210.

30 Maas, "History and Ideology" 17-31.

31 ibid., 25ff.; see also Chapter 1 (14-23).

32 Maas, "History and Ideology" 19.

33 ibid., 20, for full documentation and discussion.

34 *NJ* 72. See also *NJ* 7; Maas, "History and Ideology" 25.

35 Maas, "History and Ideology" 29-31.

36 See also *NJ* 49 (AD 537) and *NJ* 69 (AD 538) .

37 *NJ* 49, *NJ* 74.

38 *NJ* 28.

39 *NJ* 6.

40 Maas, "History and Ideology" 31.

41 David Wright, "Justinian and an Archangel", in Otto Feld and Urs Peschlow, eds, *Studien zur spätantiken und byzantinischen Kunst. Friedrich Wilhelm Deichmann gewidmet*, vol.III (Bonn, 1986) 75-80.

42 Sabine MacCormack, *Art and Ceremony in Late Antiquity* 77.

43 "When classical culture came back into fashion, after the years of struggle, it was less of a real alternative than a scholarly revival" (Cameron, "Images of Authority" 4).

44 Walter E. Kaegi, Jr, *Byzantium and the Decline of Rome* (Princeton, 1968) 59-175.

45 Walter Goffart "Zosimus, the First Historian of Rome's Fall", *AHR* 76 (1971) 412-41, here 430; Paul Alexander, "Medieval Apocalypses as Historical Sources", *AHR* 73 (1968) 997-1018 [= *Religious and Political History and Thought in the Byzantine Empire* (London, 1978) art. 13].

46 Ammianus Marcellinus, *History*, ed. C. U. Clark, L. Traube and W. Heraeus, 2 vols (Berlin, 1910-15) 31.5.11.

47 Ilsetraut Hadot, *Le Problème du néoplatonisme alexandrin. Hiéroclès et Simplicius* (Paris, 1978) 37-40, for citations and discussion.

48 e.g. Procopius, *Anecdota, Historia Arcana (Opera Omnia*, vol. 3, ed. J. Haury and G. Wirth, Leipzig, 1963) 12.16.

49 Pierre de Labriolle, *La Réaction païenne. Études sur la polémique antichrétienne du Ier au VIe siècle* (Paris, 1924) 335ff.; François Paschoud, *Cinq études sur Zosime* (Paris, 1975) 10ff.; Lellia Cracco Ruggini, "Simboli di battaglia ideologica nel tardo ellenismo", *Studi storici in honore di Ottorino Bertolini* I (Pisa, 1972) 177-300; Kaegi, *Byzantium and the Decline of Rome*.

50 There has been considerable debate on the date of composition of Zosimus' work, which stops unfinished in the sixth book. Goffart, "Zosimus" 421, accepts a date after 502. For bibliography and discussion of Zosimus, see *Zosimus. New History*, trans. with a commentary by Ronald T. Ridley (Byzantina Australiensia 2; Melbourne, 1982) xi-xv. See note 58 below.

51 *Zosimus*, trans. Ridley xiii.

52 Evagrius Scholasticus, *The Ecclesiastical History of Evagrius with the Scholia*, ed. J. Bidez and L. Parmentier (London, 1898, repr. Amsterdam, 1964) III.40-1, refutes Zosimus' arguments of Christian responsibility for the decline of Rome. Pauline Allen, *Evagrius Scholasticus. The Church Historian* (Louvain, 1981) 159-61, believes that Evagrius' refutation reflects literary concerns, not the need to combat a real pagan presence.

53 "comes et ex advocato fisci" (*PLRE* II "Zosimus 6" 1206).

54 Goffart, "Zosimus" 423; Averil Cameron, *Agathias* (Oxford, 1976) 76-9, for discussion of these glosses as a literary convention. Ronald T. Ridley, 'The Fourth and Fifth Century Civil and Military Hierarchy in Zosimus", *Byzantion* 40 (1970) 91-104, discusses Zosimus' interest in magistracies and the accuracy of his information.

55 *Zosimus*, trans. Ridley, notes 6 and 7; see also Kaegi, *Byzantium and the Decline of Rome* 67; Paschoud, *Cinq études* 10.

56 *Zosimus*, trans. Ridley xiii.

57 Goffart, "Zosimus" 424.

58 He also does not discuss the extent to which Zosimus' attitudes were derived from his sources. Zosimus relied heavily upon Eunapius for most of Books II-V.27, and there are indications in his differing evaluations of Stilicho to suggest that Zosimus was insufficiently critical of his sources, sometimes to the point of self-contradiction.: see Ronald T. Ridley,

"Eunapius and Zosimus", *Helikon* 9–10 (1969–70) 574–92. Zosimus does not criticize Constantine with the venom of Eunapius. I assume that even if Zosimus did owe a debt to Eunapius, he used Eunapius selectively, as did many other late-antique authors, and in his selections revealed his own views. See also Roger Blockley, "Was the First Book of Zosimus' New History Based on More than Two Sources?", *Byzantion* 50 (1980) 393–402; Kenneth Sacks, "The Meaning of Eunapius' History", *History and Theory* 25 (1986) 52–67, here 59ff.

59 Zosimus, *Historia Nova*, ed. L. Mendelssohn (Leipzig, 1887) 2.7.1, trans. Goffart, "Zosimus" 417.

60 Goffart, "Zosimus" 417.

61 Kaegi, *Byzantium and the Decline of Rome* 116–18.

62 *de Mag.* II.10; III.31; III.33; III.40. The loss of Moesia/Scythia was rectified by Justinian, and it is the first of Justinian's reconquests to be mentioned by Lydus; cf. Ammianus Marcellinus, *History* 21.10.8.

63 Zosimus, *Historia Nova* 2.33.3.

64 Theodor Ernst Mommsen, "St. Augustine and the Christian Idea of Progress: The Background of the City of God", *Journal of the History of Ideas* 12 (1951) 346–74; and Robert Markus, *Saeculum: History and Society in the Theology of St Augustine* (Cambridge, 1970), 1–21; 231–2.

65 *NJ* 30.11; *NJ* 80.10; Goffart, "Zosimus" 432 note 88; *de Mag.* II.15; III.39; III.55.

66 *de Mag.* III.39.

67 cf. *de Mag. proem.* "Those who were later magistrates of the state of the Romans had formerly been priests" and "civil powers . . . evolved from a priestly character to the civil form".

68 Goffart, "Zosimus" 431.

4 *DE MENSIBUS* AND THE ANTIQUARIAN TRADITION

1 For similar reasons, the reform laws of Justinian sought to combat the constant innovations wrought by time: see Michael Maas, "Roman History and Christian Ideology in Justinianic Reform Legislation" *DOP* 40 (1986) 17–31, here 29ff.

2 Herbert Hunger, *Die hochsprachliche profane Literatur der Byzantiner* (HAW 12.5.1; Munich, 1978) 250.

3 Arnaldo Momigliano, "Lydus", in *Oxford Classical Dictionary* (Oxford, 1970) 2nd edn, 630.

4 Paolo Mastandrea, *Un neoplatonico latino. Cornelio Labeone* (Leiden, 1979) 72–3.

5 See Averil Cameron, *Procopius and the Sixth Century* (Berkeley, 1985) 19–32; 37ff; 134ff; Robert Browning, "The Language of Byzantine Literature", in Spyros Vryonis, Jr. ed., *The "Past" in Medieval and Modern Greek Culture*, (Malibu, 1978) [= *Byzantina kai Metabyzantina* 1] 103–33, here 106–12.

6 This seems to be the meaning of *de Mag.* I.12.54; see Chapter 3, notes 25 and 26.

7 Michael McCormick, *Eternal Victory. Triumphal Rulership in Late Antiquity, Byzantium, and the Medieval West* (Cambridge, 1986) 65-6, 125-7.

8 Judith Herrin, *The Formation of Christendom* (Princeton, 1987) 3-14.

9 Brian Croke, "The Origins of the Christian World Chronicle", in Brian Croke and Alanna M. Emmett, eds, *History and Historians in Late Antiquity* (Sydney, 1983) 116-31; Brian Croke, "The Early Development of Byzantine Chronicles", in Elizabeth Jeffreys, with Brian Croke and Roger Scott, eds, *Studies in John Malalas* (Byzantina Australiensia 6; Sydney, 1990) 27-38.

10 On the continuity of the kalends, etc., in the west, see F.K. Ginzel, *Handbuch der mathematischen und technischen Chronologie*, vol. III (Leipzig, 1914) 115-16; on inscriptions in the Greek east, ibid., 298; on Heraclius, Novel 4 (AD 629) *de clericis conveniendis*, in J. Konidaris, "Die Novellen des Kaisers Herakleios", in *Fontes Minores* 5 (1982) 33-106, here 94; Lydus mentions the celebration of the kalends at *de Mens.* IV.4. On these celebrations, see Michel Meslin, *La Fête des kalendes de janvier dans l'empire romain* (Collection Latomus, 115; Brussels, 1970).

11 On indifferent compliance with these commands in Egypt, Roger S. Bagnall and K.A. Worp, "Chronological Reckoning in Byzantine Egypt", *GRBS* 20 (1979) 279-95, here 285; on the end of the consulate, Stein, 461-2; Roger Bagnall *et al.*, *Consuls of the Later Roman Empire* (APA Monograph 36, Atlanta, 1987) 11-12 suggests the consulship was ended because of Justinian's fear of rivals. The consulship was resumed by Justin II in 566 and held by emperors until 642; E. Stein, "Post-consulat et αὐτοκρατορία" in *Annuaire de l'Institut de Philologie et d'Histoire Orientales et Slaves* ii (1933-4) [= *Mélanges J. Bidez*] 869-912, esp. 894-9 [= *Opera Minora Selecta*, ed. J.-R. Palanque (Amsterdam, 1968) 315-58].

12 Philip Grierson, "The Date of Theoderic's Gold Medallion", *Hikuin* 11 (1985) 19-26.

13 Herrin, *Formation of Christendom* 11-13; Bruno Krusch, *Studien zur christlich-mittelalterlichen Chronologie: die Entstehung unserer heutigen Zeitrechnung*, 2 vols (Berlin, 1938) II.59-62.

14 *de Mens.* IV.103; see Demetrios Constantelos, "The Term 'Neoterikoi' (Innovators) in the *Exabiblos* of Constantine Armenopoulos and its Cultural-Linguistic Implications", in A.E. Laiou-Thomadakis, ed., *Charanis Studies* (New Brunswick, NJ, 1980) 1-17, esp. 2-8; Maas, "History and Ideology" 28-9.

15 Manfred Fuhrmann, *Das systematische Lehrbuch. Ein Beitrag zur Geschichte der Wissenschaften in der Antike*, (Göttingen, 1960) 122ff. (origins); 144ff. (Hellenistic); 156 ff. (Roman and Hellenistic models); Nicholas Horsfall, "Prose and Mime", in E.J. Kenney and W.V. Clausen eds, *The Cambridge History of Classical Literature, II. Latin Literature* (Cambridge, 1982) 286-90; Arnaldo Momigliano, "Ancient History and the Antiquarian", *Journal of the Warburg and Courtauld Institutes* 13 (1950) 285-315 [=*Studies in Historiography* (London, 1966) 1-39; = *Contributo alla storia degli studi classici* (Rome, 1955; repr. 1979) 67-106].

160

16 Momigliano, "Ancient History and the Antiquarian" 287; on the antiquarian tradition in general, Robert Browning, "Learning and the Past", in Kenney and Clausen, eds, *The Cambridge History of Classical Literature II* 762–73; Elizabeth Rawson, *Intellectual Life in the Late Roman Republic* (Baltimore, 1985) 233–49.

17 The *antiquarii* who he says "are called *calligraphoi* among the Greeks" (*de Mens.* I.33) were simply calligraphers: see, e.g., *CJ* 12.19.10 (*antiquarii* in the *scrinium memoriae* under Leo).

18 See Appendix for a list of his sources.

19 *de Mag.*III.63. mentions the epitome of his work *On the Physical Nature of Fishes*; works by this author were still current in the twelfth century, N.G. Wilson, *Scholars of Byzantium* (Baltimore, 1983) 199.

20 *de Mag.* III.63.

21 *de Mag.* I.5 (a criticism) and I.17.

22 Lydus had a good knowledge of Varro's major and minor works (Everard Flintoff, "Varro in the works of John of Lydia", in *Atti del Congresso Internazionale di Studi Varroniani II* (Rieti, 1976) 365–77). He cites Varro twenty times throughout his books, who is the only Latin author cited in all of them (ibid., 367). Varro devoted several books of his massive *Antiquitates Rerum Humanarum et Divinarum* to matters directly relevant to *de Mens.* (Book 17, *de annis*; Book 18, *de mensibus*; Book 19, *de diebus*); Hellfried Dahlmann, "M. Terentius Varro (Antiqu.)", *RE*, suppl. 6 (1935) 1172–277, here 1233; O. Gruppe, "Über die Bücher XIIII bis XVIIII der *antiquitates humanae* des Varro", *Hermes* 10 (1876) 51–60, esp. 54–6. Unfortunately these books no longer survive, though we do know something of them from Censorinus (*De Die Natali Liber*, ed. Fridericus Hultsch, (Leipzig, 1867); see G. Wissowa, "Censorinus 7", *RE* III.2 (1899) 1908–10).

23 *On Roman Antiquities*, see *de Mag.* I.5.

24 *de Mag.* I.14, derived from the *Digest*, I.11.1; on Aurelius Arcadius Charisius, see D. Liebs, "Aurelius Arcadius Charisius" in R. Herzog and Peter L. Schmidt, eds, *HAW. Lateinische Literatur der Antike 5. Restauration und Erneurung. Die lateinische Literatur von 284 bis 374 n.Chr.* (Munich, 1989) 69–71.

25 "Antiquarian knowledge formed part of the equipment of any contemporary orator", T. Barnes, "Tertullian the Antiquarian", *Studia Patristica* XIV (Texte und Untersuchungen zur Geschichte der altchristlichen Literatur 117; Berlin, 1976) 3–20, here 19 [=*Early Christianity and the Roman Empire* (London, 1984) ch.14]; on survival of classical oratory, Herrin, *Formation of Christendom*, 83–4; Lydus was asked by Justinian to deliver a panegyric in his honor, *de Mag.* III.28.

26 *de Mag.* II.25–6.

27 Hunger, *Literatur* 250; Wilson, *Scholars of Byzantium* 57; Roger D. Scott, "Malalas and his Contemporaries", in Elizabeth Jeffreys *et al. Studies in John Malalas* 67–86, here 69; Gilbert Dagron, *Constantinople imaginaire. Études sur le recueil des "Patria"* (Paris, 1984) 55–60, discusses similarities between Lydus and Hesychius.

28 Wilson, *Scholars of Byzantium* 55.

29 Cameron, *Procopius* 249; Carlo Maria Mazzucchi, "Per una rilettura del

palinseto vaticano 'sulla scienza politica' del tempo di Giustiniano", in
G.G. Archi, ed., *L'imperatore Giustiniano. Storia e mito* (Milan, 1978)
237-47, here p.246; *Menae patricii cum Thoma referendario De scientia
politica dialogus quae exstant in codice Vaticano palimpsesto*, ed. Carlo
Maria Mazzucchi (Milan, 1982); cf. *Des Byzantiner anonymus
Kriegswissenschaft*, eds H. Köchly and W. Rüstow, vol.II (Leipzig, 1855)
82-197; *Three Byzantine Military Treatises*, ed. George T. Dennis
(*CFHB* 25; Dumbarton Oaks, 1985).

30 Mary Beard, "A complex of times: no more sheep on Romulus'
   birthday", *PCPS* 213, n.s. 33 (1987) 1-15, here 7.
31 ibid., 1.
32 *On Powers or the Magistracies of the Roman State*, ed. Anastasius C.
   Bandy (American Philosophical Society Memoirs 149; Philadelphia,
   1982) xxvii-xxix; *Liber de Mensibus*, ed. Richard Wuensch (Leipzig,
   1898, repr. 1967) viii; Fridericus Bluhme, *De Ioannis Laurentii Lydi
   Libris Περὶ μηνῶν Observationum Capita Duo* (Diss., University of
   Halle, 1906) 1-3.
33 Bluhme, *De Libris*, 5-6.
34 Fr. Börtzler, "Zum Texte des Johannes Laurentius Lydus 'De
   mensibus' ", *Philologus* n.s.31 (1921) 364-79 accuses Wuensch of giving
   a false coherence to the work (364-5). A new edition is sorely needed.
35 *de Mens.* lxxx; *On Powers*, ed. Bandy xxviii; on Numa's calendar: Agnes
   Kirsopp Michels, "The 'Calendar of Numa' and the Pre-Julian Calendar",
   TAPA 80 (1949) 320-46.
36 See below, 58-60.
37 *de Mens.* I.17.
38 *de Mens.* II.1-2.
39 *de Mens.* II.3-4.
40 Henri Stern, *Le Calendrier de 354. Études sur son texte et sur les
   illustrations* (Paris, 1953) 51; Michele Salzman, *On Roman Time: the
   Codex Calendar of 354 and the Rhythms of Late Antique Urban Life*
   (Berkeley, 1991). Varro is the ultimate source for all such discussions.
41 James Caimi, *Burocrazia e diritto nel de Magistratibus di Giovanni Lido*
   (Milan, 1984) 70.
42 On non-Christian writers of late antiquity who did the same, see Emil
   Schürer, "Die siebentägige Woche im Gebrauche der christlichen Kirche
   der ersten Jahrhunderte", *ZNW* 6 (1905) 1-66, esp. 38ff.
43 Willy Rordorf, *Sunday. The History of the Day of Rest and Worship in
   the Earliest Centuries of the Christian Church*, trans. A.A.K. Graham
   (London and Philadelphia, 1968) 9-42; still useful is F.H. Colson, *The
   Week. An Essay on the Origin and Development of the Seven-Day Cycle*
   (Cambridge, 1926) esp. pp.18-61; Eviatar Zerubavel, *The Seven Day
   Circle. The History and Meaning of the Week* (Chicago, 1985) 5-26.
44 Lydus mentions Dositheus, a grammarian possibly of the fourth century
   AD (*de Mens.* IV.128) whose bilingual *Ars Grammatica* (ed. Gottfried
   Keil, *Grammatici Latini* vii (Leipzig, 1880) 363-436) includes a list of
   seven planets (Colson, *Week* 24). Lydus does not follow this order,
   however.
45 *CTh.*2.8.1; Rordorf, *Sunday* 162-6.

46 Willy Rordorf, "Sunday: The Fullness of Christian Liturgical Time", *Studia Liturgica* 14 (1982) 90-6.
47 *de Mens.* II.4; Lydus neglected to mention that the Chaldeans and Egyptians did not associate the first day with the sun.
48 Dominic J. O'Meara, *Pythagoras Revived. Mathematics and Philosophy in Late Antiquity* (Oxford, 1989).
49 Porphyry: O'Meara, *Pythagoras Revived* 25-9; Iamblichus: ibid., 30-108; Jacques Flamant, *Macrobe et le néo-platonisme latin à la fin du IVᵉ siècle* (Leiden, 1977) 310.
50 *Nicomachus of Gerasa. Introduction to Mathematics*, trans. and ed. Martin Luther D'Ooge, Frank E. Robbins, and Louis C. Karpinski (New York, 1926) 125ff.; John Philoponus wrote a commentary on Nichomachus' *Introduction to Arithmetic*, the standard textbook in neoplatonic schools; on Damascius: O'Meara, *Pythagoras Revived* 210.
51 O'Meara, *Pythagoras Revived* 53-69.
52 Walter Burkert, *Lore and Science in Ancient Pythagoreanism*, trans. Edwin L. Minar, Jr (Cambridge, Mass., 1972) 10, notes that late tradition often attributed to Pythagoras material that earlier writers did not.
53 Numbers exist in the mind of God: A.H. Armstrong, *Cambridge History of Later Greek and Early Medieval Philosophy* (Cambridge, 1967) 96; F.E. Robbins, "The Tradition of Greek Arithmology", *CP* 16.2 (1921) 97-123, here 121; O'Meara, *Pythagoras Revived* 79-81.
54 Burkert, *Lore and Science* 40-2.
55 Armand Delatte, *Études sur la littérature pythagoricienne* (Paris, 1915) 139.
56 D'Ooge *et al.*, *Nicomachus* 122.
57 Flamant, *Macrobe* 308-10.
58 Robbins, "Greek Arithmology" 97-112.
59 ibid.
60 ibid., 123.
61 ibid., 103, note 1.
62 *Introductionis Arithmeticae*, Libri II ed. Ricardus Hoche (Leipzig, 1866).
63 Photius, *Bibliotheca*, ed. René Henry, 8 vols (Paris, 1959-77) cod. 187; fragments collected ed. V. de Falco (Leipzig, 1922).
64 Daniélou, Jean, "La typologie de la semaine au IVᵉ siècle", *Recherches de Science Religieuse* 35 (1948) 382-411.
65 For the association of ten numbers with divinity, see Delatte, *Études* 141ff.; *de Mens.* I.15; III.4.
66 Bluhme, *De Libris* 13-15, on his pattern in discussing each month.
67 ibid. 5.
68 e.g., *de Mens.* IV.35.
69 *de Mens.*, III.4-9.
70 *de Mens.*, III.16.
71 *de Mens.*, III.22.
72 Bluhme, *De Libris* 13-14.
73 Beard, "A complex of times" 1; Mastandrea, *Un neoplatonico latino* 14-73.
74 On Lydus' sources, see Bluhme, *De Libris, passim*, esp. ch.II; and Appendix, above.
75 Theodorus Litt, *De Verrii Flacci et Cornelii Labeonis Fastorum Libris*

(Bonn, 1904) 5-6. He mentions Fulvius Nobilior, Junius Gracchanus, Cincius Nisus, Masurius Sabinus, Cornelius Labeo. Lydus mentions Cincius and Labeo in *de Mens.*, and a work of Gracchanus not dealing with calendars in *de Mag.* proem. and I.24.

76 See notes 15 and 22.

77 *de Mens.* IV.144; on Cincius, Henry Bardon, *La Littérature latine inconnue* II. *L'époque impériale* (Paris, 1956) 108-109.

78 *de Mens.* I.21.

79 ibid., I.21, III.10, IV.1, IV.25. See Mastandrea, *Un neoplatonico latino* 10-13; 21-47; 56-65; 72-3.

80 *de Mens.* IV.2.

81 Bluhme, *De Libris* 21ff.

82 See *Inscriptiones Italiae*, vol.XIII. *Fasti et Elogia*, ed. Attilio Degrassi, (Rome, 1963) esp. 263-77; *CIL* (Fasti Anni Iuliani) 254; Konrat Ziegler, "Polemius Silvius", *RE* 21.1 (1951) 1260-3; Filocalus: P.L. Schmidt, in R. Herzog and Peter L. Schmidt, eds, *HAW. Lateinische Literatur der Antike* 5. *Restauration und Erneurung. Die lateinische Literatur von 284 bis 374 n.Chr.* (1989) Munich 178-80.

83 *Inscriptiones Italiae. Fasti et Elogia*, ed. Degrassi, 263.

84 Derived from Columella.

85 *CIL* I.1 285.

86 Robin Lane Fox, *Pagans and Christians* (New York, 1987) 66-8; 90-2 for a colorful introduction.

87 John F. Baldovin, *The Urban Character of Christian Worship. The Origins, Development, and Meaning of Stational Liturgy* (Orientalia Christiana Analecta 228; Rome, 1987); the status of pagan festivals in the sixth century requires monographic study.

88 At IV.7; Caesar, IV.102; Augustus IV.124; Claudius, IV.59.

89 His list is full of errors and odd omissions: the Saturnalia, for example, is excluded, and he gets wrong the nature of the Ovatio.

90 Peter Schreiner, "Historisches und liturgisches zum byzantinischen Neujahr", *Rivista di Studi Bizantini e Slavi* 2 (1982) 13-23, here 14-15.

91 *de Mens.* IV.158.

92 *de Mens.* IV.158.6.

93 *de Mens.* IV.158.23.

94 Agathias, *History*, ed. Rudolf Keydell (Berlin, 1967) V.3.

95 "Because of this Romus [*sic*] devised what is known as the Brumalia, declaring, it is said, that the emperor of the time must entertain his entire senate and officials and all who serve in the palace, since they are persons of consequence, during the winter when there is a respite from fighting. He began by inviting and entertaining those whose names began with alpha, and so on, right up to the last letter; he ordered the senate to entertain in the same way. They too entertained the whole army and those they wanted. . . . This custom of the Brumalia has persisted in the Roman state to the present day." (John Malalas, *The Chronicle of John Malalas*, trans. E. Jeffreys *et al*, (Byzantina Australiensia 4; Melbourne, 1986) par. 179 (Bk 7.7) 95.

96 John R. Crawford, "De Bruma et Brumalibus Festis", *BZ* 23 (1914-19) 365-96; Ph. Koukoules, Βυζαντινῶν βίος καὶ πολιτισμός (Athens,

1948) II. 1, 25-9 and 36-8; Fotios Litsas, "Choricius of Gaza: an Approach to his Work. Introduction, Translation, and Commentary" (Diss., University of Chicago, 1980) 94, 310ff. (commentary); Albin Haebler, "Bruma", *RE* 3 (1897) 901-2; Choricius, *Oratio in Justiniani Brumalia*, in *Choricii Gazaei Opera*, ed. Richard Förster and Eberhard Richtseig (Leipzig, 1929) 175-9.

97 Litsas, "Choricius" 94.

98 Although the preface makes the reference to the consulship in ancient times, it avoids any mention of the close connection between the consul and the religious celebrations of the pagan new year, the very object of Lydus' concern at this point in *de Mens.*; on the possibility of a reflection of *NJ* 105 in *de Mag.* II.8, see Caimi, *Burocrazia*, 119-20.

99 See Chapter 5.

100 Péricles-Pierre Joannou, *Discipline générale antique (IIe-IXe s.)* (Rome, 1962) I.i, p.198; Frank R. Trombley, "The Survival of Paganism in the Byzantine Empire during the Pre-Iconoclastic Period (540-727)" (Diss., UCLA, 1981) 102-48, esp. 118ff.; *idem*, "The Council in Trullo (691-692): A Study of the Canons Relating to Paganism, Heresy, and the Invasions", *Comitatus* 9 (1978) 2-18, here 5-6 (Canon 62 specifies the Panegyris in March, but Lydus puts it in May).

101 The Brumalia continued at court, at least until the reign of Constantine Porphyrogenitus: Crawford, "De Bruma" 390.

5 PAGANISM AND POLITICS

1 *de Mens.* IV.24 (Isaiah I.11-14).

2 It is possible that *de Mens.* may have been expanded already in the sixth century: Fr. Börtzler, "Zum Texte des Johannes Laurentius Lydus 'de Mensibus' ", *Philologus* 77 (1921) 364-79; Arthur Darby Nock, "A Vision of Mandulis Aion", *HTR* 27 (1934) 53-104, here 95-6 [= *Essays on Religion and the Ancient World*, ed. Zeph Stewart, vol.1 (Oxford, 1972) 356-400, here 392-3].

3 Kenneth Harl, "Sacrifice and Pagan Belief in Fifth- and Sixth- Century Byzantium", *Past and Present* 128 (August, 1990) 7-27; Pierre Chuvin, *A Chronicle of the Last Pagans*, trans. B.A. Archer (Cambridge, Mass., 1990), surveys the decline of the pagan establishment.

4 Chuvin, *Chronicle* 134.

5 Gilbert Dagron, *Naissance d'une capitale. Constantinople et ses institutions de 330 à 451* (Paris, 1974) 378-80; Chuvin, *Chronicle* 91ff.

6 Paul Lemerle, *Byzantine Humanism. The First Phase*, trans. Helen Lindsay and Ann Moffatt (Byzantina Australiensia 3; Canberra, 1986) 73.

7 Harl, "Sacrifice and Pagan Belief " *passim*.

8 On the date of the beginning of the purge and its relation to the first Codex that appeared on 7 April 529, see Tony Honoré, *Tribonian* (London, 1978) 46-7.

9 Walter E. Kaegi, Jr, "The Fifth-Century Twilight of Byzantine Paganism", *Classica et Mediaevalia* 27 (1966) 243-75, here 271.

10 "crimen publicum", *CJ* 1.11.8 [= Leo and Anthemius, AD 472?].

11 *CJ* I.11.10.

12 Harl, "Sacrifice" 7-27.

13 *CJ* I.ll.4 = *CTh*. 16.10.17 (AD 399); earlier emperors had permitted pagan temples to stand "as sites of the traditional amusements of the Roman people" *CTh*. 16.10.3, AD 342; Michele Salzman, *On Roman Time: The Codex Calendar of 354 and the Rhythms of Urban Life in Late Antiquity* (Berkeley, l990) ch.5 on the context of the initial anti-pagan legislation of the fourth century.

14 See Chapter 4, note 100, on Trullo.

15 See Chapter 7.

16 John Malalas, *The Chronicle of John Malalas*, ed. and trans. Elizabeth Jeffreys, Michael Jeffreys, Roger Scott *et al.* (Byzantina Australiensia 4; Melbourne, 1986) 18.42; on date, Honoré, *Tribonian* 46-7; Johannes Irmscher, "Heidnische Kontinuität im justinianischen Staat", *The 17th International Byzantine Studies Conference. Major Papers.* Washington, D.C., 3-8 August 1986 (New Rochelle, 1986) 17-30.

17 *CJ*. I.11.9

18 Theophanes, *Chronographia*, ed. C. de Boor (Leipzig, 1883, repr. 1963) AM 6022, (p. 180); Malalas, *Chronicle* 18.42: "In that year there was a great persecution of Hellenes. Many had their property confiscated. Some of them died: Macedonius, Asclepiodotus, Phocas the son of Craterus, and Thomas the quaestor. This caused great fear. The emperor decreed that those who held Hellenic beliefs should not perform any state office .... This sacred decree was displayed in all provincial cities."; but Theophanes says only that Asclepiodatus killed himself and that the others were caught. Procopius mentions no executions, *Historia Arcana* (*Opera Omnia* vol.3, ed. J. Haury and G. Wirth, Leipzig, 1963) 11.31; Thomas was still Quaestor in 529 (see J.B. Bury, *History of the Later Roman Empire from the Death of Theodosius I to the Death of Justinian*, 2 vols (London, 1923, repr. 1958) II.367-8; Honoré, *Tribonian* 47 n. 65).

19 *CJ* I.11.10.

20 W.H. Buckler and David Robinson, *Sardis*, vol.7 (Leiden, 1932) 43-4 for text and commentary; more recently Clive Foss (*Byzantine and Turkish Sardis* (Cambridge, Mass., 1976) 29) has given it the date "after 539".

21 Buckler and Robinson, *Sardis* 43: "The names of other persons sentenced to confinement or internment must have been inscribed on the blocks which originally lay below this stone."

22 Malalas, *Chronicle* 18.42.

23 Procopius, *Historia Arcana* 11.31-2.

24 Frank R. Trombley, "The Survival of Paganism in the Byzantine Empire during the Pre-Iconoclastic Period (540-727)" (Diss. UCLA, 1981) 18-22, and his "Paganism in the Greek World at the End of Antiquity: The Case of Rural Anatolia and Greece", *HTR*, 78.3-4 (1985) 327-52; Chuvin, *Chronicle* 143-8; Glenn Bowersock, *Hellenism in Late Antiquity* (Ann Arbor, 1990) 1-4, 35-9; Harl, "Sacrifice" 20; John of Ephesus, *Historia Ecclesiastica* 3.3.36, *CSCO* 106, Scrip. Syri 55:169 (Syriac).

25 John of Ephesus, in F. Nau, "Analyse de la seconde partie inédite de l'histoire ecclésiastique de Jean d'Asie, patriarche jacobite de Constantinople (†585)", *Revue de l'Orient Chrétien* 2 (1897) 480ff.
26 John of Ephesus, in Nau "Analyse" 482; Charles Diehl, *Justinien et la civilisation byzantine au VIe siècle* (Paris, 1901, repr. 1969) 557.
27 Stein 373, 799–800.
28 Dagron, *Naissance* 17, note 2.
29 Malalas, *Chronicle* XVIII.136 (p.300).
30 *Vita S. Symeon Stylitae junioris*, ed. P. van den Ven, vol. 1 (Subsidia Hagiographica 32; Brussels, 1962) 161 (p.143), 164–5 (pp.145-8); Dorothy Abrahamse, "Hagiographic Sources for Byzantine Cities, 500–900 AD" (Diss., University of Michigan, 1967) 145–6.
31 Karl Krumbacher, *Geschichte der byzantinischen Literatur* (2nd edn, Berlin, 1897) 405.
32 John of Ephesus in *Chronique de Michel le Syrien, Patriarche Jacobite d'Antioche* (1166–1199), ed. J.-B. Chabot, vol. 2 (Paris, 1901) ix.33. (pp.268-70) [=*CSCO* vol.106, Scrip. Syri 55:169]; Ilse Rochow, "Die Heidenprozesse unter den Kaisern Tiberios II. Konstantinos und Maurikios", in *Studien zum 7. Jahrhundert in Byzanz (Berliner Byzantinistische Arbeiten* 47 (1976) 120–30, here 120–2; and *eadem*, "Zur Rolle der Anhänger antiker Kulte und Brauche" in F. Winkelmann *et al.*, eds, *Byzantium in 7. Jahrhundert* (Berlin, 1978), 227–55, esp. 229–33, 243–4.
33 Rochow, "Die Heidenprozesse" 120–30.
34 Trombley has shown the "mechanics of conversion" in the countryside during the late sixth century and afterwards: see his "Survival of Paganism", "Paganism in the Greek World", and "Monastic Foundations in Sixth-century Anatolia and their Role in the Social and Economic Life of the Countryside", *Greek Orthodox Theological Review* 30.1 (1985) 45–59; Harl, "Sacrifice" 20ff.; Bowersock, *Hellenism* 1–4.
35 Trombley, "Paganism in the Greek World" 327–52; Johannes Geffcken, *The Last Days of Greco-Roman Paganism*, trans. Sabine MacCormack (Amsterdam/New York/Oxford, 1978) 223–80.
36 J.A.S. Evans, "Christianity and Paganism in Procopius of Caesarea", *GRBS* 12 (1971) 81–100.
37 Walter E. Kaegi, Jr, *Byzantium and the Decline of Rome* (Princeton, 1968) 59–145.
38 Note the comment of John Dillon: "It is precisely in Iamblichus' time that the role of the philosopher . . . undergoes a significant change. With the imperial court gone over to Christianity, the philosopher becomes the champion of a rearguard action for the preservation of Hellenic values, and is ultimately driven underground by ever intensifying persecution", in Peter Brown, *The Philosopher and Society in Late Antiquity* (Berkeley, 1980) 24.
39 Damascius, *Life of Isidore*, ed. C. Zintzen (Hildesheim, 1967) 175 (= fragment 202, from the *Suda*, ed. Ada Adler, 5 vols (Leipzig, 1928-38) II.35,22); see C. Roueché, *Aphrodisias in Late Antiquity (Journal of Roman Studies Monograph* 5; London, 1989) 91.
40 Dagron, *Naissance* 377; Chuvin, *Chronicle* 101–18.
41 On cultic worship at Constantinople before Constantine, see Dagron,

Naissance 367–74, after Constantine, ibid. 374ff., Harl, "Sacrifice and Pagan Belief" *passim*.

42 Procopius, *Historia Arcana*, 11.32.
43 *CJ* I.11.10.
44 ibid.
45 Harl, "Sacrifice" 22–5.
46 Pauline Allen, *Evagrius Scholasticus. The Church Historian* (Louvain, 1981) 229–30.
47 ibid., 230–1: "There is a liberal number of references to paganism and crypto-paganism at this time in our sources, but they so often serve as polemic or to bolster a hagiographic eulogy that it is difficult to gauge the reality behind them."
48 The *Suda*, vol.4, p.588, T956: "This Tribonian was a Hellene and atheist and opposed the Christian faith in every particular." The charge has been refuted by Honoré: *Tribonian* 64–7.
49 Honoré, *Tribonian* 66.
50 Procopius, *De Bello Persico (Opera Omnia*, vol. 1, ed. J. Haury and G. Wirth, Leipzig, 1962) 1.24.10.
51 John of Ephesus, *Historica Ecclesiastica* III 27–34, V.17; Allen, *Evagrius*, 250.
52 Other examples: Anastasius, Quaestor of Justin I, ostensibly Christian, used his office "on every pretext to smite the Christians", Evagrius, Scholasticus, *The Ecclesiastical History with the Scholia*, ed. J. Bidez and L. Parmentier (London, 1898, repr. Amsterdam, 1964) III.27, 31, 34; II.29 (discussed Allen, *Evagrius* 231); in 580, Sebastianus the Praefectus Urbis Constantinopoleos (Urban Prefect) was suspected of paganism when riots broke out over the acquittal of men accused of paganism; in the reign of Maurice, the commander of Carrhae, Ascundynus, was denounced by his secretary as a secret pagan and crucified. I thank John Martindale for providing me these last two names in advance of publication of *PLRE* III.
53 Michael Maas, "Roman History and Christian Ideology in Justinianic Reform Legislation", *DOP* 40 (1986) 17–31, here 29–31.
54 Alan Cameron, "The Empress and the Poet: Paganism and Politics at the Court of Theodosius II", *Yale Classical Studies* 27 (1982) 217–90, re-evaluates the conventional view of Theodosius.
55 See Berthold Rubin, *Das Zeitalter Iustinians* (Berlin, 1960) 155.
56 Procopius, *Historia Arcana* 11.14-41, catalogues the various groups which Justinian sought to eliminate.
57 Honoré, *Tribonian* 14–15.
58 Maas, "History and Ideology" *passim*.
59 ibid., 29; Giuliana Lanata, *Legislazione e natura nelle novelle giustinianee* (Naples, 1984) esp. 177–8.
60 Justinian ordered his general Narses to destroy sanctuaries in Egypt and send the statues to Constantinople: Procopius, *De Bello Persico* 1.19.37; Harl, "Sacrifice" 21.
61 Demetrios Constantelos, "Paganism and the State in the Age of Justinian", *CHR* 50 (1964) 372–80, here 374.
62 Alan Cameron, "The Last Days of the Academy at Athens", *PCPS* 15

(1969) 7–29; John Patrick Lynch, *Aristotle's School. A Study of a Greek Educational Institution* (Berkeley, 1972) 163–87; Alison Frantz, "Pagan Philosophers in Christian Athens", *PAPS* 119 (1975) 29–38; H.J. Blumenthal, "529 and its Sequel: What Happened to the Academy?", *Byzantion* 48 (1978) 369–385; John Glucker, *Antiochus and the Late Academy* (*Hypomnemata* 56; Göttingen, 1978) 322–9.

63 *de Mag.* III.12.

64 See Chapter 1, note 15.

65 See note 60 above.

66 See Chapter 1, note 90.

67 Malalas, *Chronicle* 18.132–5; Stein 799–800.

68 Malalas, *Chronicle* 18.141.

69 Procopius, *Historia Arcana* 11.31; Irmscher, "Heidnische Kontinuität", 17–30, suggests that the accusations represent a struggle between the parvenu Justinian and the established aristocracy.

70 Maria Cesa, "La politica di Giustiniano verso l'occidente nel giudizio di Procopio", *Athenaeum* n.s. 59 (1981) 389–409, here 406–7.

71 Peter Charanis, "Hellas in Greek Sources of the Sixth, Seventh, and Eighth Centuries", in Kurt Weitzmann, ed., *Late Classical and Mediaeval Studies in Honor of Albert Mathias Friend, Jr* (Princeton, 1955) 161–76, discusses "Hellas" and "Hellene" as geographical and ethnic names not equivalent to "pagan"; Chuvin, *Chronicle* 7, 121, 133; Bowersock, *Hellenism* 9–11.

72 See note 34 above.

73 Dagron, *Naissance* 383–5; *CTh.* 16.10.21.

74 On the varieties and wide extent of paganism, see Geffcken, *Last Days* 223–80; Bowersock, *Hellenism* 1–70; Chuvin, *Chronicle* 73ff.

75 Dagron, *Naissance* 378; on the urban development of Constantinople during this period, see Cyril Mango, *Le Développement urbain de Constantinople (IVe-VIIe siècles)* (Travaux et Mémoires Monographies 2, Paris, 1985) 23–53.

76 Gilbert Dagron, *L'Empire romain d'orient au IVe siècle et les traditions politiques de l'hellénisme. Le témoignage de Thémistios* (Travaux et Mémoires 3; Paris, 1968) 1–242, is an excellent introduction; ibid., *Naissance* 379.

77 Pierre Chuvin, "Nonnos de Panopolis entre paganisme et christianisme", *Bulletin de l'Association Guillaume Budé* XLV.4 (1986) 387–96, discusses some of these issues in the context of the preceding century; Dagron, *Naissance* 385.

78 *de Mag.* III.76; *PLRE* II "Phocas 5" 881 and *PLRE* III (forthcoming); for his full titles found on a bronze weight, see A. de Ridder, *Les Bronzes antiques du Louvre*, vol.II (Paris, 1915), 172, no.3411. I am grateful to John Martindale for this information; *PLRE* II "Craterus" 328.

79 On his sponsorship of Speciosus, a Libyan grammarian, see *de Mag.* III.73, and Robert Kaster, *Guardians of Language: The Grammarian and Society in Late Antiquity* (Berkeley, 1988) 360, no.138.

80 Which Procopius defines (*De Bello Persico* II.21.2; James Caimi, *Burocrazia e diritto nel de Magistratibus di Giovanni Lido* (Milan, 1984) 264) as one who when in the palace serves the emperor as privy

councillor. The position did not preclude holding other office or military command simultaneously.

81 Malalas, *Chronicle* 422; Theophanes, *Chronographia* AM 6019.

82 He calls it the "Temple of the Great God", affecting ignorance of Christian terminology.

83 Oddly, Procopius does not mention Phocas' role in the building of the great church in *De Aedificiis* (*Opera Omnia*, vol.4, ed. J. Haury and G. Wirth, Leipzig, 1964) at I.1.22ff., even though he mentions others involved in the planning and construction. Perhaps Lydus somewhat exaggerated the significance of Phocas' contribution, or perhaps Procopius was reluctant to mention a man who had fallen into disfavor with Justinian.

84 *NJ* 82.1; on his reputation for justice, Procopius, *De Bello Persico* I.24.18, *Historica Arcana* 21.6.

85 Malalas, fr. 47 (= Constantine Porphyrogenitus, *Excerpta de insidiis*, in *Excerpta Historica*, ed C. de Boor (Berlin, 1905) 151–76, here p.173); cf. Malalas, *Chronicle* 480; Procopius, *De Bello Persico* I.25.40, cf. Malalas, *Chronicle* 480.

86 Theophanes, AM 6022; cf. Malalas, *Chronicle* 449, who erroneously says he died at this time. *PLRE* II plausibly suggests that Malalas has conflated the two persecutions, and so listed Phocas' death too early (p.882).

87 John of Ephesus, in Nau, "Analyse" 481.

88 *de Mag.* III.72.

89 *de Mag.* III.65.

90 *de Mag.* III.76.

91 *de Mag.* III.38.

92 R.M. Harrison, "The Church of St. Polyeuktos in Istanbul and the Temple of Solomon", in Cyril Mango and Omeljan Pritsak, eds, *Okeanos. Essays Presented to Ihor Ševčenko on his Sixtieth Birthday* (*Harvard Ukrainian Studies* 7; 1983) 276–9, here 277–8; Richard Krautheimer, *Early Christian and Byzantine Architecture* (Baltimore, 1975) 230; Averil Cameron, *Procopius and the Sixth Century* (Berkeley, 1985) 104, note 151; Judith Herrin, *The Formation of Christendom* (Princeton, 1987) 40.

93 Procopius, *De Aedificiis* I.8.5; Cameron, *Procopius* 104.

94 *de Mag.* I.20.

95 *de Mag.* III.72, Lydus' clumsy – and false – archaism for "patrician".

96 John Philip Thomas, *Private Religious Foundations in the Byzantine Empire*, (Dumbarton Oaks Studies 24; Washington, DC, 1987) 46–7.

97 *de Mag.* III.74.

98 e.g. Ellamus donated 20 pounds of gold. *De Mag.* III. 74.

99 Luigi Amirante, "Appunti per la storia della 'Redemptio ab Hostibus' ", *Labeo* 3 (1957) 171–220, here 213–18.

100 *de Mag.* III.76.

101 Anastasius C. Bandy, in *On Powers or the Magistracies of the Roman State* (American Philosophical Society Memoirs 149; Philadelphia, 1982) 343 (note on 250.1), accepts Lydus' explanation of Phocas' kindly subterfuge.

102 *de Mag.* III.76.
103 ibid.

6 *DE MAGISTRATIBUS* AND THE THEORY OF IMPERIAL RESTORATION

1 Magnus Aurelius Cassiodorus, *Variarum Libri XII*, ed. A.J. Fridh (Corpus Christianorum: Series Latina 96, Turnhout, 1973) 226.
2 *de Mag.* II.5; cf. III.9.9.
3 *de Mag.* II.7; Lydus quotes *Iliad* 21.196; Erik Peterson, "Die Bedeutung der ὠκεανέ-Akklamation", *Rheinisches Museum* 78 (1929) 221-3, for the late-antique use of the image of the ocean to represent the boundless generosity of a civic benefactor. Lydus has transferred a human epithet to a magistracy. See also Louis Robert, *Hellenica* VII (1949) 81 note 4 and XII 570.
4 e.g. *de Mag.* II.27.
5 *de Mag.* I.36.
6 *de Mag.* I.39ff.
7 *de Mag.* I.44ff.
8 *de Mag.* I.3 .
9 *de Mag.*
10 *de Mag.* II.1.
11 *de Mag.* II.24-30.
12 *de Mag.* III.1.
13 *de Mag.* III.68.
14 *de Mag.* III.1.
15 ibid.
16 *de Mag.* III.2-3.
17 *de Mag.* III.39.
18 ibid.
19 e.g., *Digest* I.16.10 (citing Ulpian).
20 *de Mag.* II.5.
21 *de Mag.* III.40.
22 ibid.
23 ibid; see also II.10.
24 *de Mag.* III.41; II.11 gives a slightly different version of these events, explaining that Theodosius I, in an effort to protect his sons, established that only generals might conduct wars and limited the scope of the Prefecture to affairs of the palace.
25 *de Mag.* III.42.
26 ibid.; Alan Cameron, "The Empress and the Poet: Paganism and Politics at the Court of Theodosius II", *Yale Classical Studies* 27 (1982) 217-89 (on Cyrus' career, 221-5).
27 *de Mag.* III.42.
28 *de Mag.* III.43.
29 *de Mag.* III.44.
30 *de Mag.* III.45; see also II.27.
31 *de Mag.* III.45ff.

32 *de Mag.* III.49ff.; compare the positive assessment of Marinus by Zachariah of Mitylene, *The Syriac Chronicle* (trans. F.J. Hamilton and E.W. Brooks (London, 1899, repr. 1979) 9.

33 *de Mag.* III.57 and 65-9; James Caimi, *Burocrazia e diritto nel de Magistratibus di Giovanni Lido* (Milan, 1984). 243-57.

34 *de Mag.* III.57.

35 *de Mag.* III. 56-9.

36 *de Mag.* III.65-6; Caimi, *Burocrazia* 251.

37 *de Mag.* II.68.

38 *palingenesia . . . kardokein* (*de Mag.* II.5.3) or *eita . . . genesis* (II.23). He uses the verb *anakaleo* most frequently (II.28; III.71).

39 An epigram of Agathias suggests that there may have been a literary convention of describing rebuilding that did not use the language of inscriptions: "We erect this marble statue to the Proconsul Theodosius, Governor of Asia, mighty in councils, because he raised up Smyrna and led it to the light again", Louis Robert, *Hellenica*, vol.IV, *Epigrammes du Bas-Empire* (Paris, 1948) 62 [= *Anthologia Palatina* XVI.43]. The image of return to daylight matches Lydus' description of an object's essence returning to itself: "Decay generates the return since Nature of her own accord watches over it and leads it forth again to the light of existence", *de Mag.* II.23.

40 Compare Justinian's legal theory, Michael Maas, "Roman History and Christian Ideology in Justinianic Reform Legislation", *DOP* 40 (1986) 17-31, here 29-31.

41 Livy, I.15.8 speaks of Romulus' bodyguard as "celeres". Lydus drew on a source that misunderstood Livy.

42 *de Mag.* I.14; in the eastern empire, *Eparch* was the standard Greek equivalent of Praetorian Prefect, and *Hipparch* of Master of Horse.

43 *de Mag.* I.15.

44 T. Robert S. Broughton, *The Magistrates of the Roman Republic* (New York, 1952) I.9, for citations.

45 Cf. *Digest*, 1.11.

46 *de Mag.* I.37.

47 *On Powers or the Magistracies of the Roman State*, ed. Anastasius C. Bandy (American Philosophical Society Memoirs 149; Philadelphia, 1982) 298.

48 *de Mag.* II.24.

49 Appendix, "Aurelius Arcadius Charisius"; Otto Karlowa, *Römische Rechtsgeschichte* I (Leipzig, 1885) 754; Arcadius Charisius, "de officio praefecti praetorio liber singularis", in *Palingenesia Iuris Civilis*, ed. Otto Lenel and Lorenz Sierl, vol.1 (Graz, 1889, repr., 1960) col.59; D. Liebs, "Aurelius Arcadius Charisius", in R. Herzog and Peter L. Schmidt, eds, *HAW. Lateinische Literatur der Antike Restauration und Erneuerung. Die Lateinische Literatur von 284 bis 374 n.Chr.* vol. 5 (Munich, 1989) 69-71.

50 *de Mag.* II.10.

51 *de Mag.* II.23.

52 *de Mag.* II.10.

53 *de Mag.* III.22.

54 *de Mag.* III.55.
55 *de Mag.* II.28; cf. Constantine's view of Constantinople as an image of Rome (*de Mag.* II.30).
56 Cf. Zosimus, *New History* trans. with a commentary by Ronald T. Ridley (Byzantina Australiensia 2; Melbourne, 1982) 1.7, discussing the "good" Antonine emperors: "they set right many wrongs and not only did they regain what their predecessors had lost, but they made some new acquisitions [of territory]."
57 *de Mag.* III.1.
58 *de Mag.* II.5; III.9.
59 *de Mag.* II.5.
60 *de Mag.* III.55; proem.; cf. III.71 where the rebuilding of Constantinople after the Nika riots is compared to an act of the Demiurge; II.15, the inscription in the church of Sts Sergius and Bacchus calls him "the emperor who sleeps the least". See Jean Ebersolt and Adolph Thiers, *Les Églises de Constantinople* (Paris, 1913, repr. London, 1979) 24; Berthold Rubin, *Das Zeitalter Iustinians* (Berlin, 1960) 170; cf. Procopius, *Historia Arcana* (*Opera Omnia*, vol.3, ed. J. Haury and G. Wirth, Leipzig, 1963) 12.21.
61 *de Mag.* III.33; compare Sozomen's description of Theodosius II's physical and intellectual training: *Historia Ecclesiastica*, ed. Joseph Bidez (Berlin, 1960) dedication 7-8. In this case, however, intellectual training is associated with religious piety, not historical knowledge. See Glenn Chesnut, *The First Christian Histories. Eusebius, Socrates, Sozomen, Theodoret, and Evagrius* (2nd edn, Macon, Georgia, 1986) 247-8; Glanville Downey, "Themistius and the Defense of Hellenism in the Fourth Century", *HTR* 50.4 (1957) 259-74. It is amusing to note that Lydus describes the bureaucracy of the rosy past in the same terms: "The people who ran the administration in those days were wise and educated" (*de Mag.* III.15).
62 *CTh.* 14.1.1; Ramsay MacMullen, "Roman Bureaucratese", *Traditio* 18 (1962) 364-78, here 367-8.
63 *CTh.* 6.26.1; MacMullen, "Roman Bureaucratese" 367-8.
64 Themistius, *Oration* 11, 144C-145A, in *Orationes quae Supersunt*, vol. 1, ed. G. Downey (Leipzig, 1965).
65 Plutarch, *Moralia* 10.X.3, 780f. (Cambridge, Mass., 1936, trans. Harold Fowler).
66 *de Mag.* III.30.
67 *de Mag.* II.28; compare the provincial reform legislation of the 530s: Maas, "History and Ideology" *passim.*
68 Gerhard Rösch, *ONOMA ΒΑΣΙΛΕΙΑΣ. Studien zum offiziellen Gebrauch der Kaisertitel in spätantiker und frühbyzantinischer Zeit* (Byzantina Vindobonensia 10; Vienna, 1978) 130 (Coins), 40 (*Kyrios*).
69 *de Mag.* III.1.
70 ibid.
71 *de Mag.* III.39.
72 *de Mag.* III.69.
73 *de Mag.* II.19, III.22.
74 *de Mag.* II.19; compare Procopius, *Historia Arcana* 8.13-21; for Domitian

as tyrant before the sixth century, see Rubin, *Zeitalter* 445; Lydus attributes such behavior to Romulus (I.5.1).

75 *de Mag.* III.1, III.55.

76 Lydus never suggested that the appointment of Phocas solved all the ills of the office; *de Mag.* was predicated on the assumption that the Prefecture remained in decline.

7 LYDUS AND THE PHILOSOPHERS

1 Fridericus Bluhme, *De Ioannis Laurentii Lydi Libris Περὶ μηνῶν Observationum Capita Duo* (Diss., University of Halle, 1906) 21-46; Johannes F. Schultze, *Quaestionum Lydianarum Particula Prior* (Diss., University of Greifswald, 1862) esp. 11ff.; Curt Wittig, *Quaestiones Lydianae* (Diss., University of Königsberg, 1910) *passim*; Wilhelm Christ, W. Schmid and O. Stählin, *Geschichte der griechischen Literatur. Die nachklassische Periode von 100 bis 530 nach Christus* (*HAW* 7.2.2; ed. I. Müller, rev. W. Otto *et al.*, Munich, 1924) 849-51. On florilegia see Curt Wachsmuth, *Studien zu den griechischen Florilegien* (Berlin, 1882, repr. Amsterdam, 1971).

2 Bluhme, *De Libris*, remains the fundamental study: see esp. pp.7 and 33 for convenient lists of citations. See the "Index Auctorum", in *Liber de Mensibus*, ed. Richard Wuensch (Leipzig, 1898, repr. 1967) 185-8; Thomas Carney, *Bureaucracy in Traditional Society: Romano-Byzantine Bureaucracies Viewed from within* II. *Byzantine bureaucracy from within* (Lawrence, Kansas, 1971) 47-76; see Appendix above.

3 Lydus knew a book written by Christodorus about the students of Proclus: see Appendix (Christodorus).

4 Lydus derived his view of matter from the *Timaeus* (in *Platonis Opera*, ed. J. Burnet, vol. 4, Oxford, 1904) 27D-28: "about which Plato speaks in the *Timaeus*, 'What always exists has no origin, what has an origin does not exist forever'" (*de Mens.* III.53).

5 The *Timaeus* makes "the classic Platonic distinction between being and becoming – between ideal, intelligible reality, and the material, sensible world of change": John Whittaker, "Plutarch, Platonism, and Christianity", in Henry J. Blumenthal and Robert A. Markus, eds, *Neoplatonism and Early Christian Thought. Essays in honour of A. H. Armstrong* (London, 1981) 50-63, here 54; see also his "Timaeus 27D 5ff" *Phoenix* 23 (1969) 181-5 [= *Studies in Platonism and Patristic Thought* (London, 1984) art. 2].

6 *de Mens.* III.8, IV.37; *de Ost.* 9.

7 *de Mag.* III.71.

8 *de Mens.* III.1.

9 *de Mag.* II.23.

10 *de Mens.* III.8.

11 ibid.

12 *de Mens.* III.18 [= Aristotle, *De Generatione et Corruptione*: *On Coming-to-be and passing-away*, ed. Harold H. Joachim (Oxford, 1922) II.l0 (336ᵃ, 26ff.); *de Ost.* 16a.

13 e.g.: Aristotle, *de Caelo*, ed. D.J. Allan (Oxford, 1936) I.l0; Richard Sorabji, *Time, Creation and the Continuum. Theories in Antiquity and the Early Middle Ages* (Ithaca, 1983) 193ff.

14 Aristotle, *De Gen. et Cor.* 318^b-320^a.

15 *De Caelo* I.3; Philippe Hoffmann, "Simplicius' Polemics", in Richard Sorabji, ed., *Philoponus and the Rejection of Aristotelian Science*, (London, 1987) 57–83, here 77ff.; C. Wildberg, *John Philoponus' Criticism of Aristotle's Theory of Aether* (Berlin, New York, 1988); H. H. Joachim, ed., *On Coming-to-be*, xxxii–xxxvi.

16 *De Gen. et Cor.* II.10.

17 *De Gen. et Cor.* II.11.

18 *Phthora* and *palingenesia* were important terms in Stoic philosophy for the decay and rebirth of the cosmos after a conflagration in its cyclical process: see *Stoicorum Veterum Fragmenta*, ed. Joannes von Arnim, vol.II (Leipzig, 1903, repr. 1964) 183–91. The word *palingenesia* (used by Lydus, *de Mag.* II.5) is not used by Aristotle but enters the writings of later neoplatonists via Stoic and neo-Pythagorean writers. R.T. Wallis, *Neoplatonism* (London, 1972) 77; Jaap Mansfeld, "Bad World and Demiurge: a 'Gnostic' Motif from Parmenides and Empedocles to Lucretius and Philo", in R. van den Broek and M.J. Vermaseren, eds, *Studies in Gnosticism and Hellenistic Religions: presented to Gilles Quispel on the Occasion of his 65th Birthday* (Leiden, 1981) 261–314, here 304ff.; *phthora* and *palingenesia* were also used for the new cycle in late neoplatonism. *De Mag.* does not discuss the frequency or the scale of the cycles affecting magistracies. He further differs from the Stoics and Plotinus, who believed that the cosmic cycle would repeat the same events of the past cycle. Lydus never claims that a restored office will be precisely as it had been, nor does he indicate that present circumstances are replicas of past ones. In short, as with Aristotle, Lydus owes a debt to the Stoics in his choice of a few terms, but not in their precise usage. Lydus' awareness of Stoic doctrine: Chrysippus at *de Mens.* IV.64, Chrysippus and Poseidonius at *de Mens.* IV.71.

19 e.g. *de Mens.* III.18 [= *de Gen. et Cor.* II.10]; see Appendix for other citations; Bluhme, *De Libris* 36, 37; *de Mag.* does not explicitly develop Aristotle's idea that the eternal circular movement of the sun causes generation; rather he shows that human activity as expressed in the needs of the Roman state has caused the generation and corruption of particular state offices – and by implication, the Roman state itself.

20 John H. Randall, Jr, *Aristotle* (New York, 1960) 207–18; Gérard Verbeke, 'The Aristotelian Doctrine of Qualitative Change in Physics VIII.3", in John P. Anton and George L. Kustas, eds, *Essays in Ancient Greek Philosophy* (Albany, 1971) 546–65, esp. 552ff. Aristotle would not have considered the creation of offices to be true genesis. Sarah Waterlow, *Nature, Change, and Agency in Aristotle's Physics* (Oxford, 1982) esp. ch.III, "The Analysis of Change" 93–158.

21 Carlos G. Steel, *The Changing Self. A Study on the Soul in Later Neoplatonism: Iamblichus, Damascius, and Priscianus* (Verhandelingen van de koninklijke Academie voor Wetenschappen, Letteren en Schone Kunsten van België. Klasse der Letteren XL, no.85, 1978) 115ff.

22 A.H. Armstrong, ed., *The Cambridge History of Later Greek and Early Medieval Philosophy* (Cambridge, 1967) 316.

23 Henri-Dominique Saffrey, "Le chrétien Jean Philopon et la survivance de l'École d'Alexandrie au VIᵉ siècle", *REG* 67 (1954) 396-410; K. Verrycken, "The development of Philoponus' thought and its chronology", in R. Sorabji, ed., *Aristotle Transformed* (London/Ithaca, 1990) 233-74; Henry Blumenthal, "John Philoponus and Stephanus of Alexandria: Two Neoplatonic Commentators on Aristotle?", in Dominic J. O'Meara, ed., *Neoplatonism and Christian Thought* (Albany, 1982) 54-63. This latter article questions the influence of Christianity on Philoponus' thought. See also Armstrong, ed., *Cambridge History of Later Greek and Early Medieval Philosophy* 477-83; Sorabji, ed., *Philoponus and the Rejection of Aristotelian Science.*

24 Étienne Évrard, "Jean Philopon, son *Commentaire sur Nicomaque* et ses rapports avec Ammonius", *REG* 78 (1965) 592-8, opposes this view (p.595). For arguments supporting Ammonius' role as official editor, see Saffrey, "Survivance" 405ff. The problem is that not all the mss of Philoponus mention a commentary of Ammonius in the title. On Philoponus' divergences from Aristotle: Armstrong, ed., *Cambridge History of Later Greek and Early Medieval Philosophy* 316; Gérard Verbeke, "Some Later Neoplatonic Views of Divine Creation and the Eternity of the World", in O'Meara, ed., *Neoplatonism and Christian Thought* 45-53, which is especially clear in explaining how Philoponus used Aristotelian philosophy to refute Aristotle; Verbeke, "Later Views" 47-52. On Philoponus as a "model of correctness" in interpretation of Aristotle, see S. Sambursky, *The Physical World of Late Antiquity* (Princeton, 1962) 156ff.

25 L.G. Westerink, *The Greek Commentaries on Plato's Phaedo,* 1. *Olympiodorus* (New York/Amsterdam/Oxford, 1976) 21.

26 Johannes Irmscher, "Die spätantiken Aristoteleskommentatoren in ihrer geschichtlichen Umwelt", in Gerhard Wirth, Karl-Heinz Schwarte, Johannes Heinrichs, eds, *Romanitas-Christianitas. Untersuchungen zur Geschichte und Literatur der römischen Kaiserzeit. Johannes Straub zum 70. Geburtstag am 18. Oktober 1982 gewidmet* (Berlin/New York, 1982) 411-25, esp. 422-3 on Philoponus.

27 Matthias Baltes, *Die Weltentstehung des platonischen Timaios nach den antiken Interpreten* (Leiden, 1978); Whittaker, "Plutarch, Platonism, and Christianity" 57ff.; Sorabji, *Time* 268-83; *idem*, "Infinity and the Creation", in Sorabji, ed., *Philoponus and the Rejection of Aristotelian Science* 164-78.

28 For example, Simplicius said "it is necessary . . . when Aristotle disagrees with Plato, not merely to look at the letter of the text, and condemn the discord between the two philosophers, but to consider the spirit and track down the agreement between them on the majority of points" (*In Aristotelis Categorias Commentarium*, ed. C. Kalbfleisch [= *CAG* 8, Berlin, 1907] 7, 29-32 (trans. Hoffmann, "Simplicius' Polemics" 77); Richard Sorabji, "General Introduction" to John Philoponus, *Against Aristotle on the Eternity of the World*, trans. Christian Wildberg (Ithaca 1987) 7; Ilsetraut Hadot, *Le Problème du néoplatonisme alexandrin.*

Hiéroclès et Simplicius (Paris, 1978) 195; on the hypothesis of complete doctrinal agreement between Plato and Aristotle, widely accepted by neoplatonists after Porphyry, see Whittaker, "Plutarch, Platonism, and Christianity" 59.

29 Whittaker, "Plutarch, Platonism, and Christianity" 59-61.

30 Richard Sorabji, "John Philoponus", in Sorabji, ed., *Philoponus and the Rejection of Aristotelian Science* 1-40, here 6.

31 For the development of Christian views see Robert M. Grant, *Miracle and Natural Law in Graeco-Roman and Early Christian Thought* (Amsterdam, 1952) ch.10, "Creation" pp.135-52; Philip Merlan, "Ammonius Hermiae, Zacharias Scholasticus and Boethius", *GRBS* 9.2 (1968) 193-203, offers several useful examples of the debate; Sorabji, "John Philoponus" 6-7.

32 Sorabji, *Time* 193.

33 Synesius, *Epistolae* 105, discussed by Sorabji, *Time* 196.

34 Elias, *In Cat.* 120.16-17; 187. 6-7; Sorabji, *Time* 196; Anonymous, *Prolegomena to Platonic Philosophy*, ed. L.G. Westerink (Amsterdam, 1962) xxii-xxiii suggests that "as a rule, however, he does not allow his Christianity to interfere with his philosophy. . . . This complete personal freedom of thought coupled with an outward conformist attitude must have been common enough among the intelligentsia of Justinian's reign. Its most outstanding representative is of course Procopius of Caesarea." We may add Lydus to this list.

35 Agathias, *History*, ed. Rudolf Keydell (Berlin, 1967) II.30.

36 ibid., II.29.11; see Sorabji, *Time* 193-283, esp. 199; Verbeke, "Later Views" 45-53.

37 Michel Tardieu, "Sabiens coraniques et 'Sâbiens' de Hârrân', *Journal Asiatique* 274 (1986) 1-44, esp. 22ff.

38 Sorabji, ed., *Philoponus and the Rejection of Aristotelian Science* is now the place to begin; see also Wanda Wolska, *La Topographie chrétienne de Cosmas Indicopleustès. Théologie et science au VIe siècle* (Paris, 1962) esp. chs 5-8; K. Verrycken, "The development of Philoponus' thought and its chronology" 233ff.

39 Justinian persecuted Nestorians in an effort to placate the Monophysites, but his stated objections were based on Christological differences, not cosmological ones: see Milton V. Anastos, "The Immutability of Christ and Justinian's Condemnation of Theodore of Mopsuestia", *Dumbarton Oaks Papers* 6 (1951) 125-60 [=*Studies in Byzantine Intellectual History*, (London, 1979) art.7].

40 Sorabji, "John Philoponus" 2.

41 ibid.

42 Shmuel Sambursky, "Note on John Philoponus' Rejection of the Infinite", in S.M. Stern, Albert Hourani and Vivian Brown, eds, *Islamic Philosophy and the Classical Tradition. Essays Presented by his Friends and Pupils to Richard Walzer on his Seventieth Birthday* (Columbia, South Carolina, 1973) 351-4, here 351; Sorabji, "John Philoponus" 1-40 and "Infinity and the Creation" 164-78. In part due to the efforts of Philoponus, commentary on Aristotle's works ceased between the seventh century and the eleventh: Francis Dvornik, "The Patriarch Photius in Light of Recent

Research", *Berichte zum XI. Internationalen Byzantinisten-Kongress* (Munich, 1958) III.2, 1–56, here 8.

43 Verbeke, "Later Views" 48ff., discusses Simplicius, *In Phys. VIII.1 (Aristotle 252ª 3) contra Philoponum*, ed. H. Diels [= *CAG*, vol. 10] (Berlin, 1895) 1, p.1177.

44 Sorabji, *Philoponus and the Rejection of Aristotelian Science* 233–4, for a list of his writings on the creation and destructibility of the universe.

45 Sorabji, *Time* 198; Herbert A. Davidson, "John Philoponus as a Source of Medieval Islamic and Jewish Proofs of Creation", *JAOS* 89 (1969) 357–91.

46 Johannes Philoponus, *De Aeternitate Mundi contra Aristotelem*, fragments collected and trans. C. Wildberg (Ithaca, 1987).

47 e.g., *de Aeternitate Mundi contra Proclum*, ed. Hugo Rabe (Leipzig, 1899, repr. Hildesheim, 1963) 272.11ff.; 480.12–14, 24–7; 493.25ff., 504.28–505.10; Milton V. Anastos, "Aristotle and Cosmas Indicopleustes on the Void: A Note on Theology and Science in the Sixth Century", in Προσφορά εἰς Στίλπωνα Π. Κυριακίδην. Ἑλληνικά 4; (Thessaloniki, 1953) 35–50 [= *Studies in Byzantine Intellectual History* (London, 1979) art. 14].

48 Ilsetraut Hadot, "La vie et l'oeuvre de Simplicius d'après des sources grecques et arabes", in Ilsetraut Hadot, ed., *Simplicius: sa vie, son oeuvre, sa survie. Actes du Colloque International de Paris (28 Sept.-1ᵉʳ Oct. 1985)* (Berlin/New York, 1987) 3–39.

49 Hoffmann, "Simplicius' Polemics" 61; Sorabji, "John Philoponus" 7; Sambursky, *Physical World* 154–65.

50 Hoffmann, "Simplicius' Polemics" 69 for citations.

51 Sorabji, *Time* 216, 225.

52 As Verbeke has noted, Simplicius "emphasizes the difference betweeen a process of generation and a creation out of nothing: what is generated proceeds from what already exists and passes away also into what exists; moreover, any change occurs through the action of an eternal factor": Verbeke, "Later Views" 51 (he cites Simplicius, *in Phys.* VIII.1, 1177).

53 *Simplicius, in Aristotelis de Caelo Commentaria*, ed. J.L. Heiberg, (Berlin, 1894) [= *CAG*, vol.7.]; Hoffmann, "Simplicius' Polemics" 57–83.

54 Philoponus, *De Aeternitate Mundi contra Aristotelem* 84.15–22; Hoffmann, "Simplicius' Polemics" 77; Edouard Zeller, *Die Philosophie der Griechen in ihrer geschichtlichen Entwicklung. II.2 Die nacharistotelische Philosophie* (Leipzig, 1923, repr. 1963) 912 [= 846, in 1923 edition), discusses Simplicius on *de Caelo* 103.1; ibid. 911–12 on Simplicius' efforts to reconcile the two philosophers; Sorabji, in Philoponus, *Against Aristotle*, ed. Wildberg "General Introduction" here 7–11.

55 Simplicius, *In Phys. VIII (Aristotle 252ª 3) contra Philoponum*, lines 26ff.

56 There is no obvious link between Lydus and the pagan Academy at Harrān in northern Syria that Tardieu proposes was established by Simplicius when he left Ctesiphon.

57 Whittaker, "Plutarch, Platonism, and Christianity" 57–61; Sorabji, *Time* 193–209.

58 Agathias, *History* II.30–1; see above Chapter 5, note 62 for references.

59 Steel, *Changing Self* 20.

60 ibid., 112ff.
61 ibid., 16. Steel places the origin of this notion in Plato's *Phaedo*.
62 See 93 above.
63 Iamblichus, *Les Mystères d'Égypte*, ed. and trans. É. des Places (Paris, 1966) II.11; Wallis, *Neoplatonism* 3-4; Eric R. Dodds, "Theurgy and its Relationship to Neoplatonism", *JRS* 37 (1947) 55-69; Gregory Shaw, "Theurgy: Rituals of Unification in the Neoplatonism of Iamblichus", *Traditio* 41 (1985) 1-28; Kenneth Harl, "Sacrifice and Pagan Belief in Fifth- and Sixth-Century Byzantium", *Past and Present* 128 (August, 1990) 7-27, here 13.

8 *DE OSTENTIS*: PORTENTS AND THE ENEMIES OF PTOLEMY

1 Ch. 9.
2 Procopius, *Historia Arcana* (*Opera Omnia*, vol. 3, ed. J. Haury and G. Wirth, Leipzig, 1963) 11.37; see Frederick H. Cramer, *Astrology in Roman Law and Politics* (American Philosophical Society Memoirs 37, Philadelphia, 1954), for the early empire; on the status of astrologers in Alexandria, see Garth Fowden, *The Egyptian Hermes. An Historical Approach to the Late Pagan Mind* (Cambridge, 1986) 91-4.
3 See Introduction, note 47; *de Mag.* III.38.
4 Ptolemy, *Almagest*, ed. and trans. G. J. Toomer (London, 1984); David Pingree, "Ptolemy", *Dictionary of Scientific Biography*, vol.XI (New York, 1975) 186-206, here 198.
5 David Pingree, "Ptolemy" 198.
6 *de Ost.* 4.
7 Ptolemy, *Tetrabiblos*, ed. and trans. Frank E. Robbins (London/Cambridge, Mass., 1940, repr. 1956) I.1; A.A. Long, "Astrology: Arguments Pro and Contra", in Jonathan Barnes, Jacques Brunschwig, Myles Burnyeat, Malcolm Schofield, eds, *Science and Speculation: Studies in Hellenistic Theory and Practice* (Cambridge, 1982) 165-92, here 179.
8 *Almagest* I.1.
9 *Tetrabiblos* I.1; Long, "Astrology" 179.
10 Pingree, "Ptolemy" 198; *Tetrabiblos* I.2.
11 *Tetrabiblos*, I.2; Long, "Astrology" 181.
12 e.g. Ptolemy explains that: "a certain power emanating from the eternal ethereal substance is dispersed through and permeates the whole region about the earth which throughout is subject to change, since, of the primary sublunar elements, fire and air are encompassed and changed by the motions in the ether and in turn encompass and change all else, earth and water and the plants and animals therein. For the sun . . . is always in some way affecting everything on earth. . . . The moon too, as the heavenly body nearest the earth, bestows her effluence most abundantly upon mundane things, for most of them, animate or inanimate, are sympathetic to her and change in company with her. . . . Moreover the passages of the fixed stars and the planets through the sky often signify hot, windy, and snowy conditions of the air, and mundane things are affected accordingly. Then, too, their aspects to one another, by the

meeting and mingling of their dispensations, bring about many complicated changes." (*Tetrabiblos* I.2; trans. Robbins; see also Long, "Astrology" 181).

13 *Tetrabiblos* I.2.

14 For discussion of these texts and their sources, see James Caimi, *Burocrazia e diritto nel de Magistratibus di Giovanni Lido* (Milan, 1984) 73-9.

15 e.g. Campester on comets, *de Ost.* 11ff.

16 A version of this section was presented at the annual meeting of the American Philological Association in 1986.

17 *de Mag.* III.54.

18 *de Ost.*, proem., 6.

19 *PLRE* II "Fl. Vitalianus 2" 1171-6; Peter Charanis, *Church and State in the Later Roman Empire. The Religious Policy of Anastasius the First, 491-518* (Madison, 1939) 51-65. Charanis suggests 514 as the beginning date of the revolt.

20 Charanis, *Church and State* 52, analyses his motives and discusses the primary sources.

21 V. Grumel, *Traité d'études byzantines* 1, *La chronologie* (Paris, 1958) 460.

22 ibid.

23 Charanis, *Church and State* 49, note 66 for sources.

24 ibid.

25 The connection between Vitalian and the Huns' attack is disputed: see Charanis, *Church and State* 53-4.

26 *de Mag.* III.46; III.49-51.

27 Ptolemy, *Tetrabiblos*, ed. Robbins, 5, note 4. Ptolemy's answers are largely drawn from Posidonius the Stoic, as shown by Franz Boll, *Studien über Claudius Ptolemäus. Ein Beitrag zur Geschichte der griechischen Philosophie und Astrologie (Jahrbuch für classische Philologie Suppl.* 21, Leipzig, 1894) 51-243, here 134ff.; Long, "Astrology" 179.

28 See Appendix.

29 Cosmas Indicopleustes, *Topographie chrétienne*, ed. and trans. Wanda Wolska-Conus, (Paris 1968-73).

30 Wanda Wolska, *La Topographie chrétienne de Cosmas Indicopleustès. Théologie et science au VIe siècle* (Paris, 1962) 134; cf. *de Mens.* II.9.

31 Milton V. Anastos, "Aristotle and Cosmas Indicopleustes on the Void. A Note on Theology and Science in the Sixth Century", in Προσφορά εἰς Στίλπωνα Π. Κυριακίδην. Ἑλληνικά 4; Thessaloniki, 1953) 35-50, here 38-9 [= *Studies in Byzantine Intellectual History* (London, 1979) art. XIV].

32 Anastos, "Aristotle" 43-4.

33 Wolska, *Théologie et science* 194-6.

34 ibid., 63-85; Antoine Guillaumont, "Justinien et l'Église de Perse", *DOP* 23 (1969) 41-66, here 45-7; Khalil Georr, *Les Catégories d'Aristote dans leurs versions syro-arabes* (Beirut, 1948) 1-32, for discussion and bibliography of Aristotelian studies among the Nestorians and other Syriac speakers; Robert Devréesse, *Essai sur Théodore de Mopsueste* (Studi e Testi, 141; Vatican City, 1948) 273; Anton Baumstark, *Geschichte der syrischen Literatur mit Ausschluss der christlich-palästinensischen Texte*

NOTES TO PAGES 110-13

(Bonn, 1922, repr. Berlin, 1968) 119.

35 Wolska's reservations on the influence of Mar Aba on Cosmas, *Théologie et science* 105; Robert Macina feels the influence of another Nestorian, Abraham of Bet Rabban, to have been greater than Mar Aba's ("L'homme à l'école de Dieu- D'Antioche à Nisibe. Profil herméneutique, théologique et kérygmatique de la mouvement scoliaste nestorien", *Proche-Orient Chrétien* 32 (1982) 86–121, here pp 115–17 ; Cosmas' Nestorianism, Wolska, *Théologie et science* 31, 63–85, 105–11.

36 Wolska, *Théologie et science* 63–85 discusses the relation of Cosmas to Nestorian doctrine.

37 Anastos, "Aristotle" 46–50.

38 Wolska, *Théologie et science* 148–9; 193–218 for Cosmas' interpretation of Hellenic cosmology.

39 Tony Honoré, *Tribonian* (London, 1978) 237–40.

40 Procopius, *Historia Arcana* XX.17ff.; Heinrich Kihn, *Theodor von Mopsuestia und Junilius Africanus als Exegeten. Nebst einer kritischen Textausgabe von des letzteren. Instituta Regularia Divinae Legis* (Freiburg im Breisgau, 1880) esp. pp.216–89; Guillaumont, "Justinien et l'Église de Perse" 47–8; on the variant spelling of his name, see Honoré, *Tribonian* 238.

41 Guillaumont, "Justinien et l'Église de Perse" 45; Honoré suggests that composition of the treatise may have won him imperial favor and his government job: *Tribonian* 238–9.

42 This man was probably the theologian active at the Persian court and not the Nestorian called Paul the Persian who in 527 had debated against Manichaeism at Constantinople: Kihn, *Theodor von Mopsuestia und Junilius Africanus* 244–8; on the difficulty of identifying Paul, see Dimitri Gutas, "Paul the Persian on the Classification of the Parts of Aristotle's Philosophy: A Milestone between Alexandria and Bagdad", *Der Islam* 60 (1983) 230–67, here 238 9; Guillaumont, "Justinien et l'Église de Perse" 47.

43 Guillaumont, "Justinien et l'Église de Perse" 48.

44 Kihn, *Theodor von Mopsuestia und Junilius Africanus* 468.

45 Junillus, *Instituta Regularia Divinae Legis*, ed. Heinrich Kiln in *Theodor von Mopsuestia und Junilius Africanus*, IV, 473.

46 ibid., 474.

47 ibid., 475.

48 I follow closely the discussion of Elizabeth Jeffreys, Michael Jeffreys, Roger Scott *et al.*, in *The Chronicle of John Malalas* (Byzantina Australiensia 4; Melbourne, 1986) xxii–xxiii; see also Brian Croke, "Malalas, the Man and His Work", in Elizabeth Jeffreys, with Brian Croke and Roger Scott, eds, *Studies in John Malalas* (Byzantina Australiensia 6; Sydney, 1990) 1–26.

49 Malalas, *Chronicle* VI.4, VI.27, VII.3, VII.7, VII.9.

50 ibid., XIV.42.

51 e.g., X.28.

52 Malalas, XVIII.52.

53 *de Ost.* 16.

54 ibid., 16a.

BIBLIOGRAPHY

PRIMARY SOURCES

Agapetus the Deacon, *Expositio Capitum Admonitorium*, ed. J.-P. Migne (Patrologiae Cursus Completus: Series Graeca 86.1; Paris, 1867).

Agathias of Myrine, *Historiarum Libri V*, ed. Rudolf Keydell (Berlin, 1967).

Ammianus Marcellinus, *History*, ed. C.U. Clark, L. Traube and W. Heraeus, 2 vols (Berlin, 1910–15).

Anecdota graecae codicibus manuscriptis bibliothecarum, ed. J.A. Cramer, 4 vols (Oxford, 1835–7).

Anonymous, *Des Byzantiner anonymus Kriegswissenschaft*, ed. H. Köchly and W. Rüstow, vol. II (Leipzig, 1855).

Anonymous, *Menae patricii cum Thoma referendario de scientia politica dialogus quae exstant in codice Vaticano palimpsesto*, ed. Carlo Maria Mazzucchi (Milan, 1982).

Anonymous, *Prolegomena to Platonic Philosophy*, ed. L.G. Westerink (Amsterdam, 1962).

Aristotle, *De Caelo*, ed. D.J. Allan (Oxford, 1936).

Aristotle, *On Coming-to-be and Passing-away*, trans. and ed. Harold H. Joachim (Oxford, 1922).

Asclepius of Tralles, *Commentary to Nicomachus' Introduction to Arithmetic*, ed. Leonardo Taran, *TAPS* 59.4 (1969).

Asterios of Amasea, *Sermon IV against the Festival of the Kalends* (Patrologiae Cursus Completus: Series Graeca 40; 1863) 216–25.

Cassiodorus, Magnus Aurelius, *Variarum Libri XII*, ed. A.J. Fridh (Corpus Christianorum. Series Latina 96; Turnhout, 1973).

Censorinus, *De die natali liber*, ed. Fridericus Hultsch (Leipzig, 1867).

Choricius of Gaza, *Opera*, ed. Richard Förster and Eberhard Richtseig (Leipzig, 1929).

Constantine Porphyrogenitus, *De Ceremoniis Aulae Byzantinae*, ed. J.J. Reiske (Bonn, 1830).

Constantine Porphyrogenitus, *Excerpta de insidiis*, in *Excerpta Historica*, ed. C. de Boor (Berlin, 1905).

Constantine Porphyrogenitus, *De Thematibus*, ed. A. Pertusi (Vatican City, 1952).

BIBLIOGRAPHY

Constantine Porphyrogenitus, *Vita Basilii* in *Theophanes Continuatus*, ed. Immanuel Bekker (CSHB 33; Bonn, 1838).
Cosmas Indicopleustes, *Topographie chrétienne*, ed. and trans. Wanda Wolska-Conus, 3 vols (Paris, 1968–73).
Damascius, *Life of Isidore*, ed. C. Zintzen (Hildesheim, 1967).
Dositheus, *Ars Grammatica*, in *Grammatici Latini*, vol. vii, ed. Gottfried Keil (Leipzig, 1880) 363–436.
Eusebius, *De Laudibus Constantini Oratio in Eius Tricennalibus Habita*, ed. Ivar A. Heikel. (GCS VII; Leipzig, 1902).
Eusebius, *Vita Constantini*, in *Eusebius Werke*, I.1, ed. Friedhelm Winkelmann (GCS VII.2; Berlin, 1975).
Evagrius Scholasticus, *The Ecclesiastical History with the Scholia*, ed. J. Bidez and L. Parmentier (London, 1898, repr. Amsterdam, 1964).
Iamblichus, *Les Mystères d'Égypte*, ed. and trans. É. des Places (Paris, 1966).
Inscriptiones Italiae, vol.XIII, *Fasti et Elogia*, ed. Atilio Degrassi, Fasciculus II. Fasti Anni Numani et Iuliani (Rome, 1963).
Ioannes Lydus, *see* Lydus, John.
Ius Graecoromanum: Novellae et Aureae Bullae Imperatorum post Justinianum ex editione C.E. Zachariae von Lingenthal, vol. 1, eds I. and P. Zepos (Athens, 1931).
John of Ephesus, *The Third Part of the Ecclesiastical History of John of Ephesus*, trans. R. Payne-Smith (Oxford, 1860).
John of Ephesus, *Historia Ecclesiastica*, ed., E.W. Brooks, CSCO 106, Scrip. Syri 55:169 (1936, repr.1952).
Junilius Africanus [Junillus], *Instituta Regularia Divinae Legis. Libri Duo*, ed. Heinrich Kihn, in *Theodor von Mopsuestia und Junilius Africanus als Exegeten* (Freiburg im Breisgau, 1880) 465–527.
Justinian, *Corpus Iuris Civilis*, vol.I: *Institutiones* and *Digesta*; vol.II: *Codex*; vol. III: *Novellae*, ed. P. Krüger, T. Mommsen, R. Schoell and W. Kroll (Berlin, 1915).
Justinian, *Drei dogmatische Schriften Justinians*, 2nd edn, ed. Mario Amelotti, Rosangela Albertella and Livia Migliardi (Legum Iustiniani Imperatoris Vocabularium Subsidia II; Milan, 1973).
Justinian, *Scritti teologici ed ecclesiastici de Giustiniano*, ed. Mario Amelotti and Livia Migliardi Zingale (Legum Iustiniani Imperatoris Vocabularium Subsidia III; Milan, 1977).
Justinian, *Le costituzione giustinianee nei papiri e nelle epigrafi*, ed. Mario Amelotti and Livia Migliardi Zingale (Legum Iustiniani Imperatoris Vocabularium Subsidia I; 2nd edn Milan, 1985).
Leo, *Tactica. Epilog.*, ed. J.P. Migne, PG 107. 1092b (Paris, 1863).
Léo, *Les Nouvelles de Léon le Sage*, ed. and trans. P. Noailles and A. Dain (Paris, 1944).
Libanius, *Opera* vol. VI (Orationes 13–30), ed. Richard Förster (Leipzig, 1911).
Lydus, John, *De Magistratibus Rei Publicae Romanae*, ed. I.D. Fuss (Paris, 1812).
Lydus, John, *On Powers or the Magistracies of the Roman State*, ed. Anastasius C. Bandy (American Philosophical Society Memoirs 149; Philadelphia, 1983).

Lydus, John, *De Magistratibus Populi Romani Libri Tres*, ed. Richard Wuensch (Leipzig, 1903, repr. 1967).

Lydus, John, *Liber de Mensibus*, ed. Richard Wuensch (Leipzig, 1898, repr. 1967).

Lydus, John, *Liber de Ostentis et Calendaria Omnia*, ed. Curt Wachsmuth (2nd edn, Leipzig, 1897).

Malalas, John, *The Chronicle of John Malalas*, ed. and trans. Elizabeth Jeffreys, Michael Jeffreys, Roger Scott et al. (Byzantina Australiensia 4; Melbourne, 1986).

Michael the Syrian, *Chronique de Michel le Syrien, Patriarche Jacobite d'Antioche (1166-1199)*, ed. and trans. J.-B. Chabot, 4 vols (Paris, 1899-1924).

Nicomachus, *Introductionis Arithmeticae*, ed. Ricardus Hoche (Leipzig, 1866).

Nicomachus, *Introduction to Mathematics*, ed. and trans. Martin Luther D'Ooge, Frank E. Robbins, and Louis C. Karpinski (New York, 1926).

Nicomachus, *Theologoumena arithmeticae*, ed. V. de Falco (Leipzig, 1922).

Olympiodorus, in Westerink, L.G., *The Greek Commentaries on Plato's Phaedo* vol.I (New York/Amsterdam/Oxford, 1976).

Palingenesia Iuris Civilis I, ed. Otto Lenel and Lorenz Sierl (Graz, 1889, repr. 1960).

(Parastaseis). Constantinople in the Early Eighth Century: The Parastaseis Syntomoi Chronikai, ed. Averil Cameron, Judith Herrin, et al. (Leiden, 1984).

Philoponus, John, *De Aeternitate Mundi contra Aristotelem*, fragments collected and trans. C. Wildberg (Ithaca, 1987).

Philoponus, John, *De Aeternitate Mundi Contra Proclum*, ed. Hugo Rabe (Leipzig, 1899, repr. Olms, 1963).

Philoponus, John, *In Aristotelis Libros de Generatione et Corruptione Commentaria*, ed. Hieronymus Vitelli (Berlin, 1897) [= *CAG* X.IV.2].

Photius, *Bibliothèque*, ed. René Henry, 8 vols (Paris, 1959-77).

Photius, *Fragmenta*, ed. V. de Falco (Leipzig, 1922).

Plato, *Plato's Cosmology. The Timaeus*, translated with a running commentary by F.M. Cornford (Oxford, 1937).

Plato, *Timaeus*, in *Opera*, ed. John Burnet, vol.4 (Oxford, 1904).

Plotinus, *Enneades*, ed. P. Henry and H.R. Schwyzer (Brussels/Paris/London, 1951-73).

Plutarch, *Oeuvres morales* vol.2 (essays 10-14), ed. and trans. J. Defradas et al. (Paris, 1985).

Polemius Silvius, *Fasti*, in *Corpus Inscriptionum Latinarum* I.1, ed. Theodor Mommsen (Berlin, 1893) 254-79.

Proclus, *Elements of Theology*, ed. E.R. Dodds (Oxford, 1963).

Proclus, *Hypotyposis Astronomicarum Positionum*, ed. Carolus Manitius (Leipzig 1909, repr. 1974).

Procopius, *Opera Omnia*, ed. J. Haury and G. Wirth, 4 vols (Leipzig, 1962).

Prudentius. Aurelius Prudentius Clemens, *Contra Symmachum*, in

BIBLIOGRAPHY

Carmina, ed. Maurice P. Cunningham (Corpus Christianorum. Series Latina 126; Turnhout, 1966) 209–50.

Ptolemy, *Almagest*, trans. and ed. G.J. Toomer (London, 1984).

Ptolemy, *Tetrabiblos*, ed. and trans. F.E. Robbins (London/Cambridge, Mass., 1940, repr. 1956).

Romanos, *Sancti Romani Melodi Cantica. Cantica Genuina*, ed. Paul Maas and C.A. Trypanis (Oxford, 1963).

Simplicius, *In Aristotelis Physicorum Libros Quattuor Priores Commentaria*, ed. Herman Diels (Berlin, 1882) [= *Commentaria in Aristotelem Graeca*, vol.9].

Simplicius, *In Aristotelis De Caelo Commentaria*, ed. J.L. Heiberg (Berlin, 1894) [= *Commentaria in Aristotelem Graeca*, vol.7].

Simplicius, *In Phys. VIII (Aristotle p.252ᵃ 3) contra Philoponum*, ed. H. Diels [= *Commentaria in Aristotelem Graeca*, vol. 10] (Berlin, 1895).

Simplicius, *In Aristotelis Categorias Commentarium*, ed. C. Kalbfleisch [= *Commentaria in Aristotelem Graeca*, vol.8] (Berlin, 1907).

Sozomenus, *Kirchengeschichte*, ed. Joseph Bidez (Berlin, 1960).

Stoicorum Veterum Fragmenta, ed. Johannes von Arnim, 3 vols (Leipzig, 1903–5, repr. 1964); *Indices*, ed. Maximilianus Adler (Leipzig, 1924).

Strabo, *Geography*, ed. H.L. Jones (Cambridge, Mass., 1929).

Suidas [= the *Suda*], *Lexicon (Sudae Lexicon)*, ed. Ada Adler, 5 vols (Leipzig, 1928–38).

Aurelius Symmachus, *Libri quae Supersunt*, ed. Otto Seeck (Berlin, 1883, repr. 1961).

Synesius, *Letters*, in *Epistolographi Graeci*, ed. R. Hercher (Paris, 1879) 638–739.

Themistius, *Orationes quae supersunt*, 3 vols, ed. H. Schenkl, G. Downey and A.F. Norman (Leipzig, 1965–74).

Theodore of Mopsuestia, *Le Commentaire sur les psaumes (I-LXXX)*, ed. R. Devreesse (Vatican City, 1939).

Theodosius, *Code (Libri XVI cum Constitutionibus Sirmondianis)*, ed. T. Mommsen and P. Krüger, 2 vols (Berlin, 1905, repr. 1970).

Theophanes, *Chronographia*, ed. C. de Boor (Leipzig, 1883, repr. 1963).

Theophylactus Simocatta, *Historia*, ed. C. de Boor (Leipzig, 1887).

Vita S. Symeon Stylitae Junioris, in *La Vie ancienne de S. Syméon Stylite le jeune (521-592)*, ed. Paul van den Ven, vol.1 (Subsidia Hagiographica 32; Brussels, 1962).

Zacharias of Mitylene, *The Syriac Chronicle*, trans. F.J. Hamilton and E.W. Brooks (London, 1899, repr. 1979).

Zacharias Rhetor, *Ammonius*, ed. J.P. Migne, (Patrologiae Graecae 85; Paris, 1864) 1011–44.

Zacharias Rhetor, *Vita Severi*, ed. and trans. M.-A. Kugener (Patrologia Orientalis 2; Turnhout, 1907) 7–115.

Zonaras, John, *Epitomae Historiarum Libri XIII-XVIII*, ed. T. Büttner-Wobst (Bonn, 1897).

Zosimus, *Historia Nova*, ed. L. Mendelssohn (Leipzig, 1887).

Zosimus, *New History*, trans. with a commentary by Ronald T. Ridley (Byzantina Australiensia 2; Melbourne, 1982).

SECONDARY SOURCES

Aalders, G.J.D., "ΝΟΜΟΣ ΕΜΨΥΧΟΣ in Politeia und Res Publica", in *Beiträge dem Andenken R. Starks gewidmet* (*Palingenesia* 4; 1969) 315–29.

Abrahamse, Dorothy, "Hagiographic Sources for Byzantine Cities 500–900 AD". (Diss., University of Michigan, 1967).

Alexander, Paul, J., "The Strength of Empire and Capital as Seen through Byzantine Eyes", *Speculum* 37 (1962) 339–57 [= *Religious and Political History and Thought in the Byzantine Empire* (London, 1978) art. 3].

Alexander, Paul, "Medieval Apocalypses as Historical Sources", *AHR* 73 (1968) 997–1018 [= *Religious and Political History and Thought in the Byzantine Empire* (London, 1978) art. 13].

Allen, Pauline, "The Justinianic Plague", *Byzantion* 49 (1979) 5–20.

Allen, Pauline, *Evagrius Scholasticus. The Church Historian* (Louvain, 1981).

Amelotti, Mario, "Giustiniano tra Teologia e Diritto", in G.G. Archi, ed., *L'Imperatore Giustiniano, Storia e Mito* (Milan, 1978) 133–60.

Amirante, Luigi, "Appunti per la storia della 'Redemptio ab Hostibus' ", *Labeo* 3 (1957) 171–220.

Anastos, Milton V., "The Immutability of Christ and Justinian's Condemnation of Theodore of Mopsuestia", *Dumbarton Oaks Papers* 6 (1951) 125–60 [= *Studies in Byzantine Intellectual History* (London, 1979) art.7].

Anastos, Milton V., "Aristotle and Cosmas Indicopleustes on the Void. A Note on Theology and Science in the Sixth Century", in Προσφορά είς Στίλπωνα Π. Κυριακίδην 'Ελληνικά 4; (Thessaloniki, 1953) 35–50 [= *Studies in Byzantine Intellectual History* (London, 1979) art.14].

Andreades, A., "Le recruitment des fonctionaires et les universités dans l'Empire Byzantine", in *Mélanges Byzantines présentées à M. Cornil* vol.1. (Paris, 1926) 17–40.

Andrei, Osvalda, *A. Claudius Charax di Pergamo. Interessi antiquari e antichità cittadine nell'età degli Antonini* (Bologna, 1984)

Archi, G.G., ed., *L'imperatore Giustiniano. Storia e Mito* (Milan, 1978).

Armstrong, A.H., ed., *Cambridge History of Later Greek and Early Medieval Philosophy* (Cambridge, 1967).

Atiya, A.S., *A History of Eastern Christianity* (London, 1968).

Bagnall, Roger, Cameron, Alan, Schwartz, Seth and Worp, K.A., *Consuls of the Later Roman Empire* (APA Monograph 36; Atlanta, 1987).

Bagnall, Roger and Worp, K.A., "Chronological Reckoning in Byzantine Egypt", *GRBS* 20 (1979) 279–95.

Baldovin, John F., *The Urban Character of Christian Worship. The Origins, Development, and Meaning of Stational Liturgy* (Orientalia Christiana Analecta 228, Rome, 1987).

Baltes, Matthias, *Die Weltentstehung des platonischen Timaios nach den antiken Interpreten* (Leiden, 1978).

Bardon, Henry, *La Littérature latine inconnue, II. L'époque impériale* (Paris, 1956).

Barnes, Jonathan, *Aristotle* (Oxford, 1982).

Barnes, Timothy, "Tertullian the Antiquarian", *Studia Patristica* XIV (Untersuchungen zur Geschichte der altchristlichen Literatur 117, Berlin,

1976) 3–20 [= *Early Christianity and the Roman Empire* (London, 1984) art.14].

Baumstark, Anton, *Geschichte der syrischen Literatur mit Ausschluss der christlich-palästinensischen Texte* (Bonn, 1922, repr. Berlin, 1968).

Baynes, Norman, "Eusebius and the Christian Empire", *Annuaire de l'Institut de Philologie et d'Histoire Orientales* ii (1933–4) 13–18 [= *Byzantine Studies and Other Essays* (London, 1960) 168–72].

Beard, Mary, "A Complex of Times: No More Sheep on Romulus' Birthday", *PCPS* 213, n.s. 33. (1987) 1–15.

Beck, Hans-Georg, "Konstantinopel: das neue Rom", *Gymnasium* 71 (1964) 166–74.

Beck, Hans-Georg, *Senat und Volk von Konstantinopel: Probleme der byzantinischen Verfassungsgeschichte* (Sitzungsberichte der bayerischen Akademie der Wissenschaften, Phil.-Hist. Klasse 6; 1966).

Beck, Hans-Georg, *Die Byzantiner und ihr Jenseits* (Sitzungsberichte der bayerischen Akademie der Wissenschaften, Phil.-Hist. Klasse 1979) Heft 6, 3–75.

Bellinger, Alfred, *Catalogue of the Byzantine Coins in the Dumbarton Oaks Collection and in the Whittemore Collection*, I. *Anastasius to Maurice (491-602)* (Dumbarton Oaks, 1966).

Bengston, H., "Kosmas Indikopleustes und die Ptolemäer", *Historia* 4.2–3 (1955) 151–6.

Biraban, J.N. and le Goff, Jacques, "The Plague in the Early Middle Ages", trans. Elborg Forster and Patricia Ranum, in Robert Forster and Orest Ranum, eds, *Biology of Man in History* (Baltimore, 1975) [= *Annales ESC* 24 (Nov./Dec. 1969) 1484–510].

Blockley, Roger, "Was the First Book of Zosimus' New History Based on More than Two Sources?", *Byzantion* 50 (1980) 393–402.

Bluhme, Fridericus, *De Ioannis Laurentii Lydi Libris Περὶ μηνῶν Observationum Capita Duo* (Diss., University of Halle, 1906).

Blumenthal, Henry J., "529 and its sequel: What Happened to the Academy?", *Byzantion* 48 (1978) 369–85.

Blumenthal, Henry J., "John Philoponus and Stephanus of Alexandria: Two Neoplatonic Commentators on Aristotle?", in Dominic J. O'Meara, ed., *Neoplatonism and Christian Thought* (Albany, 1982) 54–63.

Boak, A.E.R., "Imperial Coronation Ceremonies of the Fifth and Sixth Centuries", *HSCP* 30 (1919) 37–47.

Boak, A.E.R., *The Master of the Offices in the Later Roman and Byzantine Empires* (University of Michigan Studies, Humanistic Series 14; New York, 1924).

Boll, Franz, *Studien über Claudius Ptolemäus. Ein Beitrag zur Geschichte der griechischen Philosophie und Astrologie (Jahrbuch für classische Philologie Suppl.* 21; Leipzig, 1894) 51–243.

Boll, Franz, ed., *Griechische Kalender* (Heidelberg, 1910–20).

Boll, Franz, "Hebdomas", *RE* VII (1912) 2558.

Börtzler, Fr., "Zum Texte des Johannes Laurentius Lydus 'De Mensibus' ", *Philologus* n.s. 77 (1921) 364–79.

Bouché-Leclercq, Auguste, *Histoire de la divination dans l'antiquité* (Paris, 1882, repr. Brussels, 1963).

Bowersock, Glenn, *Hellenism in Late Antiquity* (Ann Arbor, 1990).

Bowie, E.L., "Greeks and their Past in the Second Sophistic", *Past and Present* 46 (1970) 3–41.

Broughton, T. Robert S., *The Magistrates of the Roman Republic*, 3 vols (New York, 1952).

Brown, Peter, "Aspects of the Christianisation of the Roman Aristocracy", *JRS* 51 (1961) 1–11 [= *Religion and Society in the Age of St. Augustine* (New York, 1972) 161–82].

Brown, Peter, "Art and Society in Late Antiquity", in K. Weitzmann, ed., *The Age of Spirituality: A Symposium* (New York, 1980) 17–28.

Brown, Peter, *The Philosopher and Society in Late Antiquity* (Berkeley, 1980).

Browning, Robert, "The Language of Byzantine Literature", in Spyros Vryonis, Jr, ed., *The "Past", in Medieval and Modern Greek Culture* (Malibu, 1978) [= *Byzantina kai Metabyzantina* I] 103–33.

Browning, Robert, "Learning and the Past" in E.J. Kenney and W.V. Clausen, eds, *The Cambridge History of Classical Literature* II, *Latin Literature* (Cambridge, 1982) 762–73.

Browning, Robert, *Justinian and Theodora* (2nd edn, London, 1987).

Buckler, W.H. and Robinson, David, *Sardis* vol. 7 (Leiden, 1932).

Burkert, Walter, *Lore and Science in Ancient Pythagoreanism*, trans. E.L. Minar Jr (Cambridge, Mass., 1972).

Bury, J.B., "The Nika Revolt", *JHS* 17 (1897) 92–119.

Bury, J.B., *History of the Later Roman Empire from the Death of Theodosius I to the Death of Justinian*, 2 vols (London, 1923, repr. 1958).

Caimi, James, "Ioannis Lydi *de Magistratibus* III 70. Note esegetiche e spunti in tema di fiscalità e legislazione protobizantine", in *Miscellanea Agostino Pertusi* I [= *Rivista di Studi Bizantini e Slavi* I (1981)] 317–61.

Caimi, James, "Per l'esegesi di Giovanni Lido 'de Magistratibus' III,9", in *Studi in onore di Arnaldo Biscardi* VI (Milan, 1982) 1–20.

Caimi, James, *Burocrazia e diritto nel de Magistratibus di Giovanni Lido* (Milan, 1984).

Caimi, James, "Una citazione da Pomponio in Lido *Mag.* I.48", *Diritto e Società nel Mondo Romano* (Como, 1988) 213–37.

Cameron, Alan, "Wandering Poets: a Literary Movement in Byzantine Egypt", *Historia* 14 (1965) 470–509 [= *Literature and Society in the Early Byzantine World* (London, 1985) art.1].

Cameron, Alan, "The Last Days of the Academy at Athens", *PCPS* 15 (1969) 7–29.

Cameron, Alan, *Circus Factions. Blues and Greens at Rome and Byzantium* (Oxford, 1976).

Cameron, Alan, "The Empress and the Poet: Paganism and Politics at the Court of Theodosius II", *Yale Classical Studies* 27 (1982) 217–89.

Cameron, Averil, *Agathias* (Oxford, 1970).

Cameron, Averil, "Corippus' Poem on Justin II: A Terminus of Antique Art?", *Annali della Scuola Normale di Pisa* ser. 3, 51 (1975) 129–65.

Cameron, Averil, "The Early Religious Policies of Justin II", in D. Baker, ed., *The Orthodox Churches and the West* (Studies in Church History 13; Oxford, 1976) 51–67.

Cameron, Averil, "Images of Authority: Élites and Icons in Late Sixth-Century Byzantium", *Past and Present* 84 (1979) 3–35 [= *Byzantium and the Classical Tradition* (Birmingham, 1981) 205–34.

Cameron, Averil, *Procopius and the Sixth Century* (Berkeley, 1985).

Cameron, Averil, "The Construction of Court Ritual: The Byzantine *Book of Ceremonies*", in David Cannadine and Simon Price, eds, *Rituals of Royalty. Power and Ceremonial in Traditional Societies* (Cambridge, 1987) 106–36.

Capdeville, Gérard, "Jean Lydus, *Les Mois* (Livre IV, Sections 1–3). Texte établi, traduit et commenté", *Annuaire 1970–1971* (École pratique des Hautes Études, IVe Section; Paris, 1971) 823–6.

Capizzi, Carmelo, "Potere e ideologia imperiale da Zenone a Giustiniano" in G.G. Archi, ed., *L'imperatore Giustiniano. Storia e Mito* (Milan, 1978) 3–35.

Carney, Thomas F., "Looking for a Writer's Picture of Reality", *Revue de l'Organisation Internationale pour l'Étude des langues anciennes par ordinateur* (Liège, 1968) 35–81.

Carney, Thomas F., "Lydos", *RE* Suppl. 12 (1970) 521–3.

Carney, Thomas F., *Bureaucracy in Traditional Society: Romano-Byzantine Bureaucracies Viewed from within* II. *Byzantine Bureaucracy from within* (Lawrence, Kansas, 1971).

Catafygiotu-Topping, Eva, "On Earthquakes and Fires: Romanos' Encomium to Justinian", *BZ* 71 (1978) 22–35.

Cavallo, Guglielmo, "Libri e publico al fine del Mondo Antico", in G. Cavallo, ed., *Libri, editori e pubblico nel Mondo Antico. Guida storica e critica* (Rome/Bari, 1975) 83–162.

Cavallo, Guglielmo, "La circolazione libraria nell'età di Giustiniano" in G.G. Archi, ed., *L'imperatore Giustiniano. Storia e Mito* (Milan, 1978 201–36.

Cesa, Maria, "La politica di Giustiniano verso l'occidente nel giudizio di Procopio", *Athenaeum* n.s. 59 (1981) 389–409.

Cesa, Maria, "Tendenze della storiografia profana in lingua greca tra il IV e il VI secolo d.C.", *Annali dell'Istituto Italiano per gli Studi Storici* 8 (1983/4) 93–114.

Charanis, Peter, *Church and State in the Later Roman Empire. The Religious Policy of Anastasius I, 491–518* (Madison, 1939).

Charanis, Peter, "Hellas in Greek Sources of the Sixth, Seventh, and Eighth Centuries", in Kurt Weitzmann, ed., *Late Classical and Mediaeval Studies in Honor of Albert Mathias Friend, Jr* (Princeton, 1955) 161–76.

Chesnut, Glenn, *The First Christian Histories. Eusebius, Socrates, Sozomen, Theodoret, and Evagrius* (Paris, 1977; 2nd edn, Macon, Georgia, 1986).

Christ, Wilhelm, Schmid, W. and Stählin, O. *Geschichte der griechischen Literatur. Die nachklassiche Periode von 100 bis 530 nach Christus* (*HAW*, 7.2.2; ed. I. Müller, rev. W. Otto *et al*; Munich, 1924).

Chrysos, Evangelos K., "Die angebliche Abschaffung der städtischen Kurien durch Kaiser Anastasios", *Βυζαντινά* 3 (1971) 94–122.

Chuvin, Pierre, "Nonnos de Panopolis entre paganisme et christianisme", *Bulletin de l'Association Guillaume Budé* XLV.4 (1986) 387–96.

Chuvin, Pierre, *A Chronicle of the Last Pagans*, trans. B.A. Archer (Cambridge, Mass., 1990).

Claude, Dietrich, *Die byzantinische Stadt im 6. Jahrhundert* (Byzantinisches Archiv 13; Munich, 1969).

Clauss, Manfred, *Der magister officiorum in der Spätantike (4.-6. Jahrhundert): Das Amt und sein Einfluss auf die kaiserliche Politik* (*Vestigia* 32; Munich, 1980).

Colson, F.H., *The Week. An Essay on the Origin and Development of the Seven Day Cycle* (Cambridge, 1926).

Conrad, Lawrence, "The Plague in Bilād al-Shām in Pre-Islamic Times", in Muhammed Adnan Bakhit and Muhammad Asfour, eds, *The IVth International Conference on Bilād al-Shām* (Amman, 1984) 143-63.

Constantelos, Demetrios, "Paganism and the State in the Age of Justinian", *Catholic Historical Review* 50 (1964) 372-80.

Constantelos, Demetrios, "The Term 'Neoterikoi' (Innovators) in the *Exabiblos* of Constantine Armenopoulos and its Cultural–Linguistic Implications", in A.E. Laiou-Thomadakis, ed., *Charanis Studies* (New Brunswick, NJ, 1980) 1-17.

Cracco Ruggini, Lellia, "Symboli di battaglia ideologica nel tardo ellenismo", *Studi storici in onore di Ottorino Bertolini* I (Pisa, 1972) 177-300.

Cracco Ruggini, Lellia, "Il miracolo nella cultura del tardo impero: concetto e funzione", *Hagiographie, culture et sociétés IVe-XIIe s.* (Paris, 1981) 161-204.

Cramer, Frederick H., *Astrology in Roman Law and Politics* (American Philosophical Society Memoirs 37; Philadelphia, 1954).

Cranz, F. Edward, "Kingdom and Polity in Eusebius of Caesarea", *HTR* 45 (1952) 47-56.

Crawford, John R., "De Bruma et Brumalibus Festis", *BZ* 23 (1914-19) 365-96.

Croke, Brian, "The Origins of the Christian World Chronicle", in Brian Croke and Alanna M. Emmett, eds, *History and Historians in Late Antiquity* (Sydney, 1983) 116-31.

Croke, Brian, "Malalus, the Man and His Work", in Elizabeth Jeffreys, with Brian Croke and Roger Scott, eds, *Studies in John Malalas* (Byzantina Australiensia 6; Sydney, 1990) 1-26.

Croke, Brian, "The Early Development of Byzantine Chronicles", in E. Jeffreys, with Brian Croke and Roger Scott, eds, *Studies in John Malalas* (Byzantina Australiensia 6; Sydney, 1990) 27-38.

Croke, Brian and Crow, James, "Procopius and Dara", *JRS* 73 (1983) 143-59.

Croke, Brian and Emmett, Alanna, "Historiography in Late Antiquity: an Overview", in Brian Croke and Alanna M. Emmett, eds, *History and Historians in Late Antiquity* (Sydney/New York, 1983) 1-12.

Croke, Brian and Harries, Jill, *Religious Conflict in Fourth Century Rome* (Sydney, 1982).

Dagron, Gilbert, *L'Empire romain d'orient au IVe siècle et les traditions politiques de l'hellenisme. Le témoinage de Thémistios* (Travaux et Mémoires 3; Paris, 1968) 1-242.

Dagron, Gilbert, "Aux origines de la civilisation byzantine: langue de culture et langue d'État", *Revue Historique* 489 (1969) 23-56.

Dagron, Gilbert, *Naissance d'une capitale. Constantinople et ses institutions de 330 à 451* (Paris, 1974).

Dagron, Gilbert, "Le christianisme dans la ville byzantine", *DOP* 31 (1977) 1–25.

Dagron, Gilbert, *Constantinople imaginaire. Études sur le recuil des "Patria"* (Paris, 1984).

Dahlmann, Hellfried, "M. Terentius Varro (Antiqu.)", *RE* Supplementband VI (1935) 1172–277.

Dahlmann, Hellfried, "Varroniana", in *Aufstieg and Niedergang der römischen Welt* 1.3, ed. H. Temporini *et al.* (Berlin/New York, 1973) 2–25.

Daniélou, Jean, "La typologie de la semaine au IVᵉ siècle", *Recherches de Science Religieuse* 35 (1948) 382–411.

Davidson, Herbert A., "John Philoponus as a Source of Medieval Islamic and Jewish Proofs of Creation", *JAOS* 89 (1969) 357–91.

Delatte, Armand, *Études sur la littérature pythogoricienne* (Paris, 1915).

Delatte, Louis, *Les Traités de la Royauté d'Ecphante, Diotogène et Sthénidas* (Liège, 1942).

Dennis, George, ed., *Three Byzantine Military Treatises* (CFHB 25; Dumbarton Oaks, 1985).

Devréesse, Robert, *Essai sur Théodore de Mopsueste* (Studi e Testi 141; Vatican City, 1948).

Diehl, Charles, "Rescrit des Empereurs Justin et Justinien en date de Iᵉʳ juin 527", *BCH* 17 (1893) 501–20.

Diehl, Charles, *Justinien et la civilisation Byzantine au VIᵉ siècle* (Paris, 1901, repr. 1969).

Dodds, E.R., "Theurgy and its Relationship to Neoplatonism", *JRS* 37 (1947) 55–69.

Dölger, Franz, "Rom in die Gedankenwelt der Byzantiner", in *Byzanz und die europäische Staatenwelt* (Ettal, 1953) 70–115.

Downey, Glanville, "Themistius and the Defense of Hellenism in the Fourth Century", *HTR* 50.4 (1957) 259–74.

Dufrenne, Suzy, "L'ananeôsis de Quasr el-Lebya", *Antiqutés Africaines* 16 (1980) 241–9.

Duhem, P., *Le Système du monde. Histoire des doctrines cosmographiques de Platon à Copernic*, 2 vols (Paris, 1913, repr. 1959).

Durliat, Jean, "Les dedicaces d'ouvrages de défense dans l'Afrique byzantine', *Collection de l'École Française de Rome* 49 (1981).

Dvornik, Francis, "The Patriarch Photius in Light of Recent Research", *Berichte zum XI. Internationalen Byzantinisten-Kongress* (Munich, 1958) III.2, pp.1–56.

Dvornik, Francis, *Early Christian and Byzantine Political Philosophy* II (Dumbarton Oaks Studies 9; Washington, DC, 1966).

Ebersolt, Jean and Thiers, Adolph, Les Églises de Constantinople (Paris, 1913/repr. London, 1979).

Eisenstadt, S.N., "Post-Traditional Societies and the Continuity and Reconstruction of Tradition", *Daedalus* (Winter, 1973) 1–27.

Ensslin, Wilhelm, "Gottkaiser und Kaiser von Gottes Gnaden", *Sitzungsberichte d. Bayer. Akad. d. Wiss., phil.-hist. Abt.* 6 (Munich, 1943) 1–133.

Evans, J.A.S., "Christianity and Paganism in Procopius of Caesarea", *GRBS* 12 (1971) 81–100.

Évrard, Étienne, "Jean Philopon, son *Commentaire sur Nicomaque* et ses rapports avec Ammonius", *REG* 78 (1965) 592–8.

Feissel, Denis and Kaygusuz, Ismail, "Un mandement impérial du VIᵉ siècle dans une inscription d'Hadrianoupolis d'Honoriade", *Travaux et Mémoirs* 9 (1985) 397–419.

Fenster, Erwin, *Laudes Constantinopolitanae* (Miscellanea Byzantina Monacensia 9; Munich, 1968).

Fiebiger, O., "Excubitorium" *RE* 6.2 (1909), cols 1577–8.

Flamant, Jacques, *Macrobe et le néo-platonisme latin, à la fin du IVᵉ siècle* (Leiden, 1977).

Flintoff, Everard, "Varro in the works of John of Lydia", *Atti del Congresso Internazionale di Studi Varroniani* II (Rieti, 1976) 365–77.

Flintoff, Everard, "Livy, John of Lydia and Pre-Literary *Satura*" *Collection Latomus* 196 (1986) 5–30.

Foss, Clive, "The Persians and the End of Antiquity", *English Historical Review* 90 (1975) 721–47.

Foss, Clive, *Byzantine and Turkish Sardis* (Cambridge, Mass., 1976).

Foss, Clive, "Archaeology and the 'Twenty Cities' of Byzantine Asia", *AJA* 81 (1977) 469–86.

Foss, Clive, *Ephesus after Antiquity: A Late Antique, Byzantine, and Turkish City* (Cambridge, 1979).

Fotiou, Anastasius, "Recruitment Shortages in Sixth Century Byzantium", *Byzantion* 58 (1988) 65–77.

Fowden, Garth, "Bishops and Temples in the Eastern Roman Empire A.D. 320–435", *JTS* n.s. 29.1 (1978) 53–78.

Fowden, Garth, *The Egyptian Hermes. An Historical Approach to the Late Pagan Mind* (Cambridge, 1986).

de Francisci, Pietro, *Arcana Imperii* III.2 (Milan, 1948).

Frank, R.I., *Scholae Palatinae. The Palace Guards of the Later Roman Empire* (Papers and Monographs of the American Academy in Rome 23; 1969).

Frantz, Alison, "Pagan Philosophers in Christian Athens", *PAPS* 119 (1975) 29–38.

Frend, W.H.C., "Old and New Rome in the Age of Justinian", in D. Baker, ed., *The Relations between East and West in the Middle Ages* (Edinburgh, 1973) 11–28.

Fuhrmann, Manfred, *Das systematische Lehrbuch. Ein Beitrag zur Geschichte der Wissenschaften in der Antike* (Göttingen, 1960).

Geffcken, Johannes, *The Last Days of Greco-Roman Paganism*, trans. Sabine MacCormack (Amsterdam/New York/Oxford, 1978).

Georr, Khahil, *Les Catégories d'Aristote dans leurs versions syro-arabes* (Beirut, 1948).

Ginzel, F.K., *Handbuch der mathematischen und technischen Chronologie* III (Leipzig, 1914).

Gizewski, Christian, *Zur Normativität und Struktur der Verfassungsverhältnisse in der späteren römischen Kaiserzeit* (Münchener Beitrage zur Papyrusforschung und antiken Rechtsgeschichte 81; Munich, 1988).

Glucker, John, *Antiochus and the Late Academy* (Hypomnemata 56; Göttingen, 1978) 322–9.

Goffart, Walter, "Zosimus, the First Historian of Rome's Fall", *AHR* 76 (1971) 412-41.

Goodenough, Erwin R., "The Political Philosophy of Hellenistic Kingship", *Yale Classical Studies* 1 (1928) 55-102.

Grabowski, Herman, *De Joannis Lydi Theologumenis Arithmeticae* (Diss., University of Königsberg, 1921).

Grant, Robert M., *Miracle and Natural Law in Graeco-Roman and Early Christian Thought* (Amsterdam, 1952).

Greer, R.A., *Theodore of Mopsuestia, Exegete and Theologian* (London, 1961).

Grierson, Philip, *Catalogue of the Byzantine Coins in the Dumbarton Oaks Collection and in the Whittemore Collection* II.1: *Phocas to Theodosius III, 602-717* (Dumbarton Oaks, 1968).

Grierson, Philip, "The Date of Theodoric's Gold Medallion", *Hikuin* 11 (1985) 19-26.

Grumel, V., *Traité d'études byzantines I. La chronologie* (Paris, 1958).

Grupe, E., "Zur Latinität Justinians", *Zeitschrift der Savigny-Stiftung für Rechtsgeschichte. Romanistische Abteilung* 14 (Weimar, 1893) 224-37.

Gruppe, O., "Über die Bücher XIIII bis XVIIII des *Antiquitates humanae* des Varro", *Hermes* 10 (1876) 51-60.

Guarducci, Margherita, "Teodosio 'Rinnovatore' di Corinto in una epigrafe greca di Kerchreai", in *Le Monde grec. Hommages à Claire Préaux*, ed. Jean Bingen, G. Cambies and G. Nachtergael (Brussels, 1975) 527-34.

Guillaumont, Antoine, "Justinien et l'Église de Perse", *DOP* 23 (1969) 41-66.

Guillou, André, "L'évêque dans la société méditerranéenne des VIᵉ-VIIᵉ siècles. Un modèle", *Bibliothèque de l'École des Chartres* 131 (1973) 5-19 [= *Culture et société en Italie Byzantine (VIᵉ-XIᵉ s.)* (London, 1978) ch.2].

Guillou, André, *La Civilization byzantine* (Paris, 1974).

Gutas, Dimitri, "Paul the Persian on the Classification of the Parts of Aristotle's Philosophy: A Milestone between Alexandria and Bagdad", *Der Islam* 60 (1983) 230-67.

Hadot, Ilsetraut, *Le Problème du néoplatonisme alexandrin. Hiéroclès et Simplicius* (Paris, 1978).

Hadot, Ilsetraut, ed., *Simplicius: sa vie, son oeuvre, sa survie. Actes du Colloque international de Paris (28 sept.-1ᵉʳ oct. 1985)* (Berlin/New York, 1987) [= *Peripatoi. Philologisch-historische Studien zum Aristotelismus*, ed. Paul Moraux, vol.15].

Hadot, Ilsetraut, "La vie et l'oeuvre de Simplicius d'après des sources grecques et arabes" in Ilsetraut Hadot, ed., *Simplicius: sa vie, son oeuvre, sa survie. Actes du Colloque International de Paris (28, Sept.-1ᵉʳ Oct. 1985)* (Berlin/ New York, 1987) 3-39 [= *Peripatoi, Philologisch-historische Studien zum Aristotelismus*, ed. Paul Moraux, vol.15].

Haebler, Albin, "Bruma" *RE* 3 (1897) 901-2.

Hahn, Ludwig, *Zum Sprachenkampf im römischen Reich bis auf die Zeit Justinians* (*Philologus* suppl. X.4; 1907) 675-718.

Haldon, John Frederick, "Ideology and Social Change in the Seventh Century. Military Discontent as a Barometer", *Klio* 68 (1986) 139-90.

Hanfmann, G.M.A. and Waldbaum, Jane C., *A Survey of Sardis and the Major Monuments outside the City Walls* (Cambridge, Mass., 1975).

Harl, Kenneth, "Sacrifices and Pagan Belief in Fifth- and Sixth-Century Byzantium", *Past and Present* 128 (August, 1990) 7–27.

Harris, W.V., "Lydus, *de Mag.* 1.27, a Reply", *Bulletin of the American Society of Papyrologists* 16 (1979) 199–200.

Harrison, R.M., "The Church of St. Polyeuktos in Istanbul and the Temple of Solomon", in Cyril Mango and Omeljan Pritsak, eds, *Okeanos. Essays Presented to Ihor Ševčenko on his Sixtieth Birthday* (Harvard Ukrainian Studies 7; 1983) 276–9.

Haussig, H.W., *A History of Byzantine Civilization*, trans. Joan M. Hussey (New York, 1971).

Hemmerdinger, B. "Les lettres latines à Constantinople jusqu'à Justinien", *Byz. Forsch.* 1 (1966) 174–8.

Hendy, Michael, *Studies in the Byzantine Monetary Economy, c. 300–1450* (Cambridge, 1985).

Henry, Patrick, III, "A Mirror for Justinian: The *Ekthesis* of Agapetus Diaconus", *GRBS* 8.4 (1967) 281–308.

Henry, Paul, "Une traduction grecque d'un texte de Macrobe dans le Περί μηνῶν de Lydus", *REL* II (1933) 164–71.

Hermann, Th., "Die Schule von Nisbis vom 5 bis 7 Jahrhundert. Ihre Quellen und ihre Geschichte", *Zeitschrift für die Neutestamentliche Wissenschaft* 25 (1926) 89–122.

Herrin, Judith, *The Formation of Christendom* (Princeton, 1987).

Hobsbawn, Eric, "Introduction: Inventing Tradition", in Eric Hobsbawn and Terence Ranger, eds, *The Invention of Tradition* (Cambridge, 1983) 1–14.

Hoffmann, Philippe, "Simplicius' Polemics" in R. Sorabji, ed., *Philoponus and the Rejection of Aristotelian Science* (London, 1987) 57–83.

Honoré, Tony, *Tribonian* (London, 1978).

Hopper, V.F., *Medieval Number Symbolism* (New York, 1938).

Horsfall, Nicholas, "Prose and Mime" in E.J. Kenney and W.V. Clausen, eds, *The Cambridge History of Classical Literature* II. *Latin Literature* (Cambridge, 1982) 286–90.

Hunger, Herbert, *Die hochsprachliche profane Literatur der Byzantiner* (HAW 12.5.1; Munich, 1978).

Hunt, E.D., review of S. MacCormack, *Art and Ceremony in Late Antiquity* (Berkeley, 1981), in *Classical Review* 33 (1983) 83–6.

Irmscher, Johannes, "Christliches und heidnisches in der Literatur der justinanischen Zeit", *Revue des Études Sud-Est Européennes* 18 (1980) 85–94.

Irmscher, Johannes, "Die spätantiken Aristoteleskommentatoren in ihrer geschichtlichen Umwelt", in Gerhard Wirth, Karl-Heinz Schwarte, Johannes Heinrichs, eds, *Romanitas-Christianitas. Untersuchungen zur Geschichte und Literatur der römischen Kaiserzeit. Johannes Straub zum 70 Geburstag am 18. Oktober 1982 gewidmet* (Berlin/New York, 1982) 411–25.

Irmscher, Johannes, "Heidnische Kontinuität im justinianischen Staat", *The 17th International Byzantine Congress. Major Papers. Washington D.C. (Aug. 3–8, 1986)* (New Rochelle, 1986) 17–30.

Jeffreys, Elizabeth, "The Attitude of Byzantine Chroniclers towards Ancient History", *Byzantion* 49 (1979) 199–238.

Jeffreys, Elizabeth, with Brian Croke and Roger Scott, eds, *Studies in John Malalas* (Byzantina Australiensia 6; Sydney, 1990).

Joannou, Péricles-Pierre, *Discipline générale antique (IIe-IX^{e}s.)* (Pontificia commissione per la relazione del codice di diritto canonico orientale, Fonti, 9; Rome, 1962).

Jones, A.H.M., "The Roman Civil Service (Clerical and Sub-clerical Grades)", *JRS* 39 (1949) 38–55 [= *Studies in Roman Government and Law* (Oxford, 1960) 151–175].

Jones, A.H.M., *The Later Roman Empire* (Oxford, 1964).

Jones, A.H.M., *The Cities of the Eastern Roman Provinces* (2nd edn, Oxford, 1971).

Jüthner, Julius, *Hellenen und Barbaren* (Leipzig, 1923).

Kaegi, Walter E. Jr, "The Fifth Century Twilight of Byzantine Paganism", *Classica et Mediaevalia* 27 (1966) 243–75.

Kaegi, Walter E. Jr, *Byzantium and the Decline of Rome* (Princeton, 1968).

Kaegi, Walter E. Jr, "Some Perspectives on Byzantine Bureaucracy", in *The Organisation of Power. Aspects of Bureaucracy in the Ancient Near East*, (Oriental Institute Studies in Ancient Oriental Civilization 46; Chicago 1987) 151–9.

Karayannopulos, J., "Der frühbyzantinische Kaiser", *BZ* 49.2 (1956) 369–84.

Karlowa, Otto, *Römische Rechtsgeschichte* 1 (Leipzig, 1885).

Kaster, Robert, *Guardians of Language: The Grammarian and Society in Late Antiquity* (Berkeley, 1988).

Kazhdan, Alexander and Constable, Giles, *People and Power in Byzantium. An Introduction to Modern Byzantine Studies* (Dumbarton Oaks, 1982).

Kennedy, Hugh, "From *Polis* to *Madina*: Urban Change in Late Antique and Early Islamic Syria", *Past and Present* 106 (1985) 3–27.

Kent, J.P.C., "Gold Coinage in the Later Roman Empire" in R.A.G. Carson and C.H.V. Sutherland, eds, *Essays in Roman Coinage Presented to Harold Mattingly*, (Oxford, 1956) 109–204.

Kihn, Heinrich, *Theodor von Mopsuestia und Junilius Africanus als Exegeten. Nebst einer kritischen Textausgabe von des letzteren. Instituta Regularia Divinae Legis* (Freiburg im Breisgau, 1880).

Kitzinger, Ernst, *Byzantine Art in the Making* (Cambridge, Mass., 1977).

Klotz, A., "Lydos 7", *RE* 13.2 (1927) 2210–17.

Konidaris, J. "Die Novellen des Kaisers Herakleios", *Fontes Minores* 5 (1982) 33–106.

Kornemann, Ernst, "Concilium", *RE* 4.1(1900) cols. 825–30.

Koukoules, Ph., Βυζαντινῶν βίος καὶ πολιτισμός vol.2 (Athens, 1948).

Krautheimer, Richard, *Early Christian and Byzantine Architecture* (Baltimore, 1975).

Krumbacher, Karl, *Geschichte der byzantinischen Literatur* (2nd edn, Munich, 1897).

Krusch, Bruno, *Studien zur christlich-mittelalterlichen Chronologie: die Entstehung unserer heutigen Zeitrechnung*, 2 vols (Berlin, 1938).

de Labriolle, Pierre, *La Réaction païenne. Études sur la polémique antichrétienne du Ier au VIe siècle* (Paris, 1924).

Ladner, Gerhard, review of B. Rubin, *Das Zeitalter Iustinians* (Berlin, 1960), *Traditio* 16 (1960) 430–5.

Ladner, Gerhard, *The Idea of Reform, Its Impact on Christian Thought and Action in the Age of the Fathers* (New York, 1967).

Ladner, Gerhard, "Justinian's Theory of Law and the Renewal Theory of the *Leges Barbarorum*", *PAPS*, 119.3 (1975) 191-200.

Lanata, Giuliana, *Legislazione e natura nelle novelle giustinianee* (Storia del pensiero giuridico 7; Naples, 1984).

Lane Fox, Robin, *Pagans and Christians*, (New York, 1987).

Leach, Edmund, "Melchisedech and the Emperor: Icons of Subversion and Orthodoxy", *Proceedings of the Royal Anthropological Institute for 1972* (1973) 5-14.

Lemerle, Paul, *The Agrarian History of Byzantium from its Origins to the Twelfth Century* (Galway, 1979).

Lemerle, Paul, *Byzantine Humanism. The First Phase*, trans. Helen Lindsay and Ann Moffatt (Byzantina Australiensia 3; Canberra, 1986).

Lenel, Otto and Sierl, Lorenz, eds, *Palingenesia Iuris Civilis* vol I (Graz 1889, repr. 1960).

Levin, Flora R., *The Harmonics of Nicomachus and the Pythagorean Tradition* (American Classical Studies 1, University Park, PA, 1975).

Liebs, D., "Aurelius Arcadius Charisius" in R. Herzog and Peter L. Schmidt, eds, *Handbuch der Altertums Wissenschaft. Lateinische Literatur der Antike 5. Restauration und Erneurung. Die Lateinische Literatur von 284 bis 374 n. Chr.* (Munich, 1989) 69-71.

Litsas, Fotios, "Choricius of Gaza: an Approach to his Work. Introduction, Translation and Commentary" (Diss., University of Chicago, 1980).

Litt, Theodorus, *De Verrii Flacci et Cornelii Labeonis Fastorum Libris* (Bonn, 1904).

Long, A.A., "Astrology: Arguments Pro and Contra", in Jonathan Barnes, Jacques Brunschwig, Myles Burnyeat, Malcolm Schofield, eds, *Science and Speculation Studies in Hellenistic Theory and Practice* (Cambridge, 1982) 165-92.

Lynch, John Patrick, *Aristotle's School. A Study of a Greek Educational Institution* (Berkeley, 1972).

Maas, Michael, "Innovation and Restoration in Justinianic Constantinople" (Diss., University of California at Berkeley, 1982).

Maas, Michael, review of James Caimi, *Burocrazia e diritto nel De Magistratibus di Giovanni Lido* (Milan, 1984), *CR* 36 (1986) 221-3.

Maas, Michael, "Roman History and Christian Ideology in Justinianic Reform Legislation", *DOP* 40 (1986) 17-31.

MacCormack, Sabine, *Art and Ceremony in Late Antiquity* (Berkeley, 1981).

McCormick, Michael, *Eternal Victory. Triumphal Rulership in Late Antiquity, Byzantium and the Early Medieval West* (Cambridge, 1986).

Macina, Robert, "L'homme à l'école de Dieu d'Antioche à Nisibe. Profil herméneutique, théologique et kérygmatique de mouvement scoliaste nestorien", *Proche-Orient Chrétien* 32 (1982) 86-121.

MacMullen, Ramsey, "Roman Bureaucratese", *Traditio* 18 (1962) 364-78.

McPhee, Nancy, *The Book of Insults* (London, 1978).

Magie, David, *Roman Imperial Rule in Asia Minor to the End of the Third Century after Christ* (Princeton, 1950).

Maguire, Henry, *Earth and Ocean. The Terrestrial World in Early Byzantine Art* (University Park and London, 1987).

Mango, Cyril, ed., *The Art of the Byzantine Empire 312-1453. Sources and Documents* (Englewood Cliffs, NJ, 1972).

Mango, Cyril, *Byzantium, the Empire of New Rome* (London, 1980).

Mango, Cyril, *Le Développement urbain de Constantinople (IVe-VIIe siècles)* (Travaux et Mémoires 2; Paris, 1985).

Mango, Cyril, "The Development of Constantinople as an Urban Centre", *The 17th International Byzantine Congress. Major Papers. Washington D.C. (Aug. 3-8, 1986)*, (New Rochelle, 1986) 117-36.

Mannino, Vincenzo, *Ricerche sul "Defensor Civitatis"* (Milan, 1984).

Mansfeld, Jaap, "Bad World and Demiurge: a 'Gnostic Motif' from Parmenides and Empedocles to Lucretius and Philo" in R. Van den Broek and M.J. Vermaseren, eds, *Studies in Gnosticism and Hellenistic Religions: Presented to Gilles Quispel on the Occasion of his 65th Birthday* (Leiden, 1986) 261-314.

Manucci, U., "La topografia cristiana di Cosma Indicopleuste e l'insegnamento teologico nella scuola antiochena", *Rivista storico-critica della scienza teologica* 4 (1909) 30-40.

Markus, Robert, *Saeculum: History and Society in the Theology of St Augustine* (Cambridge, 1970).

Markus, Robert, "The Sacred and the Secular: from Augustine to Gregory the Great", *JTS* 36.1 (1985) 84-96.

Martindale, J.R., *The Prosopography of the Later Roman Empire* II. AD 395-527 (Cambridge, 1980).

Maspero, Jean, "Horapollon et la fin du paganisme égyptien", *Bulletin de l'Institut Français d'Archéologie Orientale* II (1914) 163-95.

Mastandrea, Paolo, *Un neoplatonico latino. Cornelio Labeone* (Leiden, 1979).

Mazzucchi, Carlo Maria, "Per una rilettura del palinseto vaticano 'sulla scienza politica' del tempo di Giustiniano", in G.G. Archi, ed., *L'imperatore Giustiniano. Storia e Mito* (Milan, 1978) 237-47.

Mazzucchi, Carlo Maria and Matelli, Elisabetta, "La dottrina dello Stato nel dialogo 'Sulla Scienza Politica' e il suo autore", in G.G. Archi, ed., *Il mondo del diritto nell'epoca giustinianea. Caratteri e problematiche* (Ravenna, 1985) 209-23.

Mercati, G., "Cosmas Indicopleustes and the Paschal Chronicle", in *Opere Minori* 2. 1897-1906 (Vatican City, 1937) 470-9.

Merlan, Philip, "Johannes Lydos", *Lexikon der alten Welt* (Zurich/Stuttgart, 1965) 1390.

Merlan, Philip, "Ammonius Hermiae, Zacharias Scholasticus and Boethius", *GRBS* 9.2 (1968) 193-203.

Meslin, Michel, "Persistances païennes en Galice, vers la fin du VIe siècle", *Hommage à Marcel Renard*, vol. II (Brussels, 1969) 512-24.

Meslin, Michel, *La Fête des kalendes de janvier dans l'empire romain* (Collection Latomus 115, Brussels, 1970).

Michels, Agnes K., "The 'Calendar of Numa' and the Pre-Julian Calendar", *TAPA* 80 (1949) 320-46.

Millar, Fergus, "Empire and City, Augustus to Julian: Obligations, Excuses, and Status", *JRS* 73 (1983) 76–96.

Momigliano, Arnaldo, "Ancient History and the Antiquarian", *Journal of the Warburg and Courtauld Institutes* 13 (1950) 285–315 [= *Studies in Ancient Historiography* (London, 1966) 1–39; = *Contributo alla storia degli studi classici* (Rome, 1955; repr. 1979) 67–106].

Momigliano, Arnaldo, "L'età trapasso fra storiografia medievale (320–550 d.C.)", *Rivista Storica Italiana* 81 (1969) 286–303 [= *Quinto contributo alla storia degli studi classici e del mondo antico*, vol.2 (Rome, 1975) 49–71].

Momigliano, Arnaldo, "Lydus", in *Oxford Classical Dictionary* (2nd edn, Oxford, 1970) 630.

Momigliano, Arnaldo, review of Edward Shils, *Tradition*, in *Storia della Storiografia* 9 (1986) 159–62 [= *Ottavo contributo* (Rome, 1987) 419–24].

Momigliano, Arnaldo, *The Classical Foundations of Modern Historiography* (Berkeley, 1990).

Mommsen, Theodor Ernst, "St. Augustine and the Christian Idea of Progress: The Background of the City of God", *Journal of the History of Ideas* 12 (1951) 346–74.

Moorhead, John, "The West and the Roman Past from Theodoric to Charlemagne", in Brian Croke and Alanna Emmett, eds, *History and Historians in Late Antiquity* (Sydney, 1983) 155–69.

Moravcsik, Gyula, *Byzantinoturcica* vol.1 of *Die byzantinischen Quellen der Geschichte der Türkvölker* (Berliner Byzantinische Arbeiten 10; 1958).

Morosi, Roberto, "L'*officium* del prefetto del pretorio nel VI secolo", *Romanobarbarica* 2 (1977) 103–48.

Morrison, Karl, *Tradition and Authority in the Western Church 300–1140* (Princeton, 1969).

Mossay, J., "Les fêtes de Noël et d'Épiphanie d'après les sources littéraires cappadociennes du IVe siècle", *Textes et Études liturgiques* 3 (Louvain, 1965).

Nau, F., "Analyse de la seconde partie inédite de l'histoire ecclésiastique de Jean d'Asie, patriarche jacobite de Constantinople †585" *Revue de l'Orient Chrétien* 2 (1897) 480–2.

Nicolau, Mathieu, "A propos d'un texte parallèle de Macrobe et Lydus. La doctrine astrologique de la 'collaboration des astres' ", *REL* 11 (1933) 318–21.

Nock, Arthur Darby, "A Vision of Mandulis Aion", in HTR 27 (1934) 53–104 [= Arthur Darby Nock, *Essays on Religion and the Ancient World*, ed. Zeph Stewart, vol.1 (Oxford, 1972) 356–400].

O'Donnell, James, "Paganus", *Classical Folia* 31 (1977) 163–9.

O'Donnell, James, "The Demise of Paganism", *Traditio* 35 (1979) 45–88.

O'Meara, Dominic J., *Pythagoras Revived. Mathematics and Philosophy in Late Antiquity* (Oxford, 1989).

Ommeslaeghe, Florent van, "Le dernier mot sur Romanos le Mélode?", *Analecta Bollandiana* 97 (1979) 417–21.

Paschoud, François, *Cinq études sur Zosime* (Paris, 1975).

Patlagean, Evelyne, "La pauvreté à Byzance au VIe siècle et la législation de Justinien: les origines d'un modèle politique" in M. Mollat, ed., *Études sur l'histoire de la pauvreté (Moyen Age-XVIe siècle)* (Paris, 1974) vol.1, 59–81.

Patlagean, Evelyne, *Pauvreté économique et pauvreté sociale à Byzance 4ᵉ-7ᵉ siècles* (Paris, 1977).

Pedersen, Fritz Saaby, *Late Roman Public Professionalism* (Odense 1976).

Pedersen, Olaf, "The Ecclesiastical Calendar and the Life of the Church", in G.V. Coyne, M.A. Hoskin and O. Pedersen, eds, *Gregorian Reform of the Calendar. Proceedings of the Vatican Conference to commemorate the 400th anniversary, 1582-1982,* (Vatican City, 1983) 17–74.

Pertusi, Agostino, "Storia del pensiero politico", in *La civiltà bizantina dal IV al IX secolo. Aspetti e problemi* (Rome, 1977) 33–85.

Peterson, Erik, "Die Bedeutung der ὠκεανέ - Akklamation", *Rheinisches Museum* 78 (1929) 221-3.

Piganiol, André, "Sur le calendrier brontoscopique de Nigidius Figulus", in *Studies in Roman Economic and Social History in Honour of Allan Charter Johnson,* ed. P.R. Coleman-Norton *et al.* (Princeton, 1951) 79–87.

Pralong, Annie, "Les remparts de Philadelphie", in *Philadelphie et autres études* (Byzantina Sorbonensia 4; Paris, 1984) 101-25.

Pringsheim, Fritz, "Justinian's Prohibition of Commentaries to the Digest", *RIDA* 5 (1950) 383-415.

Purpura, G., "Giovanni di Cappadocia e la composizione della comissione del primo Codice di Giustinianeo", *Annali del Seminario Giuridico di Palermo* 36 (1976) 49–67.

Randall, John Herman, Jr, *Aristotle* (New York, 1960).

Rautman, Marcus, "Problems of Land Use and Water Supply in Late Antique Lydia", *Abstracts of Papers, Thirteenth Annual Byzantine Studies Conference Nov. 5-8, 1987, Columbus, Ohio,* 6-7.

Rawson, Elizabeth, *Intellectual Life in the Late Roman Republic* (Baltimore, 1985).

de Ridder, A., *Les Bronzes antiques du Louvre* II (Paris, 1915).

Ridley, Ronald T., "Eunapius and Zosimus", *Helikon* 9-10 (1969-70) 574-92.

Ridley, Ronald T., "The Fourth and Fifth Century Civil and Military Hierarchy in Zosimus", *Byzantion* 40 (1970) 91-104.

Rist, John, *Stoic Philosophy* (Cambridge, 1969).

Robbins, F.E., "Posidonius and the Sources of Pythagorean Arithmology", *CP* 15.4 (1920) 309-322.

Robbins, F.E., "The Tradition of Greek Arithmology", *CP* 16.2 (1921) 97-123.

Robert, Louis, *Hellenica: recueil d'épigraphie de numismatique et d'antiquités grecques,* vol. IV *Epigrammes du Bas-Empire* (Paris, 1948).

Rochow, Ilse, "Die Heidenprozesse unter den Kaisern Tiberios II. Konstantinos und Maurikios", *Studien zum 7. Jahrhunderten Byzanz* (Berliner Byzantinistische Arbeiten 47; 1976) 120–30.

Rochow, Ilse, "Zur Rolle der Anhänger antiker Kulte und Brauche", in *Byzanz im 7. Jahrhundert. Untersuchungen zur Herausbildung des Feudalismus,* ed. F.W. Winkelmann, H. Köpstein, H. Ditten and I. Rochow (Berlin, 1978) 227-55.

Rösch, Gerhard, *ONOMA ΒΑΣΙΛΕΙΑΣ. Studien zum offiziellen Gebrauch der Kaisertitel in spätantiker und frühbyzantinischer Zeit* (Byzantina Vindobonensia 10; Vienna, 1978).

Roman Imperial Coinage vols 5, 6, 7, 8, 9, edd. varii. (London, 1927-1986).

Rordorf, Willy, *Sunday. The History of the Day of Rest and Worship in the Earliest Centuries of the Christian Church*, trans. A.A.K. Graham (London and Philadelphia, 1968).

Rordorf, Willy, "Sunday: The Fullness of Christian Liturgical Time", *Studia Liturgica* 14 (1982) 90–6.

Roueché, Charlotte, "A New Inscription from Aphrodisias and the Title πατὴρ τῆς πόλεως", *GRBS*, 20, (1979 173–85).

Roueché, Charlotte, "Acclamations in the Later Roman Empire: New Evidence From Aphrodisias", *JRS* 74 (1984) 181–99.

Roueché, Charlotte, "Theodosius II, the Cities, and the Date of the History of Sozomen", *JTS* 37 (1986) 130–2.

Roueché, Charlotte, *Aphrodisias in Late Antiquity* (*Journal of Roman Studies* Monograph 5; London, 1989).

Roueché, Charlotte, "Cities and Imperial Government in the Byzantine Period" (forthcoming).

Rubin, Berthold, *Das Zeitalter Iustinians* (Berlin, 1960).

Sacks, Kenneth, "The Meaning of Eunapius' History", *History and Theory* 25 (1986) 52–67.

Saffrey, Henri-Dominique, "Le chrétien Jean Philopon et la survivance de l'École d'Alexandrie au VIᵉ siècle", *REG* 67 (1954) 396–410.

Salzman, Michele, *On Roman Time: The Codex Calendar of 354 and the Rhythms of Urban Life in Late Antiquity* (Berkeley, 1990).

Sambursky, Shmuel, *The Physical World of Late Antiquity* (London, 1962).

Sambursky, Shmuel, "Note on John Philoponus' Rejection of the Infinite" in S.M. Stern, Albert Hourani and Vivian Brown, eds, *Islamic Philosophy and the Classical Tradition. Essays Presented by his Friends and Pupils to Richard Walzer on his Seventieth Birthday* (Columbia, South Carolina, 1973) 351–4.

Schneider, F., "Über Kalendae Januariae und Martiae im Mittelalter", *Archiv für Religionswissenschaft* XX (1920–1) 82–134, 360–410.

Schreiner, Peter, "Historisches und liturgisches zum byzantinischen Neujahr", *Rivista di Studi Bizantini e Slavi* 2 (1982) 13–23.

Schultze, Johannes F., *Quaestionum Lydianarum Particula Prior* (Diss., University of Greifswald, 1862).

Schürer, Emil, "Die siebentägige Woche im Gebrauche der christlichen Kirche der ersten Jahrhunderte", *ZNW* 6 (1905) 1–66.

Scott, Roger D., "John Lydus on Some Procedural Changes", *Βυζαντινά* 4 (1972) 441–51.

Scott, Roger D., "Malalas and Justinian's Codification", in Elizabeth Jeffries, Michael Jeffries and Ann Moffatt, eds, *Byzantine Papers. Proceedings of the First Australian Byzantine Studies Conference. Canberra, 17-19 May, 1978* (Byzantina Australiensia 1; Canberra, 1981) 12–31.

Scott, Roger D. "Malalas and his Contemporaries", in Elizabeth Jeffreys with Brian Croke and Roger Scott, eds, *Studies in John Malalas* (Byzantina Australiensia 6; Sydney, 1990) 67–86.

Ševčenko, Ihor, "A Late Antique Epigram and the so-called Elder Magistrate from Aphrodisias", in *Synthronon: Art et archéologie de la fin d'antiquité et du moyen age* (Bibliothèque des Cahiers archéologiques 2; Paris, 1968) 29–41.

Ševčenko, Ihor, "Constantinople Viewed from the Provinces in the Middle Byzantine Period", in I. Sevcenko and F. Sysyn, eds, *Eucharisterion: Essays Presented to Omeljan Pritsak on his Sixtieth Birthday by his Colleagues and Students* (Harvard Ukranian Studies III/IV; 1979–80) part 2, 712–41.

Ševčenko, Ihor, "A Shadow Outline of Virtue: The Classical Heritage of Greek Classical Literature (Second to Seventh Century)" in K. Weitzmann, ed., *The Age of Spirituality: A Symposium* (New York, 1980) 53–73.

Shaw, Gregory, "Theurgy: Rituals of Unification in the Neoplatonism of Iamblichus", *Traditio* 41 (1985) 1–28.

Shils, Edward, "Tradition and Liberty: Antinomy and Interdependence", *Ethics* 68.3 (April 1958) 153–65.

Shils, Edward, *Tradition* (Chicago, 1981).

Skydsgaard, Jens Erik, *Varro the Scholar. Studies in the First Book of Varro's De Re Rustica* (Copenhagen, 1968).

Sorabji, Richard, *Time, Creation and the Continuum. Theories in Antiquity and the early Middle Ages* (Ithaca, 1983).

Sorabji, Richard, ed., *Philoponus and the Rejection of Aristotelian Science* (London, 1987).

Sorabji, Richard, "General Introduction" to John Philoponus, Against Aristotle on the Eternity of the World, trans. Christian Wildberg (Ithaca, 1987).

Steel, Carlos G., *The Changing Self. A Study on the Soul in Later Platonism: Iamblichus, Damascius, and Priscianus* (Verhandelingen van de koninklijke Academie voor Wetenschappen, Letteren en Schone Kunsten van België. Klasse der Lettern XL, no. 85; Brussels, 1978).

Stein, Ernest, "Post-Consulat et αὐτοκρατορία", *Annuaire de l'Institute de Philologie et d'Histoire Orientales* II (1933–4) [= *Mélanges J. Bidez*] 869–912 [= *Opera Minora Selecta*, ed. J.-R. Palanque, (Amsterdam, 1968) 315–58].

Stein, Ernest, "Le questeur Junillus et la date de ses 'Instituta' ", *Acad. de la Classe des Lettres de l'Académie Belgique* (1937) 378–83.

Stein, Ernest, *Untersuchungen über das Officium der Praetorianpräfektur seit Diokletian.* (2nd edn, Amsterdam, 1962).

Stein, Ernest, *Histoire du Bas-Empire* (Vienna, 1922; 2nd edn, J.R. Palanque; Paris/Brüges, 1949; repr. Amsterdam, 1968).

Steinwenter, Artur, "Nomos Empsychos. Zur Geschichte einer politischen Theorie", *Anzeiger Akademie der Wissenschaft, Wien, phil.-hist.- Klasse* 83 (1946) 250–68.

Stern, Henri, *Le Calendrier de 354. Études sur son texte et sur les illustrations* (Paris, 1953).

Straub, Johannes A., *Vom Herrscherideal in der Spätantike.* (Forschungen zur Kirchen- und Geistesgeschicht XVIII; Stuttgart, 1939, repr. 1964).

Tanasoca, N.-S., "J. Lydos et la *fabula* latine", *Rev. des Études Sud-Est Européennes* 7 (1969) 231–7.

Tardieu, Michel, "Sabiens coraniques et 'Ṣābiens' de Ḥārrān", *Journal Asiatique* 274 (1986) 1–44.

Tardieu, Michel, "Les calendriers en usage à Harrān d'après les sources arabes et le commentaire de Simplicius à la Physique d'Aristote", in Ilsetraut Hadot, ed., *Simplicius: sa vie, son oeuvre, sa survie*, (Berlin/New York, 1987) 40–57.

Teall, John, "Barbarians in Justinian's Armies", *Speculum* 40, 1965 294–322.

Teitler, H.C., *Notarii and Exceptores* (Amsterdam, 1985).

Thesleff, Holger, *The Pythagorean Texts of the Hellenistic Period* (Abo, 1965).

Thomas, John Philip, *Private Religious Foundations in the Byzantine Empire* (Dumbarton Oaks Studies 24; Washington, DC, 1987).

Toomer, G.J., "Ptolemy", in *Dictionary of Scientific Biography* vol.11 (New York, 1975) 186–206.

Treitinger, Otto, *Die Oströmische Kaiser und Reichsidee nach ihrer Gestaltung im höfischen Zeremoniell.* (Jena, 1938).

Trombley, Frank R., "The Council in Trullo (691–692): A Study of the Canons Relating to Paganism, Heresy, and the Invasions", *Comitatus* 9 (1978) 2–18.

Trombley, Frank R., "The Survival of Paganism in the Byzantine Empire during the Pre-Iconoclastic Period (540–727)" (Diss., UCLA, 1981).

Trombley, Frank R., "Paganism in the Greek World at the End of Antiquity: the Case of Rural Anatolia and Greece", *HTR* 78.3–4 (1985) 327–52.

Trombley, Frank R., "Monastic Foundations in Sixth-century Anatolia and their Role in the Social and Economic Life of the Countryside", *Greek Orthodox Theological Review* 30.1 (1985) 45–59 [= in N.M. Vaporis, ed., *Byzantine Saints and Monasteries*, (Brookline, Mass., 1985)].

Tsirpanlis, Constantine N., "John Lydus and the Imperial Administration", *Byzantion* 44 (1974) 479–501.

Turpin, William, "The Late Roman Law Codes: Forms and Procedures for Legislation from the Classical Age to Justinian" (Diss., University of Cambridge, 1981).

Turpin, William, "The Law Codes and Late Roman Law", *RIDA* 32 (1985) 339–53.

Vasiliev, Alexander A., *Justin the First. An Introduction to the Epoch of Justinian the Great* (Dumbarton Oaks Studies I; Cambridge, Mass., 1950).

Verbeke, Gérard, "The Aristotelian Doctrine of Qualitative Change in *Physics* VIII.3", in John P. Anton and George B. Kustas, eds, *Essays in Ancient Greek Philosophy* (Albany, 1971) 546–65.

Verbeke, Gérard, "Some Later Neoplatonic Views of Divine Creation and the Eternity of the World", in Dominic J. O'Meara, ed., *Neoplatonism and Christian Thought* (Albany, 1982) 45–53.

Verrycken, K., "The Development of Philoponus' Thought and its Chronology", in R. Sorabji, ed., *Aristotle Transformed* (London/Ithaca, 1990) 233–74.

Volbach, Wolfgang F., *Elfenbeinarbeiten der Spätantike und des frühen Mittelalters* (Mainz, 1952; 2nd edn, 1976).

Wachsmuth, Curtius, *Studien zu den griechischen Florilegien* (Berlin, 1882; repr. Amsterdam 1971).

Wachsmuth, Curtius, "Ein neues Fragment aus Lydus Schrift 'De Ostentis' ", *Rheinisches Museon* 52 (1897) 137–40.

Wallace-Hadrill, Andrew, *Suetonius: The Scholar and His Caesars* (London, 1983).

Wallis, R.T., *Neoplatonism* (London, 1972).

Waterlow, Sarah, *Nature, Change, and Agency in Aristotle's Physics* (Oxford, 1982).

Whittaker, John, "Timaeus 27D 5ff.", *Phoenix* 23 (1969) 181–5 [= *Studies in Platonism and Patristic Thought* (London, 1984) art.2].

Whittaker, John, "Plutarch, Platonism and Christianity", in H.J. Blumenthal and R.A. Markus, eds, *Neoplatonism and Early Christian Thought. Essays in Honour of A.H. Armstrong* (London, 1981) 50–63.

Whittow, Mark "Ruling the Late Roman and Early Byzantine City: A Continuous History", *Past and Present* 129 (1990) 3–29.

Wildberg, Christian, *John Philoponus' Criticism of Aristotle's Theory of Aether* (Berlin/New York, 1988).

Wilson, N.G., *Scholars of Byzantium* (Baltimore, 1983).

Wissowa, Georg, *De Macrobii Saturnaliorum Fontibus* (Bratislava,' 1880).

Wissowa, Georg, "Censorinus 7", *RE* III.2 (1899) 1908–10.

Wittig, Curtius, *Quaestiones Lydianae* (Diss., University of Königsberg, 1910).

Wolska, Wanda, *La Topographie chrétienne de Cosmas Indicopleustès. Théologie et science au VIe siècle* (Paris, 1962).

Woodward, A.M., "The Neocorate at Aegeae and Anazarbus in Cilicia", *Numismatic Chronicle* (ser. 7) 3 (1963) 5–10.

Wright, David H., "Ivories for the Emperor", *Third Annual Byzantine Studies Conference. Abstracts of Papers* (New York, 1977) 6–9.

Wright, David H., "Justinian and an Archangel", in Otto Feld and Urs Peschlow, eds, *Studien zur spätantiken und byzantinischen Kunst. Friedrich Wilhelm Deichmann gewidmet* III (Bonn, 1986) 75–80.

Wünsch, R., "Zu Lydus 'De Ostentis' ", *BZ* 5 (1896) 410–21.

Zachariae von Lingenthal, C.E., "Johannes des Philadelphiens Laurentius Sohn, genannt Lydus", *ZSS (Rom. Abt.)* 12 (1892) 79–80.

Zeller, Edouard, *Die Philosophie der Griechen in ihrer geschichtlichen Entwicklung* II.2. *Die nacharistotelische Philosophie.* (Leipzig, 1923, repr. Olms, 1963).

Zepos. See Ius.

Zerubavel, Eviatar, *The Seven Day Circle. The History and Meaning of the Week* (Chicago, 1985).

Ziegler, Konrat, "Polemius Silvius", *RE* 21.1 (1951) 1260–3.

Zilletti, Ugo, *Studi sul processo civile giustinianeo* (Milan, 1965).

INDEX

28–37; Christianity and 30, 67, 98, 113–14, 117–18, *see also* ambiguity; earlier scholars' views of 8; local patriotism of 30–1; qualities of 6, 9, 114–18; use of Bible 67, 83; use of Latin 25, 30, 32, 114; works of 9–11 and *passim*

MacCormack, S. 26, 47
McCormick, M. 45
Macedonius, *referendarius* 71
Macrobius 60
magister officiorum 27, 43, 55
magister equitum 89–92, 96
Malalas, John 41, 65, 71, 112–13
Marinus, Praetorian Prefect 19, 87, 109
Marius, C. 85
Mastandrea, P. 53–4
matricularius 34
Maurice, emperor 72
memorialis 31
Michael the Syrian 72
military, role in sixth century 13, 21
Momigliano, A.D. 53
Monophysitism, Monophysites 71, 76, 99, 109, 111

Nestorianism, Nestorians 101, 110–11
Nicomachus of Gerasa 59–60
Nigidius Figulus 107
Nika Revolt 16, 34, 44, 71, 79–80, 95
nomos empsychos 15, 75
Numa 56–7
numerology 58–60
numismatics 13, 17, 54

omens *see* portents
Ovid 8, 61–2

paganism: as cult 3, 50–1, 69–70, 74, 78; as impediment to office 3, 10, 68–9, 73, 78; extent of in sixth century 72, 77, 116
pagans 3, 25, 72–3, 116; persecutions of 70–2

Parastaseis Syntomoi Chronikai 13
past: appropriation of 2, 38, 68, 116–17; attitude toward, in sixth century 1–3, 38–41, 83–6, 116 and *passim*; Christianization of 2–3, 38–9; Justinian's views of 39–45; legitimating value of 38, 42, 68, 116; Lydus' views of 5–6, 30, 42–3, 83–92 and *passim; see also* Christianity; Justinian
Paul of Nisibis 111
Pegasius of Heliopolis 71
Peter the Patrician 29, 55, 81
Petronius of Philadelphia 6
Philadelphia 6, 22–3, 30–1, 88; Lydus' pride in 30–1
Philo 59–60
Philochristos 15
Philolaos 59
Philoponus, John 99, 101–2, 110–11
philosophy 3–4, 8, 29, 97–104, 117–18
Phlegon of Tralles 62
Phocas, Praetorian Prefect 10, 33–4, 44, 71, 77, 78–82, 94
Photius 3–4, 60
plague 18, 23–4, 47, 76
Plato 4, 48, 61, 97–8, 100–2
Plotinus 103
Plutarch 93
Polemius Silvius 62–3
Porphyry 100, 103
portents 9, 67, 105–13
Posidonius 110
poverty 25–6, 31
Praetorian Prefecture 6, 13, 27, 83–92, 115, 117; Lydus' views on decline of 7, 33, 49, 52, 86–8
Proclus 3, 30–1, 97, 101–2, 111
Procopius 8, 16–17, 19–21, 28, 45, 54, 73
Prudentius 38, 42
Psellus, Michael 58
Ptolemy 9, 11, 98, 101, 105–6, 110, 113, 116
Pythagoras 57–9

quaesitor 25, 85
Quinisext Council ("in Trullo") 65